KEY BISCAYNE

*A History of Miami's
Tropical Island and the
Cape Florida Lighthouse*

KEY

BIS

Like an exclamation point at the tip of the island, the lighthouse rises above impermanence and shifting sands to stand witness to history. The tower withstood attacks by hurricanes and men to be hailed today as the oldest standing permanent structure in the Miami area. It is listed on the National Register of Historic Places as "the oldest lighthouse station in Florida." (Ralph M. Munroe, Historical Association of Southern Florida)

'CAYNE

Joan Gill Blank

To Key Biscayne natives
Robin, Susan, and Prudence
who grew up on our beloved
coconut plantation
and
to Harvey who shares
my love for our island of bliss
and
to all who have ever lived on,
or longed for, an island
paradise,
I dedicate this book

Copyright © 1996 by Joan Gill Blank

All rights reserved. No part of this
book may be reproduced in any
form or by any means, electronic or
mechanical, including photocopy-
ing, recording, or by any information storage and retrieval system,
without permission in writing from
the publisher.

Inquiries should be addressed to:
Pineapple Press, Inc.
P.O. Box 3899
Sarasota, Florida 34230-3899

Library of Congress
Cataloging in Publication Data:

Blank, Joan,
    Key Biscayne : a history of Miami's
tropical island and the Cape Florida
lighthouse / by Joan Gill Blank.—1st
ed.
    p.   cm.—(Florida's history through
its places)
    Includes bibliographical
references and index.
    ISBN 1-56164-096-4 (alk. paper)
    1. Key Biscayne (Fla.)—History.   2.
Lighthouses—Florida—Key
Biscayne.   I. Title.   II. Series.
F317.D2B53   1996   95-47331
975.9′38-dc20   CIP

First Edition
10 9 8 7 6 5 4 3 2 1

Produced by
Octavo Design & Production
Printed and bound by
Edwards Brothers, Ann Arbor, MI

Contents

What Key Biscayne Meant To ...

For the earliest passersby, it was a sandbar, a landing inside the swift ocean river, a place to collect on its beaches or tidal pools succulents from the sea left by the tides; it was a resting place. For the Tequestas, part of the coastal Calusa Nation of the peninsula, it was a site from which they could escape the inland heat, enjoy the cool prevailing trade winds, and find food and fresh water; it was a fishing and whaling village.

... indigenous people

For Juan Ponce de León, it was a feather in his cap. Having found the long "island" he called La Florida, the peninsular gateway to the continent, he then found the key, which was five-mile-long Key Biscayne. He called it Santa Marta, and claimed it for the King of Spain in 1513. Here he found fresh water, no matter it was not the legendary Fountain of Youth (or was it?).

... Ponce de León

For Pedro Fornells, a native of the island of Minorca, it was a symbol of freedom. Historically, it was the first of the Royal Land Grants in south Florida, given by the Spanish king. For Fornells it was an acknowledgment of a dream fulfilled, or wrong righted, of justice overlong in coming to his people who had suffered in the New World as individuals and as a colony.

... Fornells

...Davis

For Mary Ann Davis, first American title holder, it was a coup to buy this subtropical island regarded as a strategic location by the U.S. government during territorial days. For her husband, the Deputy Marshall of St. Augustine, William G. Davis, it was a speculative venture, an economic stepping-stone with potential as a port town and resort to surpass all others.

...Dubose

For John Dubose, it was an opportunity to serve his country without being on a ship at sea away from his family, and a unique challenge to be the first keeper of the Cape Florida lighthouse, built to safeguard commerce and trade along the eastern seacoast. It was a viable opportunity to become a part of the new frontier where he and his wife, Margaret, could shed their Carolinian-planter background and, raising their children in the keeper's cottage, teach them the value of equality and freedom. Two of them are the first recorded children born on the island.

...Seminoles & Blacks

For the Indians taking refuge in the Everglades, it was a sign of white intrusion into their lives. During the Seminole Wars, the lighthouse became a symbol of the enemy whose declared goal was to exile or exterminate the redskins and their black-skinned allies, the latter sometimes runaway slaves. Briefly before and after the war, the island was a springboard to freedom for persecuted Seminoles and escaping blacks and black Seminoles across the Gulf Stream to the Bahamas.

...Harney

For William S. Harney, a volatile lieutenant colonel destined to be a general, the island became a military base upon which to train his dragoons to fight the Indians in the watery wilderness of the Everglades. It also was the island on which he purchased two lots from drawings of a paper town, drawn up in 1839 by Mary Ann and William Davis, which he returned to claim after retirement.

For engineers F. H. Gerdes and J. E. Hilgard, it was the ideal site for A. D. Bache's Coast Survey headquarters to triangulate and survey the entire coast and reef from Key West to Fort Lauderdale.

…Gerdes & Hilgard

For E. A. Osborn and E. T. Field, who planted thousands of coconuts in the coastal sands, it offered a means to buy up subtropical coastal property cheaply, to escape freezing northern winters for themselves and future like-minded tourists they hoped to lure to the palm-lined beaches they were creating from Key Biscayne to Jupiter, a distance of ninety miles by sea.

…Osborn & Field

For Waters Smith Davis, it was an inherited island, long set aside by his family, to which he returned with his wife, Sarah, in the late 1800s. At times it became an enchanted island for the family, but an island that absorbed much time to defend from litigation originally incited by his father in the 1840s. He repurchased the lighthouse from the U.S. government and built a Florida vacation home he called Cape House.

…Davis

For Ralph M. Munroe, Key Biscayne was his cruising ground, his island mistress, for he never owned it. He leased the lighthouse with two cohorts for the use of the new yacht club that had been established in his mainland boathouse. He was retained by Waters Davis to be superintendent of the Cape House property, overseeing the building of Davis's house and the cultivation and maintenance of the land during his absence. They became close friends. In the end, for Munroe as agent for the sale of the property, it became his poker chip.

…Munroe

...Deering

For James Deering, it was a win to buy Cape House and the southern end of the island following the death of Waters Davis. Initially it was seen as a natural hideaway, being opposite his palatial mansion, Vizcaya, on the mainland; it became a challenge, a litigator's nightmare, a dream unrealized.

...Matheson

For William J. Matheson, scientist, industrialist, and philanthropist, Key Biscayne was a beloved spot, a fantasy island, a botanical test tube and a showplace, a gift for his children, a tropical wonderland. He owned the land north of the Cape, but not the Cape itself. For Hugh Matheson, it was a lifesaver and became a lifelong commitment to oversee and instigate the building of a self-sufficient plantation and wildlife sanctuary with his father's encouragement and backing. "Matheson's Island," as naturalist David Fairchild called it in the 1920s, included the midsection of the island (the community) and the northern end (now Crandon Park). For Hugh, his brother Malcolm, and sister Anna Woods, their father's island, which they inherited, became a legacy, the northern portion of it being given to the people of Dade County in perpetuity as a county park.

...Áleman/Garcia

For exiled José Manuel Áleman, the island's southernmost tip with its lighthouse, bought from the James Deering estate, became a good land investment after he fled from Cuba. For his widow, Elena Santeiro Garcia, it was at first a financial headache until an opportunity arose to clear her reputation; ultimately, it would become a priceless piece of property when she sold it to the state of Florida for a state park. Here stands the oldest structure in Dade County: the lighthouse first built in 1825, rebuilt after the Indian attack, and currently undergoing restoration so that Cape Florida history continues into the twenty-first century, standing testimony to the past and the story we shall tell.

Foreword

Marjory Stoneman Douglas

"The history of an island and its environment are forever indivisible." So states our author in this work as one of the basics of understanding how we are going to save the small and large pieces of our planet. Rachel Carson suggests the interrelationships in her book *The Sea Around Us,* and also says, "Islands are ephemeral."

As a young adult, I often sailed with friends to a private palm-filled island, a romantic hideaway called Key Biscayne. Blooming tropical plants complemented the thick vegetation of native origin. I remember it surrounded by crystal-clear water, an aquarium with undersea gardens provided by nature. No bridge connected this sand-encircled island with any other place in the world.

I remember how marvelously isolated we felt upon arriving there, gaining a sense of freedom to behave as we wished, to explore barefoot in the shallows, to shout, to sing, to dance, even to go skinny-dipping by night. The island had a wide, flat beach backed up by low dunes along the ocean; the sand continued to weave its way among dark-green mangrove estuaries on the west where tropical birds roosted, strutted, and bred, secure in their privacy.

The island was a minuscule sanctuary, and in those days we thought of it as the apex of the chain of Florida Keys. In truth, it is a barrier island and, as Joan Gill Blank tells us, not only its composition but much of its history is quite unlike that of either the Florida Keys or the mainland. It is the southernmost barrier island in the United States, edging out by a few degrees those other hurricane-battered ones in the Gulf of Mexico.

What she shares with us is that the small island of Key Biscayne (which was briefly in the limelight as a Winter White House) is a microcosm of the large world we live in—historically, environmentally, and politically. In early 1970, the undersecretary of the interior called Florida the nation's environmental test-tube baby. Key Biscayne is a prime example, before and after the bridges connected the island to the mainland in the 1940s. Few among us took great notice when the changes came, and few chronicled the events, for there was insufficient awareness or understanding of the precarious balance of nature on such an island.

The island was the stuff of which dreams are made. The author shows us the surprising affairs that transformed the fragile slice of sand, the so-called Island Paradise, into a highly sought-after resort. She takes us along on her search for the earliest and subsequent islanders, settlers, title holders, keepers of the lighthouse, and those who changed its character and features. The book correctly interrelates the course of historical and environmental forces, combining words and many pictures never before published.

While offering a new understanding of coastal islands that deflect storm surges and hurricanes, this biography of a subtropical island underscores the crucial need to consider every inch of land on this planet—whether wetlands or dry lands—as an integral piece of the globe whose remaining resources must be better protected and, whenever possible, replenished. It is time to recognize, as did the first inhabitants of the island, that we hold this land in trust.

There is no more dynamic place on earth than a barrier island. As coastal sand islands, they are the front line of defense for storm surges, hurricanes, and rising seas. They are defenseless themselves and become sacrifices with or without rituals. Barrier islands are always at risk.

ONE

Emergence

THE RISE OF KEY BISCAYNE

In the year 2000, Key Biscayne will celebrate its fourth millennium if oceanographers and geologists have correctly measured its age. A composite of sand, shell, and marine organisms, layering one on the other, it emerged when the ocean sea-level rise accommodatingly slowed down as if to allow it to break through. We do not know what year a hurricane tore through a fringe of Florida coast to create this southernmost barrier island, but we know the island was a latecomer to the area.

When it emerged into the light, the quartz in the Carolinian sand that had washed down from rivers some thousand miles to the north tumbled together with trillions of particles of shells, sparkling in the sun like bits of magic crystal. It had made it to the surface and henceforth would continue to grow as long as the natural flow of currents carrying sand from the north was not blocked. The sand deposits would come to rest on its widening beach, a golden necklace of a beach, which would often feel the capriciousness of nature and ultimately be disturbed by humans. But that was yet to come.

In time, the western shores and edges, fronting the lagoon it helped create, would be barricaded by mangroves grown from seeds that had floated ashore, taking hold in wetlands, weaving long-legged roots and intertwining branches into elaborate labyrinths, expanding island borders. Sea oats, vines, and succulents gradually took hold to stabilize the sand.

Into the shallows came tropical fishes, shrimps, and crabs. Sea mammals cavorted nearby. A hard-packed beach and offshore grasses attracted other marine and amphibious creatures, wading and shore birds. They were the first to banquet on the key, sometimes at tidal pools which, like latter-day buffet tables, would be quickly emptied and then filled again with delicacies fresh from the sea.

Nature, of course, is in charge on barrier islands. There is no way to stabilize the fragile line where sand and water meet. On calm days they kiss like blithe lovers. In storms, when winds are rough, the angry

A violent hurricane, howling across an ancient sea, created the island of Key Biscayne. Separated from the long coastal strand to the north, it was born of Jurakan, the fierce Mayan and Caribbean god, one of the worldwide mythic spirits symbolizing the creator/destroyer of everything that lives and everything that dies.

ocean tears at the shores, and islands are defenseless. Fortunately, tropical islands do not always lie in the eye of storms. More often, they remain tranquil, remote and secluded, sought-after sanctuaries.

Poised at the top of the great Florida reef, as if the guardian protecting the dangerous entrance or gateway to the treacherous Straits of Florida, Key Biscayne for many years passed as one of the Florida Keys. Yet recently, ocean scientists made clear the differences between the nearly 120,000-year-old rock and reef keys and the more youthful barrier islands to their north. They are barely kissing cousins. In fact, Key Biscayne is balanced on the skeleton of a vestige fossil reef.

We tremble for the vulnerability of barrier islands. But has Key Biscayne no *venerability?* We probed deeper. And then we discovered its origins. We learned that while Key Biscayne may be an exceedingly young island of shifting sand, it is on the edge of a plateau millions of years old and is formed of timeless ocean sediments and the residues of ancient mountains.

The age of the oceans and the power of the mountains—those of the Appalachians whose high peaks touch the sky—are part of its heritage.

Footprints on the Sand

No one knows who made the first human footprints in the wet island sand. In our innocence we can briefly wax poetic, imagining wandering nomads, the homeless drifters of antiquity, on primitive water-borne craft carried by currents or winds to the emerging sandbar.

The peninsula of Florida, distinct from the coastal barrier islands, traces back to the Ice Age. Both animal and human remains dating back twelve thousand or more years attest to the area as one of the earliest places in America marked by footprints. Anthropologists and archaeologists do not deal in poetry; they deal in facts and findings, and when we relate their materials to the search for first island clues, we learn that the early years above sea level correspond to the Late Archaic period when Florida's prehistoric people were living in mound and village complexes of some sophistication. In fact, trade and cultural contact were taking place some twenty-five hundred years ago. But it is doubtful that these cultures or earlier hunters and foragers paid much heed to the rise of a coastal strand.

Yet as the coast became vegetated and animals occupied and ringed it, hunters and fishermen took notice. The natural mariners among them were drawn to the island at the edge of the sea.

This new island, bathed in sun and moonlight, was positioned in what one day would be called a most fortuitous location on the borderline of the tropics. With the great ocean stream to its east, at the top of a majestic reef to the south, with a newly created lagoon to its west, and laved by waters of an increasingly warming sea, it offered a pristine habitat.

And—unlike most islands in the southeast Florida chain—it had fresh water.

Sand and water meet along fragile margins of island's soft edge and ever-shifting coastline. (Joan E. Gill)

Island Village

The first people to leave a lasting imprint on the island were the Tequestas, part of the powerful Calusa Nation that dominated the Florida peninsula. Like other Glades and circum-Glades peoples inhabiting the fringes of the vast, swampy marshes of south Florida's Everglades, they were wise about the ways of coastal living. It is not unusual for those who live in water-dominant environments to establish island bases, or villages, especially if resources are available for self-sufficiency, trade, and defense.

For several centuries the East Coast barrier islands and coral keys supported active communities. On Key Biscayne, findings of shells, bones, potsherds, and other artifacts long suggested extensive prehistoric activity.

Late twentieth-century archaeological studies by Dade County archaeologist Robert S. Carr confirmed "intensive aboriginal activity" and show that an unusually large community stood on Key Biscayne between fifteen hundred and two thousand years ago. The Tequestas built their houses on island ridges and hammocks several feet above the ground on wooden posts; they used the fronds of palmetto or cabbage palms to thatch roofs. In a typical village, houses clustered together, close by a Long House used for ceremonial or other gatherings.

Native peoples navigated in hand-hewn dugout canoes made from the great swamp or bald cypress that grows with its roots in water and its feathery head reaching for the sky. In the Everglades, it can grow more than 150 feet tall and exceed 12.5 feet in diameter. Living in an environment where there is little durable building material, the Tequestas were astute in recognizing the value of the stately cypress, for its wood was light, easy to work, and remarkably resistant to water. They may have had their first clue from observing the growth of cypress knees which spring from underwater, and legend says, to breathe air for the lofty tree.

Cypress as well as pine dugouts were made by felling trees, setting fire to the heartwood, scraping with shells, sanding with file fish and other skins, and sometimes decorating with incised or carved animal figures. Expert mariners, the Tequestas maneuvered their dugouts through the reefs and dared to sail the Gulf Stream, launching whaling and fishing expeditions from the island. Trade or war between neighboring tribes—the Jeaga and Ais to the immediate north and the Caribs and Arawaks of the Caribbean—is also suggested by archaeological finds.

Arriving on the island in their canoes with an eye toward deep-sea fishes, sea mammals, and turtles, the first villagers established a fishing and whaling operation. They processed every part of their catch, using flesh and organs for food and bones for tools and weapons. Jaws, bills, and razor-sharp teeth were used for cutting, slicing, or incising. Fine bones became needles, and tendons thread. Whale and shark skin were cured, as were other animal skins found off- and onshore. Enormous sea-turtle shells served as grand bowls or decorative shields of war.

Tidal pools, beaches, and offshore reefs also provided a variety of objects for food, utility, and decoration. Conch and whelk shells became tools: attached to wooden handles, they were used as picks; others were blown as horns of communication or bugles of war. Large bivalves became scrapers, cups, and dippers.

The Tequestas left no evidence of written language, although they may have made signs and symbols in the sand and planned or commemorated important voyages and memorable ceremonies using the ancient art of pictography, as coastal and desert people, even to this day, communicate among themselves. Of course, like the impermanence of their medium, messages drawn on sand would remain only briefly.

In 1992, archaeologists, examining land laid bare by the storm surge and winds of Hurricane Andrew, found no rich deposit of metal artifacts, just one scrap of thin gold, probably used in a gorget (necklace). The only gold or silver found in Florida was usually salvaged by skilled native divers from shipwrecked plate ships from Central and South America that had ripped apart on offshore reefs or sunk during hurricanes. The scientists did find important pieces of pottery and animal bones such as deer, bear, alligator, or crocodile remains. In ongoing digs, prehistoric artifacts and other clues found by Carr throughout the island confirm that Key Biscayne, in fact, is an important pre-Columbian site. Its villages comprise the largest Tequesta community found, its size and significance previously unsuspected.

Through the years, many Indian mounds and middens had been leveled; early treasures lie under twentieth-century fill and paved roads. Artifacts have been scattered, crushed, and buried. If some of the materials were sacred and escaped the natural destruction of water, tides, and storms, the despoilers of the wild lands and wetlands did not notice or did not care. They rarely looked back. Too few understand that these

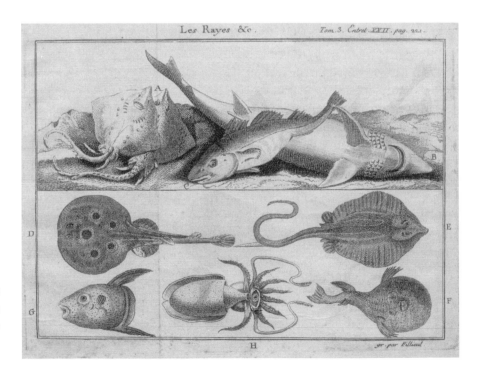

Shark, rays, and other marine fishes provided not only food but sharp teeth and barbs for tools for Tequesta. (Early 1700s engraving, Blank Collection)

are our heritage and are to be kept in trust. The history of an island and its environment are forever indivisible.

Blow Ye Whales

Dolphins and manatees are familiar in waters around Key Biscayne. Small whales sometimes wash up on the beach, but a grandiose whale is less often seen. Indeed, the practice of whaling has never been much noted by those south of New England, although long-known whaling skills date back to early Native Americans and, according to author Sandra Riley, "Almost twenty years before Nantucketers solicited help to learn the art of whale fishing, it was a rapidly expanding industry in the Bahamas," where it had been brought by the Eleutheran Adventurers, the intrepid "religious independents" who sailed south from Bermuda between 1646 and 1648.

The first planned sperm-whaling voyage was recorded in a petition sent in 1688 to the governor of Massachusetts, Sir Edmund Andros, requesting a license for twelve marines, twelve whalemen, and six divers from a New England port for "a fishing design about the Bohamas Islands, and Cap[e] Florida, for sperma Coety whales and for Racks [wrecks]."

Still earlier evidence exists of whaling in the region. In 1567, Friar Francisco Villareal, a Spanish missionary who had been escorted to the bay area by conquistador Pedro Menéndez de Avilés, broke bread with Tequesta Indians. Soon he wrote that the natives ate fruit on an island a league distant from the mouth of the Miami River where the mission was located, and that their regular diet included fish and whales. They launched their dugouts to this island not only when there was a "plague of mosquitoes" on the mainland, but to stock up on marine resources and wild plants and fruits. The friar's report was fast followed by the observations of shipwrecked Hernando d'Escalante Fontaneda who spent much time in Florida with the Calusa Indians. Upon returning to Spain, in 1575 he wrote, "Their common food is fish, turtle and snails [probably conch], and tuny and whales."

Among marine resources of the Tequesta, besides sea mammals and sea turtles, were rays, sharks, sailfish, and many other saltwater fishes and shellfishes. These they used for food, tools, utensils, weapons, and decorative and ritual purposes. Nothing was wasted by the maritime cultures; moreover, human bones were spiritual objects of great importance.

Native people believed in the power of animal spirits, and there is a tradition of ceremonies and sacrifices associated with land and sea hunts. In south Florida rituals and dances, celebrants wore decorative wooden masks that combined human and animal features. Prehistoric Florida artists, as artists of all times, were influenced by their environment. In south Florida they carved bone, shell, and wood and painted the magical dolphin, sea turtle, barracuda, pelican, Florida panther, deer, and alligator. The skills of woodworkers were heightened by their

All creatures that have a blow-hole respire and inspire. —ARISTOTLE

Whales, along with other sea mammals, were hunted off Cape Florida. (Heraldic whale emblem, National Institute of Oceanography, England)

use of particular shark and ray teeth and barbs that cut like diamond points. The wood carving of the notable effigy of the Florida panther found on Marco Island, housed at the Smithsonian Institution, is one of the oldest artifacts found in America and has been compared to those of the ancient Egyptians.

Sea Cow Hunt

In winter all the Indians go to sea in their canoes to hunt for sea cows. One of their number carries three stakes fastened to his girdle and a rope on his arm. When he discovers a sea cow he throws a rope around its neck, and as the animal sinks under the waves and the Indian drives a stake through one of its nostrils and no matter how much it may dive, the Indian never loses it because he goes on its back.

—Account from Juan Ponce de León's voyage

American Manatee (*Trichechus manatus*) of Florida and West Indian waters. Commonly known as the sea cow, the docile mammal was probable source of mermaid myths, as well as a food source for earliest people. (Blank Collection)

TWO

Key to the Continent

PONCE TASTES THE WATER

Outsmarting and outnavigating peers and predecessors who would exceed his fame for centuries, Juan Ponce de León, an accomplished and bold red-headed son of a Spanish rogue and nobleman, deftly made the first documented discovery of the turbulent and as-yet-unnamed Gulf Stream in the spring of 1513 after siting and claiming, with modest ceremony upon the sand, an unkissed continent. He called the continent La Florida, and then sailed south to discover a tiny separate island that he christened Santa Marta. Years later it would be known as Key Biscayne. Legend has it that Juan Ponce slept upon this island but did not stay long enough to discover his Fountain of Youth. Yet historian Samuel Eliot Morison tells us that on this site he "found a spring of sweet water."

Because of this natural supply of fresh water, a resource not found at all coastal landings, the island would soon be marked on sailing maps and charts. Key Biscayne water filled many a ship's barrel and went into many a sailor's parched throat, and who is to say whether or not mariners gained renewed power and longevity in the drinking?

According to the distinguished Admiral Morison, whose research and writing have helped blow away some of the cobwebs of history concerning discoveries of and voyages to America, "Juan Ponce de León is the most elusive of the early conquistadores. We know where he went and what he did, but of his personality, only the generalities."

Yet this son of a nobleman, who found his sea legs on the second voyage of Columbus, had a well-documented tenure in the New World. He discovered and settled the Caribbean island of Puerto Rico, where he brought his wife and became governor. He was buried in San Juan, under an epitaph that reads, "Beneath this structure rest the bones of a Lion."

In the year 1521, the Lion attempted to land on the west coast of Florida. He was felled by an arrow of a native intent on defending

Key Biscayne was not only a jewel for the crown, but a feather in the cap of Juan Ponce de León. Jubilant in his discovery of Florida near today's St. Augustine, he followed the coastline south to find and claim for Spain a tiny gem of an island that he named Santa Marta, a name that would not stay. (Laurence Donovan)

Calusa Nation territory. It had become apparent that the intruders were attempting to establish themselves on the peninsula. The sharp-shooting natives aborted the first attempt at European settlement on the continent, which, had it been successful, would have predated St. Augustine by forty-four years and Plymouth by ninety-nine.

Along the East Coast north of Key Biscayne there were other tribes than the Tequestas, among them the Jaega, Ais, and Timucuans. Early explorers and travelers reported native people and their villages, and some of them were friendly. But when Juan Ponce de León, the first to claim the Land of Flowers, sailed south and sent men ashore for fire-wood and fresh water, he was surprised when his Spaniards were at-tacked and murdered by the natives (Jaegas or Tequestas). He appar-ently gave no thought to the fact that he was invading their land, their property, their liberty, and their lives.

In June 1513, two months after his discovery of Key Biscayne, during an exploratory cruise of the Keys and a layover in the Dry Tortugas

(which he named), crew members captured 160 turtles, 14 seals, 7,000 pelicans, and other wild fowl.

First encounters of Native Americans and Spaniards as seen through the artist's eye. Wondrous tropical plants and feathered, furred, and finned animals of land and sea surround island as two of Juan Ponce de León's crew beach their boat on the back of an alligator. (Laurence Donovan, City of Miami)

Ponce's Seed

In an incredible turn of history, and adding to the myth, Juan Ponce de León's seed eventually sprang up on the island of Key Biscayne. After a four-hundred-year interval, a young man from an old Castilian family, tracing its lineage to the Ponce de León family, arrived at Cape Florida. Julian Caverly Gonzales conducted a ten-year courtship before he carried Emmeline Coit Davis as his bride over the threshold of a grand beach-side cottage called Cape House in 1902. The groom's father-in-law, Waters S. Davis, had been so preoccupied heading off litigation over title to the property, he did not realize that his daughter

Julian Caverly Gonzales, 7, traces his ancestry back to the family of the Spanish discoverer (Juan Ponce de Leon) and is the great-grandchild of the first American title holder (Mary Ann Davis) of Key Biscayne. The tiny island became his own winter playground in the first decade of the twentieth century. (Gonzales/Day Collection)

was marrying into a family claiming to be related to the man who in 1513 claimed the island for King Ferdinand of Spain. In the first decade of the 1900s, the island would be the winter playground for a little red-headed boy, also named Julian, and his younger sister, Edith, whose most illustrious ancestor was said to be Juan Ponce de León.

Cabot in the Rain

Controversy rumbles like thunderclouds over the Glades when weathered historians, who have written much on bronze plaques that stand in public places, are asked by latter-day scholars to change their views. According to experts Samuel Eliot Morison and Aurelio Tio, there is no validity to the belief that John Cabot, sailing for Queen Elizabeth, ever came close to Florida or Key Biscayne. Quoting dates and places carefully, they say that the claim of Cabot's son, Sebastian, who wrote the account of the discovery of the Cape of the End of April, said by some to be Key Biscayne, is preposterous. Alas, John Cabot had already been lost at sea off Newfoundland, so that the only way he could have found it was posthumously. Sebastian, they say, was a loyal son who exaggerated his father's accomplishments.

When scholars meet like thunderclaps, someone's favorite hero takes a drenching. In this case, John Cabot is left out in the rain.

Here a Cape, There a Cape

Cape Florida was put on world maps early, but it did not always mark its present site. The *Cabo de Florida* was a mapmaker's dream and later a historian's nightmare. It was the place name of choice pinned, like a donkey's tail, by cartographers at the southernmost point of many a New World map dating from the fifteenth century. It marked the Yucatán, Cuba, Cape Sable, the vast Everglades, Key Largo, Miami, Miami Beach, and all the way up to Cape Canaveral. Collectors chasing this fast-moving cape on early maps also value the roving depictions of *Florida*, which at one time designated half of the North American continent, north to Virginia. For years the present states of Georgia, the Carolinas, Alabama, Louisiana, and Texas were shown as one property called Florida, and the Cape was its farthest point south.

Cabo de Florida was a familiar name and stop-off for John Hawkins in 1565, who reported the inhabitants were fierce and warlike; Francis Drake, sailing from the West Indies on his way to sack and burn St. Augustine, chronicled fires near the cape and along the coast. The Spanish plate ships took their northings before heading east for the Azores and Spain, and West Indian hurricanes dashed more

THREE

First Royal Land Grant

PEDRO'S ISLAND

Records on the island of Minorca were searched by the author in the 1980s to discover background of first Royal Grant holder of Key Biscayne, Pedro Fornells. The first recorded settler in South Florida shared this distinction with his wife, Mariana Tuduri, who also had childhood memories of the ancient town and countryside surrounding Ciudadela. (Harvey Blank)

Pedro Fornells (1760–1807) was the youngest child of Juan Fornells and his wife, Juana Quintana, who, prior to 1768, lived in the charming walled-in city of Ciudadela on the island of Minorca. On a clear day, they could make out the coast of Spain from their two-story stone house high above the little port, behind the grand cathedral, a block from the magnificent overview of the Mediterranean Sea. The English had taken over their much-occupied-and-reoccupied island. Foreign powers coveted its port, with its deep-water harbor and natural fortifications on rocky promontories, as the best in the Mediterranean.

But in the latest exchange, Minorcans found themselves in a frightful situation. Taxes rose; unemployment rose; religious freedoms were threatened. All this might have been tolerable had not a prolonged drought caused crops to fry like fritters in fields and make harvest celebrations no longer possible. If not for the fishermen and their continuing hauls, Minorca's famine would have devastated the islanders.

Pedro Fornells was eight years old when news of an expedition to the New World rippled across the island. Large families were invited to sign aboard for resettlement in a colony in Florida, south of St. Augustine. Juan and Juana Fornells met the requirements that were being hawked from house to house across the island by galloping horsemen who traveled the stone-walled roads and rock paths from *finca* to *finca*, farm to farm. They must have smiled down at young Pedro, the seventh child of their marriage, as they envisioned a land of flowers and opportunity.

The longest contracts were for ten years, and then the indentured would receive their choice of land, divided from a portion of the original tract. Grants were being generously issued by the British Land Board to certain lords, physicians, and other speculators who asserted their interest in protecting England's newest acquisition in the

Tracing Minorcan records revealed Pedro's roots. Archival materials at the University Seminary yielded pre-1768 business transactions. Cathedral records revealed dates of births, marriages, deaths and Pedro's roots to Gabriel Fornells, who arrived in the thirteenth century in Minorca from the Province of Catalonia, Spain. (Harvey Blank)

Americas. They claimed they would do their part by developing plantations that would benefit people on both sides of the Atlantic.

At the harbor in Mahon, expedition representatives convinced 365 families to sign aboard. The Minorcans, as well as some Italians and Greeks, volunteered to become indentured servants, and they believed they had made a wise decision. They took their families and belongings on board on April Fool's Day, 1768, in what would be the largest single movement of settlers to the New World during colonial times. A count of "1,403 men, women, and children embarked for His Majesty's province of East Florida" aboard eight vessels, according to eighteenth century documents held in the British Public Record Office.

The alleged savior of the Mediterranean people was a Scottish doctor, Andrew Turnbull, who opened his purse with dreams of being the indigo, silk, and cotton king of Florida and the Carolinas. But in his desperation to make a profit, his oppression grew, and eventually he would be deposed of his Florida colony.

Pedro survived the ocean crossing, but many passengers in the ill-starred ships were buried at sea. There were some 150 casualties by the time they reached the uncleared site of the plantation at New Smyrna, and within five months, another three hundred died. Dr. Turnbull explained the wilderness conditions by saying that to prepare the land, he had shipped five hundred slaves in a vessel that had sunk at sea, which perhaps was supposed to make the survivors from the Mediterranean count their blessings.

Sorrow, grieving, and lamentation were not openly permitted. Every immigrant was immediately put to work, including children such as Pedro and Mariana Tuduri, the young girl he would eventually marry. After more than seven years of hard labor, beatings, broken promises, and deprivations, Pedro, Mariana, and the others who survived—including the Catholic priests—organized a clandestine escape from the indigo plantation in the dead of night on what might be called a Freedom March from the New Smyrna colony to St. Augustine, slipping past their guards in silent flight. It was a fearful story, one which

Stephen Vincent Benét, whose ancestors were among this group, has fictionalized in his book *Spanish Bayonette*.

The Minorcans, after much legal activity, were given room outside the city gates of St. Augustine until the Spanish once again gained control of Florida and the English rulers left. Then the refugees were allowed to move into the old city, and they did.

After Pedro's own family was gone, he moved in with a cousin, as was often the custom. His cousin, Marcos Andreu, was married to Mariana (who already had been twice widowed). The two men ran a grog shop. Marcos kept a schooner at the harbor, and together they decided to sail south toward islands they had heard of since the early years when some members of the Turnbull colony rebelled and sailed down into the Florida Keys, only to be captured and returned.

When Marcos died several years later, Pedro and Mariana were married. Pedro was 33. Not long afterward, he applied for one of the Spanish grants available for petitioners in the year 1790. Most petitioners asked for tracts near St. Augustine. Pedro already held land inside the city walls, where he and Mariana would build a house, according to records in the St. Augustine Historical Society. But Pedro's horizons went far beyond the city streets.

Pedro Fornells, after reconnoitering the area, asked for all the lands around what is now Biscayne Bay, including Key Biscayne. But in July 1803, he mistook three persons he saw on the mainland opposite the key for legitimate settlers or planters. He changed his petition to the crown to request only the island of Key Biscayne in January 1804. He received the first Royal Spanish Grant in south Florida on January 18, 1805. By this act, 175 acres, "the only cultivatable land" on Key Biscayne, moved from the status of Miscellaneous Sovereign Land into the private sector.

The terms required that the petitioner settle the area in six months. Pedro did, sailing his beloved Mariana, two stepchildren, at least two friends and a sixteen-year-old black woman the 330 miles along the coastline to their new island. It is easy to imagine him stepping ashore and kneeling down upon the sand, for it had been thirty-seven years since they had sailed away from their first island home. Now they had a new one.

No Rolling Stones on Key Biscayne

Had Pedro Fornells's grant been for one of the keys to the south, one formed of Key Largo limestone or coral rock rather than sand, there might still exist some physical evidence of the first settlement. A lasting structure might have been noted by a nineteenth-century traveler— even if a twentieth-century bulldozer would have considered it rubble and leveled it without looking back.

Had rock been available, very likely the settlers would have built with it, because they came from a Mediterranean island where rocks are in every field, caves in every cliff, boulders on every hillside. Its harbors are bulwarked with natural granite. Early Minorcans built dry stone walls that have lasted over the centuries; prehistoric stone megaliths predate these walls by thousands of years. But Key Biscayne has neither hard bedrock nor loose rock. The best the Fornells family could have found was patches of fossilized roots attached to the floor of the shallow shore, which to this day precariously survive at the north end of the island. No rolling stones here.

Exploring the interior, they would find no prehistoric megaliths or monuments although there were mounds containing shells and bones, the kitchen middens of earlier Indian villages or seasonal camps, and there were burial mounds of the ancient Tequestas. Around them were telltale tools—conch shells with holes in the top—and pieces of pottery that may have been used for cooking and drinking vessels. Perhaps they recognized fishing lures and hooks carved from mammal bones or blades from shark and other fish teeth or parts and shells. They probably considered it remarkable that the earlier people had managed at all without stone and metal. It would have seemed impossible to restore their own cosmopolitan culture with so few material resources. They may well have quoted the words from Matthew in the Bible to one another to affirm their decision to return to St. Augustine: *[He] shall be likened unto a foolish man, which built his house upon the sand.*

After the six-months residence required by the land grant, Pedro and his family returned to St. Augustine. At least in St. Augustine there was coquina rock from Anastasia Island with which to build a lasting two-story house—that, indeed, still stands, a registered historic home (known as the Fornells House) on the corner of Spanish and Hypolita Streets.

Cape Florida's First Ranger

As the first recorded settler and his small band loaded their belongings aboard the schooner for the return to St. Augustine, they left behind household goods, along with farming, hunting, and fishing tools for one man, identified only as Vincent, who remained on the island. Vincent must have watched as they hauled up the anchor and hoisted sail, heading east a distance to catch the prevailing southeast breeze at the edge of the Gulf Stream, leaving him alone on shore as caretaker and custodian.

Pedro Fornells had been clever enough to secure this grant that no other Minorcan, Spaniard, or any other had thought to apply for. He had agreed to settle the land with his family and put it under cultivation. As island settlers, they would have constructed shelters and other structures for their community of seven, undoubtedly thatching with the handy palmettos and using local timber and driftwood. Now, for the lone Vincent, this must have seemed palatial, if primitive, premises for one.

On the best land, close to a freshwater source, staples such as corn

BRICK CHIMNEY

WOOD LOUVER VENT

CHIMNEY RECENT CO

COQUINA BLOCK WALL EXPOSED

THIS PORTION NOT MEASURED BECAUSE OF ITS RECENT ADDITION TO ORIGINAL HOUSE

EXPOSED COQUINA

CONSTRUCTION JOINT VISIBLE

3-0¼   2-2

NORTH SIDE WALL ELEVATION
SCALE ¼"=1'-0"

Restoration drawing of the Don Pedro Fornells House, built of native coquina rock at 22 Spanish Street, St. Augustine. (St. Augustine Historical Society)

and coffee were cultivated. The settlers had hunted game and collected bird eggs and, in season, sea turtle eggs. To supplement these, wild sea grapes, cocoplums, and berries were gathered on land, and oysters, mussels, and other seafood offshore.

The subtropical seas where the islanders had fished and waded barefoot all day in the shallows the length of the island were a sharp contrast to the sometimes icy-cold Mediterranean, where their parents and grandparents had made their livings, many as seafarers in the Balearic Islands. Shared memories of those islands' rocky coves and steep cliffs, many ringed with deep water, must have made low-lying Key Biscayne, with its mangrove-bordered sandy beaches, seem a strange but appealing alternative.

In one sense, by coming to the island, Pedro was regaining the Minorcan independence his forerunners had lost when they signed aboard Dr. Andrew Turnbull's ships and learned too late that the Scottish physician-turned-planter was not a man of his word. They had signed away their freedom, and for islanders there is nothing worse.

Was Vincent aware that the job of being custodian of Key Biscayne meant the responsibility of guarding against the intrusion of the Bahamians, second generation- Englishmen, or British Loyalists who had already made their hostility known? The experience at New Smyrna had taught the Minorcans a degree of distrust for the English that they could not easily overcome. Too many of their families and friends had suffered and died on the voyage to Turnbull's indigo fields where they labored endlessly and often felt the overseer's whip on their bare flesh. So, like Pedro and Mariana, Vincent put up his guard.

Would the Bahamians, some of whom thought they had prior squatters' rights, persist in camping on the mainland across Biscayne Bay in between their trading trips—if that is what they were—to New

Providence and elsewhere, and try to claim Fornells's Island? Vincent, who would have to fend off any intruders, remained the sole visible reminder of lawful Spanish presence as he safeguarded the earliest Spanish Land Grant in south Florida.

There is little in the records about this unsung hero of Cape Florida who kept watch over the island. Others would follow in his footsteps, but in the year 1805, the intrepid Vincent became Cape Florida's first ranger.

Pedro Fornells and his wife did not return to live on Key Biscayne. Pedro died at their home in St. Augustine in 1807, and the island passed to Mariana, who survived him by thirteen years.

Because of the early Minorcan role on Key Biscayne, south Florida is forever bound to Minorca, the island that now calls itself the Island Paradise of the Mediterranean. After the Pedro Fornells land claim, a number of events transpired before succeeding Balearic Islanders appeared on Cape Florida and across from the key, further impacting the currents of history on Key Biscayne Bay.

FOUR

Title Changes Hands

MARY ANN DAVIS ASSUMES TITLE

Soon after Florida became a territory of the United States in 1821 and the Spanish flag was run down the pole for the final time, a young, blue-eyed, black-haired woman (who had been born in the British Isles and brought by her parents to Charleston, South Carolina, as a small child) was persuaded by her husband, an American of enormous vitality, to move to Florida.

Mary Ann Channer Davis (1793–1885) and William Goodwin Davis (1776–1853) made a good team. He would hold many appointments in St. Augustine and become Deputy Marshall of the territorial region from the St. Johns River to Cape Florida. She had learned independence and mastered mercantile skills from her widowed mother, who ran a shop in Charleston. When it came to buying, selling, or attaching worth to goods and properties, she was no hindrance to her ambitious husband. Mary Ann Davis was a match for anyone.

They worked quietly, not revealing any conflicts of interest, as they collected real estate, mainly in her name only. They had many children, one of whom became governor of Texas, while another helped build Galveston's financial district known as the "Wall Street of the Southwest." They also built in south Florida the first grand estate on the island that once had belonged to Pedro Fornells.

Leading up to the purchase of Fornells's island, there was much courting, like some drawn-out prenuptial rites known only to the partners. In a remarkable coup, after doing some extraordinary sleuthing and networking among the Minorcan population of St. Augustine—where newcomers were not easily accepted—Mary Ann Davis received a deed that would later need confirmation and rarely be out of dispute or litigation for almost a century. She bought the Key Biscayne tract for $100. The seller was an heir of the Fornells family.

Rafael Andreu was one of the children of a previous marriage of Mariana Fornells; he had no sentimental desire to keep the distant island

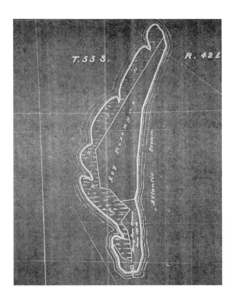

Map of Key Biscayne shows 175-acre Mary Ann Davis plat adjoining marshlands on west side of island. (National Archives)

and no need to prove himself able to fight the elements as had the older Minorcans who had been oppressed on Turnbull's plantation in New Smyrna. Perhaps he and his wife, Francesca Villalonga, wondered why the Davises wanted this unsettled island 330 miles down the coast on the open sea. He apparently did not ask. He and his brother each had inherited homes in the charming ancient city of St. Augustine; his older half-sister had married and moved to Cuba.

Actually, in earlier negotiations for a different grant, the Davises had dealings with the Villalonga family, purchasing some five hundred acres on the road near the old fort for the sum of $50. It appears that in the process of talking about available properties, the possibility of the island being available through the Villalonga connection surfaced. It seems the Davises had some inside information and were looking for the owners of the relatively unknown key.

Procuring tracts of land was difficult. Alexander Hamilton, Jr., the son of the first Secretary of the Treasury, was charged with straightening out lost papers and confusing deeds to clear American titles for former Spanish and British crown grants, a job at which he failed miserably. Yet, the Davises and hundreds of others placed their hope for the future in real estate. The Davis title was confirmed in 1824.

Adding to the Davises' interest was coastal conversation that naval officer David Porter and Washington officials were pushing to build three strategically placed lighthouses on the southern seaboard to safeguard shipping. Foreign pirates were diverting revenue across the Gulf Stream and the Florida Straits as they boarded ships—some wrecked on the reef, others in full sail—threatening the lives of passengers and appropriating goods to British-owned islands or to Cuba or beyond. If the coastal grapevine was right, pending appropriations included a lighthouse part way between Key West and St. Augustine. And so a couple of

Caroline Goodwin Davis (1817–1877) made this pencil drawing of the St. Augustine cottage where she grew up. Born in Charleston when her mother, Mary Ann, was 25 years old, Caroline never married. She moved with her family to Galveston, Texas, where she lived to be 60 years old. Few of her drawings have survived. (Blank Collection)

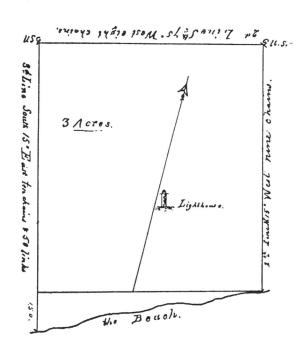

This Indenture, made the _Thirtieth_ day of _June_ in the year of our Lord one thousand eight hundred and twenty seven _Between_ _William G. Davis and Mary Ann Davis his wife, of the city of St. Augustine, in the Territory of Florida_, of the first part, and _the United States of America_ of the second part, Witnesseth, That the said part__ of the first part, for and in consideration of the sum of _Two hundred and twenty five dollars_ lawful money of the United States of America, to them in hand paid, at or before the ensealing and delivery of these presents, by the said party of the second part, the receipt whereof is hereby acknowledged, and the said party of the second part ~~heirs, executors, and administrators~~ for ever released and discharged from the same by these presents, have granted, bargained, sold, aliened, remised, released, enfeoffed, conveyed and confirmed, and by these presents do — grant, bargain, sell, alien, remise, release, enfeoff, convey and confirm unto the said party of the second part, and to their ~~heirs~~ and assigns for ever, All that certain tract or parcel of land, situate, lying and being on the island called _Key Biscayne_ near _Cape Florida_ in the Territory of Florida aforesaid, containing _three acres_, on which the _Light house_ of the United States has been built and now stands, which said three acres are bounded as follows: on the South by the beach and on North, East and West, by land belonging to the said parties of the first part ...

[survey plat labels:]
U.S.   2d Line S 4¾° West eight chains.   U.S.

3 Acres.

3d Line South 15° East ten chains & 50 links.   Lighthouse.   1st Line N 15° West nine chains.

the Beach.

I hereby certify, that at the request of John Rodman Esq. Collector of the District of St. Augustine, I have surveyed on the Island of Key Biscayne Three acres of land at the place where the Light house stands for the United States. the marks and boundaries as set forth in the above plot.
St. Augustine 25 april 1827.
signed J. N. Ives.

Warranty deed and $225 payment to Mary Ann and William G. Davis is issued June 13, 1827 after three-year bureaucratic delay during which time the United States "lighthouse has been built and now stands . . . on Key Biscayne." Survey and plat by Jeremiah Ives accompanies indenture, its accuracy would later be challenged. (National Archives)

Old prayer book of Mary Ann Davis, a member of Trinity Church, St. Augustine. (Larocca/Davis Collection)

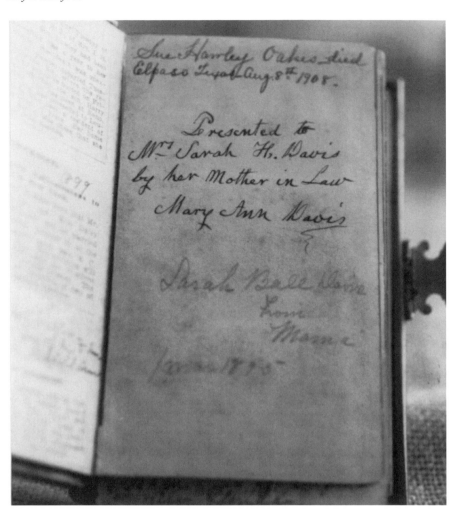

Mary Ann's daughter, and namesake, was one of six living children in 1846. (Gray/Davis Collection)

conspirators, wife and husband, made a quick decision. The outcome is history.

Mary Ann and William Davis offered three of the 175 acres on the strategic southern tip of Key Biscayne to the U.S. government for a military reservation. It took until 1827 (after the lighthouse was built) for them to collect their money, but, as discussed in handwritten letters in the National Archives and Davis documents, they were paid $225, a fine profit on their purchase price. The money was sent for safekeeping to their Charleston bank, after which Mary Ann encouraged her husband to plan for the day when they would be able to design a town and preside over a bustling port of entry on an island that would be nationally and internationally recognized as the site of the Cape Florida lighthouse.

It was a good plan, for the outer beaches all the way up to New River, at least twenty nautical miles north, offered no water passageway into the bay. However, as the Spaniards had known three hundred years earlier, channels at both ends of Key Biscayne allowed approach to the mainland, where there were springs, rivers, and pockets of rich soil being cultivated by families (their presence noted by Pedro Fornells in 1803) who for the past few years had been trying to confirm donation grants. The Davises knew about this because Marshal Waters Smith, for whom Davis worked (and after whom he named one of his sons), had made a trip to Key Biscayne in 1825. He sailed over to the mainland, marked on an 1823 map as "The Cape Florida Settlement," to confer with squatters who wanted him to represent them in court concerning their rights to ownership of land on the opposite side of the long lagoon called Key Biscayne Bay. Indeed, the location of Mary Ann's island was a good one; it was at the crossroads of history.

First Keeper of the Light

JOHN DUBOSE

Jeffroie DuBois, a Norman knight, accompanied William the Conqueror (Duke of Normandy) into England in 1066.
—TRANSACTIONS OF THE HUGUENOT SOCIETY OF SOUTH CAROLINA

When word came from Washington that the president of the United States had appointed "a man from the Territory" to be the first keeper of the Cape Florida lighthouse, the owners of all the land deemed habitable on Key Biscayne celebrated; the Davises believed they would have a personal friend, John Dubose (1779–1845), watching out for their island interests while they continued to live in St. Augustine. St. Augustine's front runner for the lighthouse post, however, had mixed feelings. Dubose had wanted an appointment as captain of a revenue cutter to enforce "energetick measures," as he called them, to rid the southern coast and keys of wreckers and pirates. As the District Inspector of Customs, he had sailed the area and proposed means of controlling international plundering of U.S. shipping by Bahamian, Spanish and Cuban pirates. (He reported seeing "120 sail of Vessels" manned by wreckers positioned on the edge of the treacherous reef about seventy miles south of Cape Florida.)

Among those who recommended him was the territorial representative Richard Keith Call (sometime Florida delegate to the U.S. Congress, later territorial governor). Also, Waters Smith, the first mayor of St. Augustine and marshal of the district from the St. Johns River to Cape Florida, spoke highly of him as "a Gentleman of intelligence with abilities fitting him for a more elevated situation." John Dubose was fortunate he was not declared overqualified. His official appointment is listed as May 7, 1825; the event meant that the former naval captain was moving ashore.

When John, his wife, Margaret, and five children moved with all their goods, they became the first American family to take up permanent residence on the key. They were accompanied by two former slaves of Margaret's brother, who (after the brief stay of the sixteen-year-old who came with the Fornells) were the first recorded blacks to live on Key Biscayne. The family Bible, which Dubose descendants (who spell their name DuBose) have carefully kept, shows the keeper's notations, including: "Sailed from St. Augustine, Wednesday 7th of December, 1825, and landed at Cape Florida on Monday 13th December 1825."

Margaret was John's cousin and also a part of the lineage that traced its ancestry from Isaac the Immigrant to the New World in the 1660s. Now, as they stepped on the beach of Key Biscayne, it was a coming home that Margaret particularly had longed for, because John had spent much of his life at sea, including chasing Barbary pirates in the Mediterranean aboard the *U.S. Constellation* (which had spent time in Mahon in the same deep-water port from which the Minorcan royal grant holders had departed years earlier). It was time John was coming ashore, for he was now forty-six years of age, and had agreed to leave behind the plantation life of their parents in Carolina to share coastal frontier life in an altogether different environment. On an unsettled subtropical island far removed from the class society of the colonial South, they were free to teach their children to follow the ocean tides, not the tides of prejudice. Gentle freedom was in the wind. There was not only a welcoming party of long-legged birds of the mangroves and beaches ringing the islands, but a brand new two-story brick house beside the sixty-five-foot-tall light tower. On December 17, 1825, four days after his arrival, John Dubose illuminated the Cape Florida light. Its glow pierced the primal darkness. Now there was a night to celebrate! What is little known, however, is that the bureaucracy chastised Dubose for the action and darkened the light. He had failed to notify proper authorities that he was ready to light up the island—first it had to be advertised! Yet early lighting was requested by construction agent Noah Humphries to assure curing of white lead glazing in the lantern.

Margaret and John parented three more children, including the island's first recorded native son and daughter. David Dubose was born in the keeper's cottage on February 19, 1826, and Jane on the night of February 27, 1829. Their little sister was born "near the Miami River," as recorded in the family Bible. Older siblings had been born at Charleston and St. Augustine. During the period they lived in this natural wilderness, their mother and father were their schoolteachers. The cottage had its own library during their tenure (descendants still own some of the books), but nature taught them much more. Key Biscayne had magnificent lessons with rookeries and wading birds everywhere, all manner of fishes and mammals of the sea, turtles seasonally leaving their eggs, and tides bringing them gifts from other continents and shores. John James Audubon came by and drew birds off Cape Florida. Dr. Benjamin Strobel, a friend of the ornithologist who knew him during his stay in Key West, sailed to the Cape where the Duboses entertained him for dinner.

During this time also, botanist, physician, and diplomat Henry Perrine sent from Mexico tropical plants, saplings, and seeds—more than one hundred at one time, including coconuts, to the care of the Duboses, who planted them on the island. Dr. Perrine is the one who introduced pure quinine as a cure for malaria. If circumstances had been different, he probably would have lived on Key Biscayne, which he seems to have favored early on. He was so impressed with the island's climate that in 1833 in a national publication he proposed that Key Biscayne be developed as a health resort, but it didn't happen.

Between Perrine's proposal and the next formal attempt at development of the island in 1839, several dramatic events occurred in south Florida. In 1835, a major hurricane swept the island, damaging the lighthouse foundation, the tower, and the keeper's cottage, and leaving three feet of water that destroyed trees and other vegetation. Later, on his last visit to Cape Florida, John Dubose wrote, "As an experiment, I planted the paper mulberry and [manila mulberry] *Morus multicaulis* at the light-house. The former grew finely, became of some size, and, in the hurricane of 1835, the sea overflowed it to the depth of three feet, and killed it." But the multicaulis made a comeback, as storm-ravaged trees often do, and it bore fruit several months later. "I saw it and three more small trees of the same kind, on my late visit to Cape Florida light, on 16th August, 1837."

The 1835 hurricane's powerful surge, followed by another in 1838, also tore into land farther north, boring through the long strip of barrier coast above Bear Cut that subsequently would form Narrows Cut and a sister island to Key Biscayne. This new island would later be known as Virginia Key.

"This lighthouse is located different from any other on the coastline in the interior of the island 1/4 of a mile from the beach in the midst of scrubs and palmettoes, without any tree to shade the house ... Wreckers generally pass by on their way for supply of water [but] ... sometimes for weeks I do not see a soul on the island," wrote John Dubose in 1826, one year after his appointment.

During his decade of service on Key Biscayne, whether up in the eagle's nest or down on the ground of the compound, Dubose took his job seriously. He was committed to fulfilling the role of the government lighthouse keeper, warning vessels of approaching dangers and assuming other responsibilities of early nineteenth-century coastal management. Because of the isolation of this post, he was fortunate to have healthy growing children, some of them old enough to assist in the fishing, hunting, and gardening necessary for provisioning his family. They also helped maintain the well some three hundred feet northeast of the house on the beach. Early on, the water supply had to be monitored; later Dubose worried about procuring the $300 needed for a cistern alongside the house, "indispensable for the comfort in dry weather." During their early years there, he was concerned, as others were in those days, that the two swampy ponds that were also close to the house were sending off unhealthy vapors, but, fortunately, this was not the case.

From the very beginning, when he had illuminated the new lighthouse without first alerting Washington through channels in Key West, this lighthouse keeper, who had served as a captain in the U.S. Navy and was used to giving orders and having them smartly carried out, was often in a jam. He earned a reputation of being Puckish, the bad boy of the Lighthouse Service. Of course, it may not have helped that he also had applied for the position in thriving Key West which was filled by his long-time antagonist, William Pinkney.

Until Pinkney's death in 1832, the Key West Collector of Customs was inclined to give Dubose short shrift and make life difficult on Cape Florida. The reputed diplomacy and patience of Stephen Pleasonton, who was in charge of lighthouses and juggled requests, complaints, and reports from his far-flung keepers along the East Coast all the way around the Gulf of Mexico, did not solve the problem. No one satisfactorily monitored the monthly slow-down or oversights of revenue cutters ferrying food, supplies, mail, other requests, and inspectors from Key West to Cape Florida. The timely arrival of the cutters was crucial to tolerable—much less comfortable—island living, especially for a family that had no neighbors—or convenience shops—in the vicinity.

Island living mandated a boat. None came with the job. How could a keeper without a boat be expected to engage in protective or rescue activities, salvage, fishing, or patrols? The day after he lighted the tower, Dubose requested his first vessel "to be used on this desolate island."

As his request was kept on hold, Dubose wrote Pleasonton directly, "the situation of this light is far different from that of any other on the American coast. There is no one so far removed from a settlers part of the country and where a Keeper has to send so far for his supplies . . . cut off from all civilized society."

After months of waiting, he was given a boat, but rarely were his requests honored at the asking. He learned to pinch-hit, jerry-rig, and improvise on this station at the top of the reef. His observations of the original contractor's shoddy workmanship on the lighthouse and keeper's house were ignored, and he seems not to have even excited a response when he wrote, "this lighthouse appears to be gradually settling and inclining to the East owing, I suppose, to want of sufficient care in fixing the foundations." It wasn't until later in the century that the contractor's corner-cutting became too obvious to ignore. During a tower rebuilding, the walls were found not to be five feet thick at the base, as specified, but hollow. John and Margaret Dubose could have attested much sooner to dirt floors in the keeper's cottage, an unwhite-washed tower, no spare glass for broken panes in the lantern room, and other oversights. Dubose was constantly repairing the structures, while the customs office in Key West played lighthouse turf wars.

It was not easy. Margaret had given up a new inheritance to come with her husband, letting go of eleven hundred acres of plantation land in Salem County, a divided share of her parents' estate and long owned by the Duboses of South Carolina (her side of the family). In the old South where cotton was king, John and Margaret had left their past. It seemed ironic, then, when John Dubose was reprimanded for failing to turn in a soggy bale of cotton that showed up on the beach, instead exchanging it for a much more critical family need—a sack of coffee beans—from a passing captain. Scandalous! In 1827, William Pinkney wrote an incriminating report of the incident. How quickly the news flew that Dubose had not turned in the bale for salvage, which was his duty. He was accused of defrauding the government. It was recommended that he be removed from his job. He appealed the dismissal. He won, but was soundly censured.

John Dubose was seldom praised for his good works. Besides safeguarding the island and constantly improving the grounds, he and his sons built a portico and a second boat, added a loft for the additional children, and kept the light in excellent shape in spite of few supplies. He also entertained and assisted passersby, and Margaret was a charming hostess and helpmate. Moreover, they assisted in some of the earliest plant introductions, setting out seeds or saplings sent to them by Perrine. They also built the first home on the Hunting Grounds, on the mainland (later determined to be Cutler), a twelve-mile sail southwest from Cape Florida.

Happy Birthday, Mr. Audubon!

Off Cape Florida, John James Audubon (1785–1851), naturalist and artist, caught his first look at the lighthouse on April 24, 1832, five days after taking passage from Charleston. Although he may not have set foot on the island, he lists sighting at least a half-dozen species of birds off Cape Florida that spring.

At Indian Key the following day, Audubon was joined by James Egan, who presented him with three specimens of young birds (one alive, two dead) that he could not identify. They headed off in a "beautiful bark," well fitted out but with minimal camping supplies. Audubon, however, carried a journal, sketchbook, pencils, and great expectations. They rowed across Florida Bay some twenty miles into a vast wilderness of water where no major ships could hope to sail. The destination was Sandy Key, a sanctuary created not by law but by location. To this day it remains a place where human intrusion is difficult, and is now protected as part of Everglades National Park.

Audubon and Egan left the anchored boat bobbing in the water and waded ashore to sleep on the sand after a long day's travel. At daybreak, Audubon awoke to a remarkable scene. The barge and crew were marooned on the flats, and before his eyes were thousands of wading birds of the most miraculous colors and physical features. They stepped agilely across the exposed and glistening mud flats as if they were walking on wildflowers sprung up after a rain. With his keen vision, Audubon followed the stilt-legged and other flocks of moving, regrouping birds who stalked their breakfast, sticking their variety of bills sub-surface to pick up hidden or exposed morsels burrowing or wiggling on the flats or in mudholes. A magnificent show! Scarlet and wood ibises hunted apart from the blue herons; white egrets and roseate terns moved at their own paces.

One group, grand and powerful, remained aloof and stood unmoving, waiting for food to come to them. Their patience was fulfilled without a step, so quick were their senses. Audubon had never heard

Audubon's shearwater, dusky petrel (*Puffinus lherminieri*). "While on board the United States' Revenue Cutter the *Marion*, and in the waters of the Gulf Stream opposite Cape Florida," Audubon wrote, "I saw a Flock of these birds, which, on sailing among them, would scarcely swim off from our bows, they being apparently gorged with food." The ship was running at about ten knots. (John James Audubon)

these incredible birds described, nor ever imagined anything like them, "their pure white plumage like beings of another world." This was the Great White Heron, which he wrote "rarely go[es] as far eastward as Cape Florida." He described it in detail as a new species *Ardea occidentalis* but it became controversial as a morphological variant, perhaps an albino, of the Great Blue (*Ardea herodias*).

Great White Heron (*Ardea occidentalis*). (John James Audubon)

When Audubon went abroad to work with his engraver and printer, he would present specimens of this unknown Florida beauty to the museum in Charleston, to the Academy of Natural Sciences in Philadelphia, and a pair of skins to His Royal Highness, the Duke of Sussex, who in turn gave them to the British Museum. The Zoological Society of London was also a recipient of one of these prizes.

Perhaps one reason the discovery of the Great White Heron loomed large in the ornithologist's eyes is that he may have wondered whether he would have a gift when he celebrated his birthday in the wilds of Florida. Although some controversy also exists about the date of Audubon's birth, biographer Kathryn Hall Proby, established in her book *Audubon in Florida,* that he was the "son of a prosperous, roving French sea captain named Jean Audubon and a French servant girl named Jeanne Rabine . . . and born on his father's plantation in Aux Cays, Santo Domingo, on April 26, 1785."

Using this date, the man who was destined to become world acclaimed first saw Key Biscayne from shipboard two days before his birthday, set off from Indian Key the following day, spending the night on the beach, and awakened to behold a most remarkable bird: apparently a new species for the books, surely a gift beyond all expectations. Amid all his findings, this one would be among his favorites. Call it frosting on the cake: Happy Birthday, Mr. Audubon.

Eggers and Sea Gull Pie

During his Florida cruise, Audubon met and wrote about a colorful group of wreckers. A few years later, one of the lighthouse keeper's sons, Johnny Dutorque Dubose, in 1837, attempting to earn his living in the Dry Tortugas, joined the wreckers. It was an experience "very much against his inclination," wrote Margaret Dubose about Johnny. "He does not like a wrecker's life. . . . His greatest complaint is idleness. He says five or six vessels lie at anchor constantly without the least thing on earth to do. He goes on a small island, in a morning catches near a hundred gulls with his hand to make a pie for dinner, and picks up five or six hundred eggs for the day and then all the work is over." So much for the idleness of wreckers, the urgency of eggers, and the culinary horror of sea gull pie.

Between preying on ships, most wreckers were not only migrant eggers but hunters and herdsmen of sea mammals and reptiles as well. Men from the Keys and Gulf of Mexico, and others from New Providence and Cuba, also made a good living from nature's larder. Besides stocking up on provisions with a surfeit of bird and turtle eggs, they collected the meat of these animals and that of larger prey such as manatees, including the plump and playful West Indian seals of Florida which ultimately were butchered to extinction. The sooty coots on Cape Sable were another case of destruction of a species as recorded by historian Charlton W. Tebeau, who noted that, in one instance, eggers collected a reported eight tons of coot eggs which they sailed to Havana to sell for seventy-five cents a gallon.

Migrating Birds

Not all birds use south Florida as rookeries. Some did not stop to lay eggs but flew right on by, seasonally migrating from north to south and back again along their traditional flyway. Others stopped to take advantage of the mild winters, flying north again in spring. Did the native people of Florida wonder where the birds disappeared to when they left in the spring? William Bartram, a botanist traveling the peninsula in the late eighteenth century, observed that "the ancients . . . seem to have been very ignorant or erroneous in their conjectures concerning what became of birds. . . . In the southern and temperate climates some imagined they went to the moon"—leaving behind their tell-tail feathers.

Feathers

Seminole fan made of turkey feathers had many uses. This was a fire fan. (Smithsonian Institution)

Feathers have long played a role in magic and medicine; they have been used decoratively and in fashions, used as probes and as pens. In fact, bird poachers—catering to high fashion—once threatened to wipe out the majestic snowy egret before it was protected by law.

Perhaps the best use of feathers was the feather fan used widely by the Seminoles. "The feathers of the wings and tail of the Roseate Spoonbill are manufactured into fans by the Indians and Negroes of Florida," wrote John James Audubon. This provided them with an environmentally harmless cooling system without the need for fluorocarbons used in the later invention of air conditioning.

Wild turkey tail feathers were chosen by earliest Floridians for ceremonial occasions. Jacques Le Moyne, artist with the Huguenot colony in Florida in the sixteenth century, drew and described a marriage ceremony in which on each side of the bride "walk two men waving elegant fans, attached on long handles, to protect her from the ardors of the sun."

The Great American Cock

The wild turkey, or as Audubon called it, the Great American Cock, found in temperate and subtropical zones, was plentiful in the Everglades. South of the Dubose mainland property, and opposite Elliott

Key, the U.S. Coast Surveyors in 1850 recorded a wild place they called Turkey Point (now the site of a nuclear power and light station). Few see or hear wild turkeys today, but had Benjamin Franklin been given his way, the bird might have been a protected species like our national emblem, the bald eagle. He wrote in a letter to his daughter, Sally Bache (who was A. D. Bache's grandmother):

> I wish the Bald Eagle had not been chosen as the Representative of our Country; he is a Bird of bad moral Character; like those among Men who live by Sharping and Robbing, he is generally poor, and often very lousy.
>
> The Turkey is a much more respectable Bird, and withal a true original Native of America.   —*January 26, 1784*

Florida wild turkey was handy game for native people and settlers. When the Duboses were lightkeepers and kept a mainland homestead, they hunted and farmed. There was an early tradition of preparing turkey, venison, squash, sweet potatoes, and pumpkins from the Everglades for a Thanksgiving Day feast at Cape Florida. Thanksgiving was first celebrated in America as recorded in 1564 by René de Laudonnière on the St. Johns River near Jacksonville, by French Huguenots, forerunners of the Duboses, joined by the Timucua Indians in Florida, fifty years before the pilgrims landed at Plymouth Rock.

The pilgrims did not add hearts of cabbage palm (described in 1841 by Dr. Samuel Forry as "bearing the taste of ripe chestnuts"), tangy sea-turtle steak, or ibis to their celebration, foods that were plentiful and popular in south Florida. A reported delicacy of lighthouse keepers' tables in the 1800s included eggs and meat of the *Phoenicopteridus ruber*, fresh from the wild flamingo rookery at Cape Florida.

Sea Turtles

In turtle season on Key Biscayne, the Duboses used their sloop as a nursery for sea-turtle hatchlings. Enormous full-grown turtles were caught on and off coastal beaches. James Dubose, son of the lighthouse keeper John, wrote of catching 210 turtles in five days "worth but 4 cents a pound."

In his *Natural History of Florida and the Carolinas*, published in 1754, American naturalist and artist Mark Catesby wrote, "of the different Kinds of Sea-Tortoise, with their Properties in general":

> The Sea-Tortoise is by our Sailors vulgarly called Turtle, whereof there are four distinct kinds: The green Turtle, the Hawks-bill, the Loggerhead Turtle and the Trunk Turtle. They are all eatable, but the green Turtle is that which all the maritime Inhabitants in America, that live between the Tropicks, subsist much upon. They much excell the other kinds of Turtle, and are in great Esteem for the wholesome and agreable Food they afford.
>
> All Sorts of Turtle except the Loggerhead Turtle are timerous and make little Resistance when taken, but in Time of Coition all the kinds

Turtles are ... to be had in plenty; those we took were of three kinds: the loggerhead, hawkbill and green; the two last are much the best.

—Andrew Ellicott, 1799

are very furious and regardless of Danger: The male Copulates by the help of two Horns or Claws under his fore-Fins, by which he holds and clings to the fleshy Part of the Neck of the Female: They usually continue in Copulation above 14 Days: They have four Legs, which are of much greater Use to them as Fins to swim with, than as Legs to walk with, which they do awkwardly and with slow Pace. They never go on Shoar but to lay their Eggs, which is in April; they then crawl up from the Sea above the flowing of high Water, and dig a Hole above two Feet deep in the Sand, into which they drop in one Night above an hundred Eggs, at which Time they are so intent on Natures Work that they regard none that approach them, but will drop their Eggs into a Hat if held under them, but if they are disturbed before they begin to lay, they will forsake the Place and seek another. They lay their Eggs at three and sometimes at four different Times, there being fourteen Days between every Time, so that they hatch and creep from their Holes into the Sea at different Times also: When they have laid their Complement of Eggs they fill the Hole with Sand, and leave them to be hatched by the heat of the Sun, which is usually performed in about three Weeks.

Dr. Strobel's Key Biscayne Operation

The sand was not the sole province of the turtles. Wind, waves, currents, and tide moved it around, sometimes taking it away, sometimes returning it to the beaches. Then came Dr. Strobel.

Key Biscayne has been a target for sandnappers since the late 1820s and early 1830s when a territorial physician of questionable reputation agreed to diagnose the condition of the sand of the south Florida Keys and coasts. With a chart in hand, Dr. Benjamin Strobel sailed from Key West with the presumptuous idea of finding the best beach extant to transport sand to Key West to use for building material. Of course, he arrived in the guise of Good Samaritan, for he and his captain and crew represented a good cause: The sand would be used in building a badly needed hospital in Key West.

How his eyes must have glinted when he saw the "fine white hard sand beach" of Key Biscayne; he had found the perfect specimen. He wrote his finding and report and, without wasting a single day, saw to it that his team began the operation. And so humans began rather early to tamper with the island's natural resources. Assault on its wildlife was less successful.

Here is Strobel's account of his visit:

[Key Biscayne] is covered with fine white sand. . . . About the middle of the Island I saw a swamp containing the saw Palmetto. The Northern and Eastern part of it is covered with Mangrove, whilst on the Southern side, a fine white hard sand beach extends from the light house . . . to Bear Cut. The beaches of the Keys generally consist of finely pulverized shell, differing in this respect from that of Key Biscayne. Having concluded that this would be a suitable place for procuring the sand which we wanted, the depth of the water back of the light, and the boldness of the shore, being such as to enable our vessel to land alongside, I ordered her to take in a cargo.

Before leaving the island with his stolen sand, Benjamin Strobel took an unscheduled moonlight walk on the beach, but it was not for romantic reasons.

> Of all the places in the world for mosquitoes, Key Biscayne is entitled to the preference, saying nothing of the sand flies. Their everlasting hum never ceases. Morning, noon and night the ear is assailed with their baleful noise. Mr. DuBose, the keeper of the light, had provided himself with a flapper, for which he found employment night and day.
>
> [At] the light house, I accepted the polite invitation of Mr. DuBose to sup with him. The table was placed in the piazza. We were surrounded with smoke pans, and enveloped in smoke, but still found it necessary to keep our hands and feet in active motion to avoid the assaults of the enemy. After supper I went on board of our sloop—our beds were brought on deck, and our mosquito nets spread. . . . But, alas, it was fruitless labor. The enemy stormed and assailed us in every direction. One of the sailors swore that they had divided into two gangs, and that one hoisted the net, whilst the other got under and fed. . . . After tossing and tumbling, slapping, scratching and grumbling, for about three hours, I gave up all prospect of sleeping, and proposed to the Captain that we should get up and take a walk on the beach, which lay to the windward. . . . He assented—we crossed the Island, and walked some four or five miles on the beach by moonlight. The breeze from the water was delightful and refreshing, and we enjoyed it until near daylight, when we returned on board, to make another effort to sleep, but we positively could not close our eyes, until we covered ourselves over head and ears, with cloaks and blankets. Of the two evils we were compelled to choose the least, and took the steam in preference to the mosquitoes.

So much for Dr. Strobel's R_x.

Key Biscayne Health Resort

The first major proposal for Key Biscayne to become an island resort was made in 1833 by Dr. Henry Perrine, physician and botanist, while John Dubose was the keeper of the light. Dr. Perrine wrote in a national journal:

> We have testimony of the healthiness (climate) of Cape Florida in its most unequivocal form. The family of J. Dubose, consisting of eleven whites, and several negroes, has not had a case of sickness during the last seven years. The tenderest and most productive vegetables of the tropics are flourishing under his care. . . . The harbor at the cape . . . is easily accessible and a voyage to and from the northern states can be made easily. . . . *Humanity requires that Key Biscayne should be made an available resort as soon as possible. . . . At Cape Florida, an association might be readily formed with a capital of a hundred thousand dollars*

[author's italics], which would furnish the buildings, gardens, and other conveniences requisite for the most squeamish visitor, and keep a packet running every month with passengers and effects to and from the north. The most luxurious accommodations could be profitably afforded at half the price paid in Havana.

And so the first syndicate was proposed to turn the key into an island resort. The first, but not the last. Why didn't it happen? Because the land was already owned by the Davises, which Perrine hadn't bothered to find out. The Seminole War was in effect, and a storm put the island under three feet of water, so that saplings Perrine had introduced were flooded out.

Perrine, while ambassador to Campeche, seized the opportunity to begin the first tropical plant introductions into the United States. An earlier proposal for Cape Florida by Peter S. Chazotte and a Philadelphia syndicate had never developed. Perrine sent more than a hundred boxes of tropical plants to John Dubose to plant on the island. Among them were sisal so that the United States would be able to grow its own hemp for ropes, also mulberry for silk production, coconut for food and oil, and all sorts of species of plants that would one day change forever American and global agriculture, industry, trade, and commerce. Perrine ended up with a grant of land from the United States on the mainland, but the station he envisioned was not to be realized during his lifetime. As Perrine himself said in the Congressional Record, before he was murdered, "The weather and the Indians contrived against me."

SIX

Warriors Converge

LIGHTHOUSE ATTACK

The Seminoles were being moved down the peninsula toward the area then known as Key Biscayne Bay and the Cape Florida Settlement, which included the mainland.

For ten years the U.S. presence at the Cape Florida lighthouse had stood unthreatened until the military began pressing the Indians from the northern and central part of the Floridas south into the swampy Everglades. The Second Seminole War was erupting and it would impact the entire territory.

The whites were trying to exterminate the people they had pushed inland and down the peninsula, including cinnamon-skinned people joined sometimes by blacks who had escaped slavery by whites, and joined also by remnants of northern nations, among them Creeks, including Red Sticks, who were being shipped West, away from the coast.

When the Seminoles could no longer tolerate the broken promises and hostility, the pummeling of their people; when they could not make the white man understand they would not leave their native soil or be forced into irons; when they saw their brothers dying of abuse or grief, their families made captive, their leaders imprisoned and killed, even the most reasonable of them no longer could say "peace."

In January 1836 the bloody massacre of the William Cooley family, settlers, and coontie-starch manufacturers, occurred on the New River, close to present-day Fort Lauderdale. When word of the tragedy reached those living along the Miami River, they decided to evacuate the mainland for Key Biscayne (a decided switch from modern-day residents, who leave the island for the mainland in times of crisis). They agreed with lighthouse keeper Dubose that the island was not the safest haven. They shipped out to Key West where many took refuge for a good length of time. Lucky they did, for Washington officials did not heed the keeper's continuing warning that the key was threatened.

From the Everglades and from the ridge, the Indians could see the lighthouse clearly, for vegetation was low and there were no obstacles to viewing. It must have seemed a disturbing silhouette against the sky by day; by night its light was unlike any star of the universe. It is likely

The situation of the inhabitants east of the St. John's and south of St. Augustine, is truly deplorable. New Smyrna has been burnt and all the fine plantations in that neighborhood are broken up. Many of the negroes have been carried off, or have joined the savages. The Indians are dispersed in small parties, and when pursued they take refuge in the thickets ... and fight with desperation, until they are dead, no matter by what numbers of troops they are assailed.

—NILES' WEEKLY REGISTER,
FEBRUARY 6, 1836

This is the last and the most desperate struggle of the Indian. He fights now gloriously and gallantly, with the spirit of a thousand lions in his breast—for the soil on which he was born, and which was his just inheritance from his ancestors.—We, by a forced and corrupt treaty, call it ours. We send armed men—men armed with the whisky-bottle, a weapon more terrible than the rifle.... Preparations are making— not for the defeat of the Seminoles, but for their extermination. Every Indian and every negro suspected of having been allied to the Indians will be slaughtered in less than two months from this time.

—NILES' WEEKLY REGISTER,
FEBRUARY 6, 1836

that they came to loathe its unnatural incandescence, destroying the canopy of darkness, intruding into nature's spaces, and seeming to spy into their retreat.

In distant Calusa legend, the island had been their island; now this symbol of the white man rose to mock them. Not only this, but also, they believed, to monitor them. The eye in the sky. The white man had seized their coastline and built upon it this tower that sent an ominous eye into the favorite path of the rising moon by night, and stared from its single orb by day, full circle round into the very heart of the wet prairies and their "hummucks," islets that became the refuge for war chiefs like Chekika.

It is probable that from camps in the Everglades, the lighthouse was the prime target of the Indians, but they had lookouts and learned from strategists like Arpeika (still camped in central Florida) that they must strike only when the coast was most vulnerable.

Lighthouse Attack: July 23, 1836

Although one other lighthouse was entered, it was the only time in history that a U.S. lighthouse was attacked by North American Indians.

Alexander J. Dallas had sailed his fleet away from south Florida waters without realizing that "a most perilous situation" was about to take place on the beach of Key Biscayne. By the time word reached him a month later that the Indians had attacked, the Commander of the Florida Squadron was far distant from Cape Florida, his ships at anchor in Pensacola Bay.

The U.S. government never admitted it, but the attack on the lighthouse took all the president's men by surprise. No one has challenged their laxity, but they did not take responsibility for the surprise attack. For months they had turned a deaf ear on warnings sent to them by John Dubose, a veteran keeper, and others who called for protection, for it had become apparent to south Floridians that as the Indians were pushed down the peninsula, their anger and resentment, like their numbers, increased.

Washington officials seemed indifferent, and annoyed. In fact, they were egged on a bit by a few customs officials in Key West, who believed wrongly that the lighthouse keeper was exaggerating the dangers, running scared, and shirking his duty. Later they tried to place the blame on him, saying he had fled the scene.

There were neither guards on shore nor ships on patrol off Cape Florida when the Indians attacked, and the warriors knew it. Nor was John Dubose there, for he had been on duty for many anxious months, sometimes with guards, sometimes not, depending on the mood and politics in play at Key West and Washington. Five days before the attack, given a brief leave, he sailed for Key West, where his family, already in the southernmost city of the United States, was planning a celebration on his fifty-seventh birthday. It became a date forever blemished on his calendar. One wonders if an Indian scout had seen him raise his sails

for the cruise south and decided that the right moment had come to strike the island. In any event, the July 23, 1836, tragedy would always haunt John Dubose, and his birthday was filled with sorrow from that year forward.

Dubose had entrusted the light to John W. Thompson and his assistant, Aaron Carter. They were all alone when, around 4:00 in the afternoon, forty to fifty warriors burst upon the compound, whooping and hollering. The two men raced for the tower in a blaze of rifle balls, some going through Thompson's clothing before he and Carter could slam the door.

The keeper fired shots from a light-tower window as the enemy tried to break in the latched door. He saw others at the dwelling house and fired at them. The Indians took aim at the lighthouse window. Thompson boarded the lower window and kept the warriors out, while they poured in heavy fire at all the windows and lanterns.

Indian scouts circled the lighthouse. They checked the house and grounds and searched the horizon for ships. There were only the two men on the premises.

The Indians kept up the attack all night. The keeper's cottage and the out buildings were burned, the tower door was set afire, and flames ringed the circular tower. Inside the tower, stored tins of oil became perforated and ignited. The keeper cursed, but thanked his stars that he had sawed away the stairs. He and Carter had managed to carry with them a keg of powder furnished to the keeper for defense. With smoke and sparks rising from below, they had to leave the unbearable heat of the lantern room and crawl onto the platform that circled the outside of the tower. Thompson was hit; a keen marksman had fired three rifle

Lighthouse attack, July 23, 1836, was a dramatic event of Second Seminole War in which the temporory white keeper was severely injured and his black assistant lost his life defending the United States lightstation at Cape Florida. (Oil painting by Kenneth Hughs. Historical Association of South Florida) balls through one of Thompson's feet, and wounded his other ankle. The next rifle ball killed Carter.

Thompson reported, "The lamps and glasses bursting and flying all directions . . . and flesh roasting." He managed to get hold of the keg of gunpowder, probably to destroy himself and the building together, and threw it roaring to the bottom of the inferno. The explosion resounded far out to sea.

The first report out of Key West to Washington says that "the US Transport Scho[oner] *Motto* was within sight of the burning buildings, but on account of light and adverse [conditions] could not approach nearer than seven miles of the scene that night. The next morning, the wind being still unfavorable, two boats were manned from the *Motto* & proceeded to the Cape. On their way they recovered a Sloop boat, which the Indians had taken & in which they had deposited their plunder." Their plunder was from looting the keeper's cottage, where the Duboses had lived for so many years. Fortunately, they had already removed to Key West some of their prized personal belongings, including their Bible, paintings, documents, and books.

Believing they were unseen, the Indians disappeared, pushing their canoes silently into the bay, some making along the beach, going in silence as they had come. Undoubtedly, they paddled along the western side of the island, threading through the mangrove shoreline until they found refuge in the same place where they had hidden prior to the attack, on the north end of the island. There a channel ran deep into a mangrove pocket where no one would follow them. They had triumphed and they would return to take possession of the island.

Thompson had survived although he had lost consciousness. From the top of the platform, he awoke in time to watch the attackers leave. Then, in great anguish, he waited for the rescue operations to begin.

The first day the rescue attempt failed. The exhausted, nearly suicidal Thompson was about fifty-five feet above the ground on the platform with no stairs and no ladder. The rescuers tried to shoot up a line on a kite to Thompson "in his elevated situation that day," but fell short of saving the wounded man, who was suffering from burns, exposure, and shock. Finally, as one story later told by John Duke (son of the next lighthouse keeper, and whose sister married one of the Dubose sons) relates: "a line was fastened on the ramrod of a musket and fired over the tower which Thompson got hold of and hauled up a block and . . . a sailor man was hoisted up, made Thompson fast and lowered him down."

When they brought down Carter's body, they dug a grave and buried him beside the lighthouse, the only person ever killed in the defense of a U.S. lighthouse attacked by Indians. If Aaron Carter was a slave, he was now free at last.

Cape Florida: Springboard to Freedom

In the early years of the nineteenth century when fugitive slaves were told to *follow the North Star* to freedom in the northern states and

Canada, runaways in Florida and even from Alabama were already secretly sailing from Cape Florida to the British Bahamas where freedom was in the wind.

Many slaves had taken refuge with Seminoles, and some intermarried, so that they were called Seminole Negroes. With their Indian allies, black Seminoles united to fight for liberty, or to escape. Those determined not to be removed or killed did not take the northern exit but stealthily moved southward down the long peninsula to Key Biscayne. There they rendezvoused with Bahamian captains, bartering on the beaches to establish the cost of passage on this perilous journey across the Gulf Stream.

It is estimated that just before the lighthouse was built at the southern end of Key Biscayne, in the early 1820s, that three hundred brave men and women, with their children, left Cape Florida to take asylum in the Bahamas. They sailed to the northwest end of Andros, the largest island, near the Tongue of the Ocean and on the edge of a magnificent coral reef, and settled at Red Bay and Nicolls Town.

The escapes did not occur all at once. Five years before the lighthouse was illuminated, one traveler reported seeing sixty Indians and sixty runaways and "27 sail of Bahamian wreckers" preparing to leave uninhabited Cape Florida. Much courage was needed to make the dangerous voyage aboard the small Bahamian sloops and sailing ships of the wreckers, although the captains knew the passage well, having been daring and aggressive privateers for years.

Not all went in a group. Some raised sails on their own dugouts and outriggers and, like Scipio Bowlegs, were victorious in their crossing. The surname Bowleg(s), a vintage Seminole name, is a familiar one in the Bahamas. In fact, a hundred years later, Scipio's grandson, interviewed at Andros Island, could still relate tales of his grandfather's crossing.

Some of those attempting escape did not make it, no more than all present-day boat people heading for our shores are successful. The record is clear that in 1841, "in sight of Cape Florida," Jonathan Walker and his sailboat, carrying seven runaways from Pensacola, were interdicted at sea. A salvage ship, on the outlook for illicit traffickers crossing the Gulf Stream, captured and took the boat in tow to Key West. The slaves were shipped back to their masters. Walker was imprisoned in Pensacola, and the initials SS for *slave stealer* burned into the flesh of his hand. When the mistreatment of this Quaker became news, American and English abolitionists rallied to free him. John Greenleaf Whittier, poet and crusading antislavery editor, wrote his poem "The Branded Hand" after he heard about the atrocity committed in Florida.

Later, writing from her home in Mandarin, Florida, author Harriet Beecher Stowe may have been unaware of the earlier Everglades underground in her own backyard. Yet "Cape Florida" was once the password, and Key Biscayne the springboard to freedom from Florida.

Between Key Biscaino and the Bahama Banks, it is about fifteen leagues broad.
—ANDREW ELLICOTT, 1799

In my conferences with the Indian chiefs in 1837, I ascertained that a constant communication had been kept up between the Seminoles and certain persons in the Bahamas, and that most of the negroes who had eloped from their masters & sought refuge among the Indians previous to the war had been taken from the Peninsula in British vessels. Key Biscayne is so situated as to command both Providence & Florida Channels, and if fortified would put an end to the communication between Islanders and the blacks on the Peninsula.
—MAJ. GEN. THOMAS S. JESUP, JANUARY 16, 1844

The Troops Come Splashing In

CAPE BEACHHEAD

When the troops came splashing in commanded by Lt. Col. James Bankhead, they were given a heavy task. In the punishing tropical sun, they sweated as they followed stern orders to make camp on the three-acre slice of scrub land bordered by blistering hot beaches and mangrove and buttonwood thickets filled with all manner of wild and fearful creatures unknown to northerners. They bravely cleared the grounds, chopping through hostile spines and spikes, burrs, and sharp-edged grasses alive with lizards, snakes, and scorpions. Mosquitoes and sand fleas tormented the troops at their hard labor. Yet the work was rewarding. When they finished, they saw that the military reservation overlooked a magnificent seascape of ever-changing blues and greens, or silver or golden in the moonlight or sunlight. The unending beauty of the tropical Atlantic on the east stretched to the indigo-blue line of the Gulf Stream. To the south, the Florida Keys dotted the crystal-clear, azure shallows and, to the west, in the lee of the island, lay the protected lagoon called Key Biscayne Bay, its far bank marked by silver bluffs fringed with greenery stretching out of sight to the Everglades. No wonder the Indians, once returned, had not wanted to give up this island beachhead and lookout point.

The first fort on Key Biscayne followed fast on the heels of the troops that landed in March 1838 beside the hollow lighthouse. It was a peripatetic fort—a fort of several locations and many names that headquartered men from all the military services. Lt. Levin Powell was the first to receive orders to set up an area fort, but later chroniclers would be filled with consternation trying to pinpoint the subsequent orders, dates, and places.

Historian Charlton W. Tebeau says, "The Navy established Fort Dallas on Key Biscayne, a post which the Army was later to move to

The fort on Cape Florida became a peripatetic fort, like the mangroves, ever walking. Fortunately, one of the officers of the Third Artillery, Capt. J. R. Vinton, was a man who carried more than the usual rations; he carried a pencil and sketch pad drawing the tents, parade grounds, fort headquarters, and blacksmith's shop beside the burned out lighthouse on Key Biscayne.

According to a letter from Maj. Gen. Thomas S. Jesup to the Adjutant General, military forces landed on Key Biscayne early in March 1838. The U.S. troops were assigned to headquarter at the fort.

In 1845, artist Vinton sent his pen-and-ink drawings to Charleston to J. Mott, who had a book in progress. He listed them separately and wrote, "The second is a view of Key Biscayne in which several persons are besieged by Indians under circumstances of thrilling interest. You must recollect this story and a graphic (narrative description) of it connected with the engraving will afford an interesting chapter to your book." Vinton's best-known work is an 1837 drawing of Osceola, the great leader of the Seminoles and symbol of resistance. (University of Miami, Archives and Special Collections, Otto G. Richter Library)

The three military officers after whom the first fort on the key and mainland was named are shown in order, Alexander James Dallas, James Bankhead, and S. L. Russel. These engraved miniatures depict them at a younger age. (Saint Memin Collection, American Portrait Gallery)

the north bank of the Miami River." Cmdr. Alexander James Dallas, after whom it was named, must have been displeased when it was moved. The Navy needed maneuvering room, but on the Miami River no ships could come in to the fort due to the mud banks and flats. What good was it to carry on with the tradition of having your fort at the mouth of a river if it was blocked by shoals and sandbars?

Fort Dallas, whether called Fort Bankhead for its original commander or Fort Russell (also spelled Russel) for a fallen hero, was better off located on Key Biscayne. "The main station was on Key Biscayne," according to a later War Department report, "which afforded a better command of the approaches from the West Indies or from the Atlantic."

Dallas was commander of the naval forces and son of former President Thomas Jefferson's Secretary of State. Lt. Col. James Bankhead, who would be promoted during his Florida duty, putting him into scrimmages with Seminoles, gave the fort its second name. This later would be changed in memory of Capt. Samuel L. Russell, killed on the Miami River when he "received two balls in his breast" and a "third in his brain." For most of its duration, it was called Fort Russell, but not always: "Camp Fort Russell, Key Biscayne E FL" was one designation used by the surgeon general's office, and there are remarkably clear daily records of the surgeons-in-charge of the hospital where many men were treated, and others, sad to say, died. The hospital took care of men from all the services except during 1840 when the Navy's Florida Squadron had a general hospital on Indian Key.

In the summer of 1839, Fort/Camp Russell hosted a sizeable command. There were thirty-eight members of the artillery; sixty infantry men, a detachment of thirty dragoons, and fifteen members from the U.S. Steamer of War, *Poinsett,* on Key Biscayne for part of the quarter. The "Strength of the Command" from July 31 to September 30 was 143 men.

First Hospital

The hospital built on Key Biscayne serviced Army, Navy, and Marine personnel during the Second Seminole War according to military records of medical historian William M. Straight, M.D. For some of them, it was rest and recovery; for a few, a final resting place. During the Seminole Wars, many American soldiers died of disease, wounds, and exhaustion. Between 1839 and 1842, there were five army surgeons assigned successively to Key Biscayne.

During the summer of 1840 through December 1841, James N. Conrad, assistant surgeon, U.S. Army, saw the sick and wounded at Ft. Russell, Key Biscayne. He sent monthly reports to Dr. Benjamin King, Acting Surgeon General in Washington, D.C.; in August 1840, Conrad treated 103 patients, twenty-three for fevers (malaria) and twenty-six for dysentery, one of whom died.

As with modern troops, headaches, constipation, and skin infections were common complaints. In the rainy season, there was ten times as much fever (malaria) as in the dry season, and three times as much dysentery. Dysentery caused the most deaths, with malaria, tuberculosis, gunshot wounds, and intemperance (alcoholism) followed by other maladies. On Key Biscayne, between 1839 and 1842, with a mean strength of two hundred men, the average mortality rate was eight per year. The records showed intemperance (alcoholism) very common; no wonder, since, according to Jim Woodman, Key Biscayne's first chronicler in 1961, those patients included members of the spirited Florida Squadron commanded by John T. McLaughlin, whose six hundred sailors consumed or disposed of half as much wine and spirits in four years as did the five thousand men in the entire U.S. Navy. In reporting this, Woodman noted that the $16,000 expenditure was "for medical purposes."

War Games

The Army divided the territory of Florida into squares; in fact, Gen. Zachary Taylor, afterwards president of the United States, set up a game board divided into 190 squares. It was drawn so that the troops, in their proper positions, would provide better protection to the white settlement—and be the winner.

May 6, 1839, the Commanding General wrote the Secretary of War from Headquarters of the Army, at Fort King: "the Indians are now operating in small parties probably because they find it dangerous longer to continue among the settlements and are making their way southerly to avoid the troops posted in the squares" adding that the Indians availed themselves "on their way of every opportunity to do all the mischief in their power by attacking defenseless and isolated individuals."

Optimism surfaced momentarily. "We are in hopes of driving them [the Indians] below the 28th degree of North Latitude and if they can be

The Indian War is about to commence again very soon—Indians have lately committed many dreadful murders—the citizens are now busily employed taking up all the publick lumber from this place to Key Biscayne to put up a barracks Hospital and other necessary houses for the troops stationed there.

—MARGARET DUBOSE, OCTOBER 15, 1839 WRITING FROM KEY WEST TO HER SON IN TEXAS

Cover of a report on the patients from the military hospital at Camp Fort Russell, Key Biscayne, to the office of the Surgeon General in Washington, D.C. (William Straight Collection)

kept there, they can hereafter do little or no injury, as the coast is now covered from St. Augustine to Key Biscayne by forts and cruisers."

General William S. Harney sits for his portrait a quarter century after training the troops on Key Biscayne during the Seminole Wars. (Mathew B. Brady, National Archives)

William Selby Harney (1800–1889)

Lt. Col. William Selby Harney replaced Lt. Col. Bankhead. A West Pointer, Harney was out to make a name for himself as an Indian fighter. Although sometimes at odds with his superiors, he managed to work around them and move up the military ladder to the rank of general. Along the way, the red-haired cavalry officer, in charge of loyal troops, built a reputation for brutality, tyranny, and mendacity, leaving a bloody trail as he relentlessly pursued Seminoles in Florida and later Sioux across the western part of the country.

When Harney arrived on Key Biscayne, he immediately set off down the bay to hunt Indians. He "came up with Appiacca [also known as Arpeika and as Sam Jones] fifteen or twenty miles southwest of Key Biscayne, attacked and beat him" That was Gen. Thomas Jesup's report to the Secretary of War, but Arpeika had out-foxed Harney and disappeared into the Everglades.

When Harney was assigned to guard a trading post on the Caloosahatchee River, he took some twenty-seven crack dragoons from Key Biscayne. On July 23, 1839 (three years to the day after the Cape Florida lighthouse attack), Arpeika's young friend Chekika, whose strength was legendary, ambushed Harney, attacking at dawn while he and his sentries were asleep. The infuriated Harney escaped in only his shirt and drawers. Chekika became his sworn enemy.

Returning to Key Biscayne, Harney plotted his course. He trained the Second Dragoons of the famed Second Cavalry. For a time he let them gallop their horses along the beaches. Then he exchanged their horses for canoes. They must learn the ways of jungle warfare. Much of the island was wetlands, tangled and impenetrable. He made his men train in the island swamps. They crawled through the labyrinthine root systems of the mangroves. They waded in chest-high water, their weapons over their heads. Then he had canoes shipped to Cape Florida. By year's end the men were tough as Indians and disciplined to slip their canoes silently through water like alligators, unseen in the sawgrass of the swamp. They had target practice on the beach. The newly invented Colt pistols with their rounds of ammunition were handed out as Harney prepared his men to do combat in the Everglades—man-to-man, if necessary.

Harney had promised his superior officer "that he would return with the scalp of that piratical savage," and according to William C. Sturtevant, who wrote of "Chakaika and the Spanish Indians," he "obtained a coil of new rope from a fisherman, to be used later in hanging Chakaika and his men."

Meanwhile, Chief Chekika [Chakaika] had plans of his own. He was waiting for the right time to attack farther south at Indian Key to restock his arsenal, previously supplied by the Bahamians and Cubans prior to the arrival of the U.S. Navy in Florida and Biscayne Bay. His target was the Indian Key warehouse overflowing with valuable salvage, including weapons stashed away by the incorrigible island proprietor and wrecker, Jacob Housman, a convicted embezzler who became a self-appointed Indian hunter.

When in the first week of August, 1840, Chief Chekika's scouts reported that Lieutenant Commander McLaughlin in his flagship, the *Flirt*, had sailed from the Navy depot a mile from Indian Key up to visit his friend Lieutenant Colonel Harney at the Key Biscayne post, Chekika attacked with some 130 warriors. They set fire to much of the island and, after a night of violence, left in twenty-eight canoes and six of Housman's boats, booty-laden as they headed for their camp in the Everglades. Housman survived, but Dr. Henry Perrine and five others did not. When the news broke nationally, Congress and national leaders wondered what was going on in the south Florida "theater of war." There was a great public outcry. The U.S. Navy was shame-faced and, once more, Harney had been caught sleeping.

Harney felt pressured to search out and destroy Chekika. He swore it was the last time his enemy would outsmart him. He waited until the rainy season ended, and then, taking his hanging rope and camouflaging his men in "Indian paint," he set off in war canoes for his revenge.

Harney's final staging platform was Fort Dallas and, in December 1840, he traveled up the Miami River to invade the Everglades. Surprising his enemy in his own camp deep in the wilderness, Harney killed the chief, scalped him, and then strung up his body from the tallest tree, and he did this in front of Chekika's wife and daughters. He took captive the chief's family and others of the group, sailing them to Key Biscayne prior to removal from Florida.

Indian indignation was immense, but the nation's jubilation rang out because Harney had demonstrated that the white man could enter and cross the "impenetrable Everglades" like an Indian or panther, fight in jungle conditions, and win. Washington would call the red-haired colonel a great hero.

The uncompromising Indian killer had emerged victorious. Harney has been credited by some historians for bringing the Second Seminole War closer to an end.

Billy Bowlegs II, Seminole warrior and Arpeika's lieutenant, had accompanied Chekika in the 1839 attack on William Harney. (Blank Collection)

The Huguenot Connection

Even as Minorcan contributions have been long overlooked in south Florida, so have those of the French Huguenot families who dared to search for freedom on the exposed coastal frontiers and islands. The three most dramatic acts of the Seminole War in south Florida involved three Huguenots on the Florida frontier. They treasured their religious and civil freedoms, for all had ancestors in centuries past who were killed in the St. Bartholomew's Day Massacre, a collective memory no French Protestant would ever be allowed to forget. They shared a common heritage, and tragedy.

The arrival of six hundred French Huguenots in north Florida in the sixteenth century incited the Spaniard Pedro Menéndez de Avilés to stage a surprise attack and massacres, near the inlet to be named Matanzas. Massacre, derived from the old French word *macecle* is translated into the Spanish *matanza*, slaughter. In the 1700s, when three to four hundred Frenchmen were shipwrecked in the Florida Keys, their mass murder, said to be by Indians, gave one of the rocky coral islands its first name, Matanzas (noted on a 1741 map by John Goggin), later changed to Indian Key.

The Huguenot connection on Key Biscayne began in 1825 when John Dubose, his pregnant wife, and children arrived. They were visited by Henry Perrine, a fellow Huguenot, who had his eye on the area as a magnificent new garden in which to introduce tropical edible and exotic plants for the U.S. government. They were also visited by Huguenot William Cooley, who would stop en route to Key West where he marketed the starch that he manufactured from wild coontie root. He and his wife and two daughters and their tutor lived on the mainland on New River, some twenty miles to the north of Key Biscayne.

The massacres continued when, in January 1836, while Cooley was away, his family was brutally murdered by a band led by Chekika. The Seminole War had moved south.

Seven months later, on July 23, the Cape Florida lighthouse was ambushed, just as John Dubose had warned it might be. He and his family were in Key West, but the substitute keeper was injured and his assistant murdered.

Seventy-five miles south of Cape Florida, and four years later, Dr. Perrine, along with several others, was slain on Indian Key (which once again lived up to its former name, Matanzas).

Indian Roundups

Bribes throw dust into cunning men's eyes. —OLD SAYING

In January 1841, the roundups seemed to be making progress, according to reports that were progressively filed under the benign heading: "Negotiations with Indians." The redskins and their black-skinned allies were either being forcefully captured by the military or, in some cases, being led or sent in.

The United States was using corrupt methods to win the war, including bounties and bribes. Capt. John Page of the Fourth Artillery sent a letter to Washington lamenting that he had run out of money to buy in the enemy: "I have got a great many in by hiring one hostile to bring in another."

Armed steamboats were dispatched to harbors and coastal lighthouses, including Cape Florida, to pick up prisoners being held under guard for out-of-state shipment. Once on board, they were put in irons, routed to New Orleans and then to Arkansas (later Oklahoma).

The same officer proudly reported to the U.S. Commander of Indian Affairs: "I have the honor to inform you that I have now within the chair of Sentinels at this post [at Jupiter], one hundred and fifty Indians, Ten of that number of Mickasuki, and the balance, of the Tallahassee tribe. This I view in a favorable light, as their principal chief Eco-emaltha is with them, and they have stated that their object in coming in is for the purpose of emigrating."

Winding up the report, on January 26, 1841, he adds, "I have despatched in a Steam Boat my Asst. Gen'l to Key Biscayne, to conduct to this post the thirty two Indians captured by Lt. Col. Harney in the Everglades." Among the captives waiting down the coast at Key Biscayne were Chekika's widow and children.

As the Second Seminole War wound down, it appears that the burned-out, hollowed-out lighthouse served as a tall stockade-in-the-round, recalled to a sorrowful duty as the last of the natives anticipated their removal from south Florida.

Even as the first people of Florida had been decimated by European diseases and conquerors, now later Indians, such as the Seminoles, were losing their right to live and die on their native soil.

Belt of Seminole chief. (Smithsonian Institution)

My father told me I was made of the sands of Florida, and that when I was placed in the ground, the Seminoles would dance and sing around my grave.

—COACOOCHEE (WILDCAT), YOUNG FRIEND OF OSCEOLA, WHO DIED EN ROUTE TO ARKANSAS

EIGHT

First Town on Key Biscayne

AN ADMIRABLE HEALTH SPA

The troops were holding down the fort when Mary Ann and William G. Davis began to scheme about their port town on Key Biscayne. Not only were the snappy Second Dragoons there under Col. William S. Harney, but the U.S. Navy was holding down the north end of the island near Bear Cut, and the Marines had landed.

Northern newspapers were calling for settlers near Cape Florida. It was time for resurrection of the Davis dream of a town with a port. They had gained experience with town development, for the Deputy Marshall and Peter Skenandoah Smith were developing North City, sometimes called the first suburb of St. Augustine, outside the gates of the ancient city.

The cape was a strategic site for the town that Mary Ann and William laid out in 1839 and had drawn by a Philadelphia printer. The lots surrounded the lighthouse reservation on the tip of the barrier island. The Davises envisioned a kind of boom town around the military base with the excitement of a port that served not only the military but also travelers, traders, respectable wreckers, and adventurers.

Street names were selected to give pleasure to immediate family members (Davis, Mary, Edmund, Waters—shortened to Water Street as in many coastal towns) and to give political patrimony to the territorial representative of Dade County, the Hon. Charles Downing (although Mary Ann could have held that it was named after Downing Street in the town of London, where she was born). Washington and Jefferson streets were named for presidents, or ships of the same names that were attached to the Florida Squadron.

William Harney, commander of the military post, bought the first two lots across from the lighthouse from the Davises for a total of $1,000. The Davises' partner, Venancio Sanchez, agreed to sell lots to Dr. William H. Simmons, who was one of two who selected Tallahassee as the capital of Florida; to Brig. Gen. Joseph Hernandez, a Minorcan who led the militia during the Seminole Wars and who, under the orders of

supplies on the island was stopped by the Indians. Standing their ground directly in the way of Washington officials, "hostile savages" sought to repossess the noble island where their ancient forerunners had lived in villages. They reclaimed the cape and the darkened coast-line as their own. During an uneasy interim, the number of shipwrecks rose dramatically due to the increased trade to and from ports in the Gulf of Mexico. Florida Indians and wreckers profited.

Between 1837 and 1841, all attempts at rebuilding the white man's totem were thwarted. Even Colonel Harney failed in his attempt to re-build during his island duty. Finally, the military withdrew from Key Biscayne as the Second Seminole War officially ended in 1842. The toll included tragic exile of nearly four thousand Indians and blacks to the West, joined by thousands who followed the "Trail of Tears" by land and by sea: native men, women, and children from other tribes and other regions. Surviving Seminoles would be known as "one of the five civilized tribes" in the reservations. Some, however, including black Seminoles, escaped to Texas and elsewhere.

Some white pioneers left Florida by choice during the 1840s. They had been targets or victims of war who had lost their homes, their land, their hopes, and their dreams in the territory. When plans to recon-struct the lighthouse and safeguard south Florida settlements were in-definitely suspended, grievances grew. Fed up with the lack of new op-portunity and impinged upon by military, economic, and political constraints, many pioneers fled Florida. Among the emigrants were the families of John Dubose and William Goodwin Davis; both chose the wide-open spaces of Texas.

Dubose had wanted to return as keeper of the lighthouse whenever it would be rebuilt. But time ran out. While waiting in Key West, he was voted to a term as Monroe County representative to the territorial leg-islature. Following his service and at the urging of their offspring, he and Margaret decided to sail across the Gulf of Mexico, disembarking at Port LaVaca. Their oldest son, Johnny, had accumulated in Texas "some of the best lands available." These included prairie and gently rolling acreage that would become cattle country (several of the boys later rode the Chisholm Trail) later studded with oil wells. The Dubose holdings included property in Gonzales and Hammon counties as well as the land upon which Rice University now stands in Houston.

The entire family emigrated, taking memories of homes on Key Bis-cayne, the Hunting Grounds, Indian Key, and Key West. Descendants still live in Texas not far from the riverside homestead where John and Margaret retired on the Guadalupe River near the town of Gonzales. To this day in Independence Park they celebrate its role in history as "the Lexington of Texas." Here the first shot of the Texas Revolution was fired in 1836. Here, too, sixty miles from San Antonio, Gen. Sam Houston first heard of the fall of the Alamo and began the Runaway Scrape, pursuing the Mexican victor, Gen. Santa Anna, and ultimately defeating him.

On Cape Florida, Davis had planned to develop his health resort and port with a newly constructed and whitewashed light tower as the cen-terpiece of the town. But when the tower was not built and disputes

over the future of all the property were unresolved, the Davis family, who had never lived on the island, decided to take passage to the barrier island of Galveston. Mary Ann and William, in their own names, began to pick up real estate, and their family settled in the community with the exception of their older son, Edmund Jackson Davis, who would move on and ultimately become the governor of Texas in Austin. Edmund's younger brother, Waters Smith Davis, kept the family together in Galveston and, in fact, covered for some of his big brother's political and other indiscretions. Their father died in 1853; Mary Ann lived to be ninety-two and left her Cape Florida property to her children and grandchildren upon her death in 1885.

In south Florida, a solitary island remained with a burned-out shell of a tower, abandoned buildings empty of troops, and a once-cleared parade ground returning to its tangled natural growth. The wide, hard beaches at low tide, so recently marked by hoofprints as reported by an officer who galloped his steed along the fringes of the surf, were now clean except for the tracks of thousands of gulls and terns and wading birds tiptoeing among scurrying crabs and other creatures to feed at the water's edge and in the shallows that teemed with fishes.

The early to mid-1840s were mostly quiet times. Yet, a front-page news item of the May 21, 1841, edition of *The Florida Herald* posted election returns from Key Biscayne. The ballots showed ten votes for Whig delegate Charles Downing, and ten for his opponent, David Levy, in their race for the U.S. Congress as territorial representatives from Florida. Later, David Yulee, aka Levy, was elected the first state representative to the U.S. Congress, where he served in the Senate.

Across from the island, a few mainland settlers returned and a few new ones arrived. When William H. English, the nephew of Richard Fitzpatrick who, prior to the attack on the lighthouse had tried to introduce the plantation system to south Florida, settled on his uncle's property on the first designated site of Fort Dallas, he figuratively followed in the footsteps of William Goodwin Davis by designing his own paper town on the mainland. He called it Miami, and explained it was located "upon Key Biscayne Bay." It would be almost a half century before it was incorporated in 1896.

The Dade County seat, which in 1836 was at Indian Key with a proviso that once a year county court would be held at Cape Florida, was moved to Miami in 1844. Just one year earlier, an optimistic editor in St. Augustine proclaimed that Miami, a rising new city, would become the hub of the bay area.

As to Key Biscayne's past and its destiny, he wrote, "A lighthouse is at Key Biscayne, which, when it shall have been repaired, will serve to guard against any danger apprehended by those unacquainted with the coast. It was at one time thought that Key Biscayne would be the place for the building of a town, and we confess we thought so too, but the golden moment has passed."

NINE

Relighting the Island

TOPOGs TO THE RESCUE

Although some dismissed the future of Key Biscayne, military men still believed it was of importance. According to Thomas S. Jesup, Quarter Master General, in a report of 1843, "Key West, the Dry Tortugas, and Key Biscayne are the great strategic points on our southern frontier; and they should be strongly fortified."

Still, for eleven long years after the lighthouse had been attacked and put out of commission, no work took place. At last it was scheduled to be "rebuilt and restored" as final bids were received September 1, 1846, at the Fifth Auditor's Office, U.S. Treasury Department. It was to be replicated according to the original published specifications:

> The tower to be round, built of hard brick, all laid in hydraulic cement, 24 feet diameter at the base, 12 feet diameter at the top, height 65 feet from the surface of the ground to the top of the deck, walls 4 feet thick at the base, to be regularly graduated to 2 feet at the top. Foundation to be laid as deep as may be necessary to make the fabric secure.

The fire-and-hurricane-damaged tower and the keeper's dwelling were to be "built up anew." Builders celebrated the arrival of new bricks from Massachusetts, because the first shipload had been turned back by the presence of Indians on shore. The specifications continued:

> The contractor to have the privilege of using the brick in the old tower, now there. None of the old bricks to be laid in outside or inside course of the tower, nor in the outside course of the dwelling house.

The building contract had gone to New Englander Leonard Hammond for a low bid of $7,995. Winslow Lewis, a crony of Pleasonton who was still in charge of lighthouse building on the East Coast, was at first given the job, but later kept only the contract for installing his patented wick lamps and reflectors, as he had done up and down the seaboard (and for which, it is recorded, he overcharged on the Cape Florida job, making an 800 percent profit).

The new lighthouse keeper, Reason Duke, appointed October 24, 1846, at $600 a year, took charge during the rebuilding of the lighthouse. Ten years earlier, after the Indian attack, he and his family, who had settled on the Miami River, had evacuated with the Duboses and others to Key West in January of 1836. They had also lived in Tampa. Their daughter, Elizabeth Duke, married James Dubose, the son of the first lighthouse keeper. (This family visited often on the key; in fact, when James was very ill, they stayed with the Dukes for some months at a time in the keeper's cottage, according to private correspondence.) Duke's son John corresponded with James Dubose's brother Elias, sending the news from Florida to Texas many years after their parents were gone.

Reason Duke's pioneering lifestyle on Biscayne, Florida, and Tampa bays prepared him for the many delays in completing the tower, including "contractors' vessels with materials having been run foul of at sea" and the installation "in an insecure manner" of the lantern, which brought some criticism of more wasteful spending of public money. Duke was appointed as a Dade County juror in 1844 before serving at Key Biscayne.

Finally, in 1847, an official U.S. notice declared that "the lighthouse, destroyed by the Indians in 1836 and recently rebuilt at Cape Florida . . . was relit for the first time on the night of April 30."

As whale oil was poured into the lamps and lighted, a keeper and his family could celebrate the illumination of the island once again, the first time since Florida had achieved statehood two years earlier in 1845, as the twenty-seventh state. Territorial days had come to a close.

From the tower watchroom, Reason Duke could see ships hugging the Florida coast far too close to the reef that paralleled the rushing Gulf Stream. The velocity of the stream was feared by captains and ship masters, especially as it began to increase where the Florida Straits narrowed from ninety miles wide between Cuba and Key West to forty-five miles between the Bahamas and Cape Florida. The ships, carrying goods from the Mississippi and Gulf of Mexico ports, New Orleans, Galveston, and Mobile, navigated with inadequate sailing directions and often misleading charts. Duke must have been concerned whether the light was powerful enough to help the passing ships whose perilous course along the reefs could easily be altered by currents and gales or pilot error. And Duke knew that six months before the Cape Florida light was put back into service, the mighty October 1846 hurricane had destroyed the Key West and Sand Key lighthouses. He must have hoped that the new statehood of Florida would result in the U.S. government improving the deteriorating lighthouse system. In fact, the Key West light was rushed to completion and was lit on February 10, 1848. In the same year, Key West's U.S. Sen. Stephen R. Mallory (who had spent a year across from Key Biscayne on the English plantation along the Miami River) urgently advocated before Congress a survey of the Florida reefs to determine how to avert further wrecks with loss of life and commercial goods, as ships continued to pile up on the rocks.

Statehood *did* matter. Washington took a hard look at the longest coastline in the continental United States and agreed with the captains and shippers, and the insurance companies, experiencing great losses from shipwrecks. Better protection must be given to the tall-masted ships of U.S. and foreign registry—their holds creaking with cargo such as cotton, tobacco, coffee, rum, and turpentine exchanged for manufactured products and goods at ports of call on the East Coast or across the ocean.

Not only was the lighthouse system lacking, but the waters were basically uncharted. Like sailors of yesteryear, navigators in the Florida Straits still checked with the stars because they were forced to work with crude nautical charts based on the Spanish and English surveys of the 1700s. This profited only the wreckers, who had a thriving business cruising and camping along the coast and beaches, lying in wait like latter-day pirates to board foundering ships (except that sometimes they saved many lives). "Wreck-ashore!" was the cry that meant lucrative salvage and unexpected gifts from hatch covers to luxury items to kegs of aged whiskey that floated ashore. In a 1944 paper in the *Florida Historical Quarterly*, Dorothy Dodd details "The Wrecking Business on the Florida Reef, 1822–1860."

By mid-century, Washington embarked on a course to determine how to make the remote coast safe for national and international shipping, and safe for "settlement and improvement." One reconnaissance team was sent to reconnoiter the reef, another the coastlands and islands including Key Biscayne. On these trips were two future generals who would become American heroes.

Robert E. Lee (1807–1870)

In early 1849, the U.S. Schooner *Phoenix* anchored off Key Biscayne in full view of the white, sixty-five-foot lighthouse, its neat brick keeper's cottage with its vegetable garden and orchard surrounded by a picket fence. Four officers came ashore, among them a tall Virginian who was a forty-year-old Army engineer.

Changes were afoot for the lighthouse system. It had come under severe criticism for becoming antiquated and ill-managed under the long rule of Fifth Auditor Stephen Pleasonton (who began in 1820 and continued his superintendency until 1852). Should the topographical bureau take charge? In fact the 1849 coastline survey, conducted by the U.S. Board of Engineers, would almost immediately not only impact the future of the Cape Florida lighthouse, so recently rebuilt to old specifications, but also affect changes in the rest of the lighthouse network.

In a report dated March 12, 1849, and written off Savannah aboard the *Phoenix*, Robert E. Lee recorded that he and other members of the U.S. Board of Engineers deemed the island of Key Biscayne "essential for defensive purposes" to be set aside as a military reservation. As a lieutenant colonel, Lee and his fellow board members visited and examined the islands and coast of Florida as far south as Key West and the Tortugas, coming ashore at Key Biscayne, and reporting to President

Robert E. Lee visited Key Biscayne as a young topographical engineer before he became a General in the Confederate Army. (Early portrait by William Edward West, Washington and Lee University)

James Knox Polk, under whose administration (1845–1849) more territory was acquired by the United States than under any other president.

The act of making Key Biscayne a military reservation would set off repercussions between public and private interests that would be argued, litigated, and only settled in the following century by Presidential Orders.

The future Superintendant of West Point, Robert E. Lee, destined to become the great Confederate general, left his footprints on the sand of Key Biscayne. He did not just sail past the rest of south Florida on

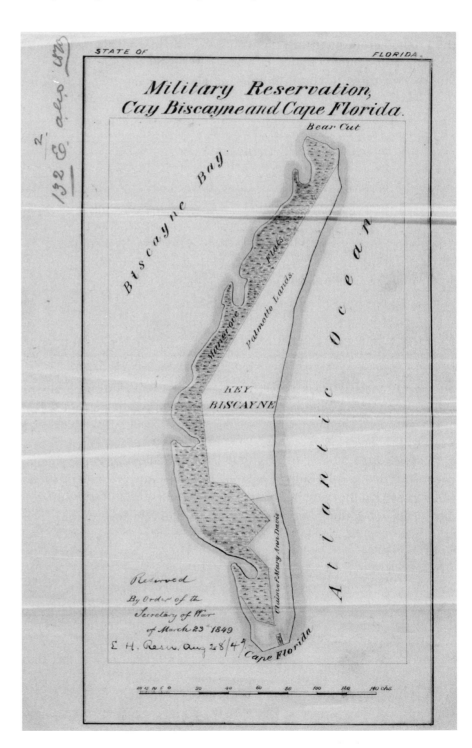

U.S. Military Reservation Cay Biscayne and Cape Florida. (National Archives)

one swift inspection tour. An engineer, he studied the design of Fort Jefferson, called the Gibraltar of the Gulf, which guarded sea lanes and traffic from the Caribbean, Gulf of Mexico, and Latin America. The Dry Tortugas previously had been a wreckers' hangout and a favorite of seal hunters, turtlers, and eggers. Fort Jefferson later became a prison holding Dr. Samuel Mudd, who helped set the broken leg of John Wilkes Booth, President Abraham Lincoln's assassin. It is now a National Monument and nature sanctuary.

When the Civil War began, and Lee was called to duty in the Confederacy, he organized the South Atlantic Coast Defenses and visited troops in East Florida. When he inspected the disarray of troops at the north Florida port town of Fernandina Beach, he said, "I hope the enemy will be polite enough to wait for us." Lee County, on Florida's West Coast, was named after him.

Before Lee surrendered to Gen. Ulysses S. Grant at Appomattox, Virginia, he was confronted and defeated at the pivitol battle at Gettysburg in 1863 by his former friend and fellow West Pointer, Gen. George G. Meade, in charge of the Army of the Potomac. Long before this fateful battle, the lives of Lee and Meade had crossed on the tiny island of Key Biscayne. While Lee and his Board surveyed the islands and coastal properties, Meade, another engineer in the Army Corps of Topographical Engineers, was sent to survey the condition of south Florida's lighthouse system to recommend alternative locations and constructions. He would come to know Key Biscayne and its environs well.

Lee and Meade had been on the same side in their efforts to defend the American coastline.

Reef Wrecks Call for Action: TOPOGs to the Rescue

The rising number of wrecks between Key Biscayne and the Dry Tortugas, and the preliminary surveys by the engineers, demonstrated the urgency of a scientific survey of the treacherous Florida reef. One of its outcomes would be to make available sound hydrographic charts for mariners. Between the late 1840s and the late 1850s, more than five hundred ships were wrecked. In one year, more than $200,000 of goods was lost off Cape Florida alone. Assistant U.S. Coast Surveyor F. H. Gerdes (1809–1884) would report: "Within the period of five years up to January, 1850, the annual value of the vessels and cargoes wrecked on this coast was nearly *one million of dollars....* The entire loss resulting from defective information would be saved by the completion of the survey, besides that from the deficiency of lights, beacons, and buoys.

Using Key Biscayne as headquarters, the U.S. surveyors of the Army Corps of Topographical Engineers (TOPOGs) set up a camp with a specially designed astronomical/magnetic station next to the lighthouse on Cape Florida. They spent thousands of hours on Key Biscayne and in the bay area. Braving many dangers on "the exposed and dangerous

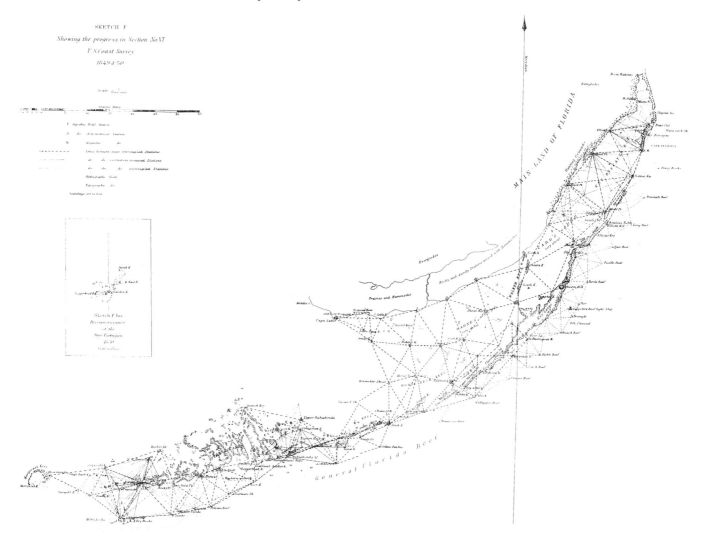

With Key Biscayne as base headquarters at top of U.S. Coast Survey (map 1849–50), the Florida Keys to the south were surveyed and measured by triangulation. (National Archives)

Tomorrow we stand for Cape Florida ... to select & measure the Base ... from Key Biscayne. I will report to you our progress.
—F. H. GERDES TO A. D. BACHE,
NOVEMBER 18, 1849

coast," the surveyors carried pistols and muskets to protect themselves from Indians whom they believed might interfere with their coastal and inland peregrinations as they began triangulating the keys.

On Mark: Key Biscayne

Hailed as "antebellum America's greatest attempt at applied science," the U.S. Coast Survey team was made up of Army and Navy men on detail. It was founded by Ferdinand Hassler, of whom it was said by his successor, "He was a man like the work itself, in advance of his times." Those were the words of Alexander Dallas Bache (1806–1867), who succeeded Hassler, serving from 1843 until his death.

A West Point graduate, A. D. Bache was a man with sound scientific training, high intelligence, and the courage to proceed innovatively. His genes weren't bad either: his great-grandfather was Benjamin Franklin. Perhaps he inherited some of his scientific boldness and curiosity. Like Franklin, he conducted fascinating Gulf Stream studies.

Nicknamed "the peripatetic superintendent" by the Secretary of the Navy, Bache spent much time away from the nation's capital on field trips. He knew the fine art of delegating hard physical work to others and challenging them mentally to great prowess. He then supervised on a drop-in basis, sometimes when he was least expected.

There were some forty members of the survey party camped west of the lighthouse in tents and offshore when Bache arrived with his own party, including his wife, to take charge of final activities. Having reached the island "after so much railroading, steamboating, and sailing," Bache wrote in a letter datelined Key Biscayne on April 6, 1855, "we are drinking in deep draughts of 'East Wind' as if it were soda water."

Bache's assistants who seem to have worked the hardest on Key Biscayne, and been disciplined as well, were both German born: Frederick H. Gerdes and Julius Erasmus Hilgard. Gerdes had begun a general reconnaissance in Florida of the keys and reefs "with a view to the surveys required by the General Land Office." His work was interrupted, however, by a severe illness while he was in Washington, D.C. He returned to his large family in Pascagoula, Mississippi, to recover. His health regained, he sailed across the Gulf of Mexico to Key West to rejoin Hilgard, who had taken charge when Gerdes became ill.

Alexander Bache, Superintendent of U.S. Coast Survey, supervised work and installation of the base marks on Key Biscayne. (Mathew B. Brady, National Portrait Gallery)

Hilgard's early work, a survey map of Key Biscayne (1848), became immensely important evidence in subsequent legal disputes through many years. He also made the first astronomical and magnetic observations—"observations for latitude and azimuth and of moon culminations for longitude"—at Cape Florida in 1849 and 1850. He spent much time with Gerdes in the early years, and in 1855 he helped welcome Bache to Cape Florida upon the arrival of Bache's party, erecting two granite monuments that bear Bache's name on the north and south ends of the island.

Bache was exceedingly proud of the work on the lower Florida East Coast where he had charged his two young protégés with a horrendous task. They had long conferences prior to beginning the remarkable endeavor to find a base of operations from which the south Florida coast, including the keys, could be accurately surveyed by triangulation. After months of sailing and surveying throughout the area, they settled on their mark: Key Biscayne, the five-mile-long island at latitude 25°39'55.8"N and longitude 80°09'24.4"W. If the island had no other claim to history, this scientific choice would place it in the bull's-eye.

Cape Florida has a "good harbor and almost unknown entrance (11 feet). . . . A Base here can be good," wrote Gerdes to his chief, Superintendent Bache. It was early 1849, and the U.S. government anticipated danger from the remaining hostile Indians along the coast. To ensure safety for the men and gear, including surveying paraphernalia and magnetic instruments of great value, the Coast Survey schooners *Nymph* and *Phoenix* were fitted out with "the greatest care and a full complement of arms!" So were the schooners *Gerdes* and *Petrel* sailed by Gerdes and Hilgard.

Gerdes found Key Biscayne "the only island" proper for a site. The keys were unfit for they were "stony, rocky, grown over with roots and stumps, and everywhere thickly wooded. On Key Biscayne, along the beach of the Atlantic Ocean, runs a wide plain from S to N. . . . [with] level and solid ground."

He described the northern end of the island as "overgrown with palmetto and small bushes and long grass . . . intersected by a small stream, which forms, to some extent, a sort of hollow." He would require "hoe, shovel and axe" to clear all the "thick and horizontally running palmetto roots, that cover the work surface like the web of a spider."

When Bache had a stroke in 1864, Hilgard took charge of the Washington office and subsequently became superintendent of the U.S. Coast Survey. Gerdes, meanwhile, remained in the field, and his service record is long, for he surveyed coasts from Long Island, New York, to the Dry Tortugas, around the Gulf of Mexico to Galveston, Texas.

Map Notations

- Northwest Point reveals the entrance to North Channel, used previously by the U.S. Navy.
- Northeast Point shows "rocks" along otherwise sandy shore. Significance of rocky area was not revealed to Gerdes, but one hundred years later scientists announced that "a unique formation" existed: a black-mangrove fossil reef.
- West Point (above center of island) is edged by mangrove shores with several lagoons. "The beaches kind of quick sand." Off West Point, fourteen feet of water.
- East side forms "The Big Bend," the curve on the seaside beach.
- South end borders the Key Biscayne Channel, variously called the Key Biscayne Inlet, "a good harbor" and "almost unknown entrance."
- Southwest Anchorage is located inside sand banks where ships Gerdes, Petrel, and others anchored safely in lee.
- South Point, the tip of Cape Florida where the south base marker was located, subsequently eroded into the sea.

Following the site visit of the U.S. Board of Engineers and the subsequent Executive Order reserving all the lands on Key Biscayne for use of the United States, J. E. Hilgard was assigned to the island to make a survey that he dated October 24, 1848, and redrew in 1870. In 1916, when private and public ownership of all the lands on Key Biscayne were in dispute, the outcome of the case hung upon the credibility of the Hilgard survey. When he sailed up from Key West past Key Largo (which he reported September 10, 1848, as "a rendezvous for Indians . . . fires all over the Island"), young Hilgard never could have imagined that his survey would become the prime exhibit in a Congressional hearing airing the first major conflict on Key Biscayne between public and private land usage in the twentieth century. So much for the power of the surveyor's plumb.

Bache Marks

His name is carved in polished granite markers shipped to the island to mark the north and south ends of the Key Biscayne base line. One 836-pound obelisk is in its original location at the north end, where it was accidentally discovered in 1970 by workers clearing woodlands and wetlands which they thought had never been disturbed. They found what they thought was the tombstone of a man named "A. D. Bache, 1855." There was much speculation, especially among surveyors and historians, until James C. Frasier, the Field Survey Supervisor of the Dade County Public Works Department, was called to investigate. He was able to read the words "U.S. Coast Survey" on the marker, and Miami historian Arva Moore Parks, writing in *Tequesta* in 1973 about the rediscovered monument, reports a recovery note was sent to the U.S. Coast and Geodetic Survey as research was begun to solve the mystery of the "lost monument."

The north marker, originally placed among "a spider web of palmettos" and in "a hammock of wood," can be seen on a green at the Key Biscayne county golf course. The existence of a south base marker was known to the property owners of Cape Florida, for it shows up on a survey as late as 1913 at the low tide line. Subsequent tides, storms, and hurricanes washed away much land south of the lighthouse, and the marker was submerged by the sea and eventually covered with sand. In 1988, the Society of Professional Land Surveyors engaged the 301st Aerospace Rescue and Recovery Squadron to salvage it from the sea. The divers recovered it intact offshore and brought it to high ground. It is protected today within the lighthouse compound in Bill Baggs Cape Florida State Park.

Perhaps for the first time, the public became aware of the extent of lost land and lost history, part of life on a sand island subject to marine and land erosion.

Gerdes Journal: Notes and Drawings

Who named Virginia Key?

"The Island above Kay Biscayne has no name, used to belong to the mainland, but the Cut (Narrows Cut) broke through about 10 or 12 years ago." Next to this notation on his 1849 map, Gerdes wrote in "Virginia Key."

Only after the hurricane of 1835, which was noted by the Cape Florida lighthouse keeper to have produced a great surge that cracked the lighthouse and damaged the keeper's house on Key Biscayne, does any island appear on maps north of the key and Bear Cut. Classically, hurricanes are noted for boring through sand spits to transform barrier coasts, making inlets and islands. The hurricane of 1835 and subsequent storm and erosion forces produced a new island which was given a new place name.

"There is only one island above Key Biscayne, which no name to be found, I have called it Virginia Key." This important reference has been overlooked. Clearly Virginia Key was a newly charted island, for Gerdes was under restraint of the 1831 memorandum of the General Land Office warning pioneering surveyors "Never to give new names to such objects where names have heretofore been given . . ." and to name the natural sites that were unidentified.

Gerdes prepared topographical sketches of the principal islands facing the reef channel including:

> *Virginia Key*—About three miles long and one mile wide, wooded, with a fine Atlantic beach; southern passage called Bear Cut, with four feet water.

> *Key Biscayne*—Southern point called Cape Florida, having a lighthouse; key five miles long, from one to two wide, with a fine Atlantic beach, and a strip of open land alongside, covered only with palmettos &c.; the rest wooded. The southern inlet (Key Biscayne inlet) has a swash channel over the reef with ten feet water. West and southwest of the island is an excellent anchorage and harbor. From here to the Miami [River] eight feet may be carried.

> *Soldier Key*—Five miles below, very small; filled with mangroves.

In preparation for later published reports, handwritten entries in his field books reveal attention to minute topographic detail but inconsistencies in spelling and so forth:

> *Island N of Kay Biscayne*—Fine seabeach, full of lagoones, some making in from Kay Biscayne Bay. Sandy soil with Palmettoes

> *Virginia Key*—mostly covered with Mangroves from S. to N about 3 miles—1–1/2 mile wide

> *Kay Biscayne*—Upper part of the Island intermixed with rocks, lower part sandy, level—fine beach, and for 300 yards from East beach open from woods, only covered with palmettoes & grapy bushes. The sandy soil (little black) produces any kind of Vegetables. The West side, from which several lagoons make in, covered with mangroves. The beaches kind of Quiksand. Southern point is called Cape Florida. Lighthouse. ±5 miles by 3 miles [*Author's Note: In the subsequent official published report in the 1850s, Gerdes states that Key Biscayne is 1 to 2 miles wide.*]

> *Soldier Kay*—about 5 miles south from Cape Florida. small, 1/2 mile diameter, rocky bottom with mangroves, level with water. The ragged Kays about 5 in number, 4 miles below Soldier Kay beginning and extending about 4 miles more. most of them rocky with Mangroves . . . sandy nature . . . some timber. Parts of beach on the Eastern shore

> *Elliots Kay*—Some very good land with timber (Dog wood & yellow Wood) . . . with Mangroves. On the land some slight elevation. Part good beach 5 miles by 1-1/3 miles

> *Small Islands*—named Black Casar, Old Rhodes, and Angle fish . . . each very small, level with the sea, rocky bottom and covered with Mangroves.

> *Kay larger*—This Island runs NE and SW and is about 25 miles long and perhaps from 1 to 2 miles average

Miami River

Across from the island, Gerdes and his team explored the narrow Miami River. From its source in the Everglades, its clear, fresh water flowed four miles to Key Biscayne Bay, where it mixed with saltwater that came in and out with the ocean tides. The Miami River running into Key Biscayne Bay was first casually sketched by Gerdes in his field journal (below), then more formally drawn for the Coast Survey publication. Early Miami settlers lived on the river, including several who served as Cape Florida lighthouse keepers.

The Miami River runs from the Everglades and empties in Key Biscayne Bay about nine miles from Biscayne light-house.
—JOHN DUKE, STATEMENT IN 1891

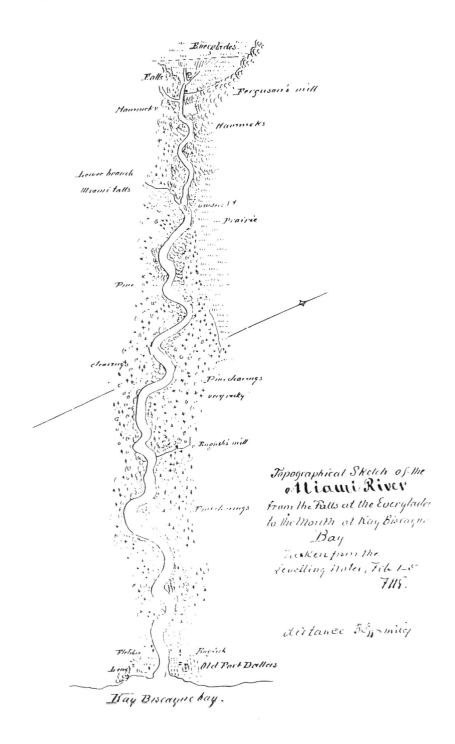

Early explorers and visitors were enchanted by The Rapids and the river's lush and fertile banks covered with magnolias, oaks, orchids, and moss. The banks had supported the early native people and, in 1567, the first south Florida mission. In the nineteenth century, its banks were settled sporadically, and several pioneers became keepers of the Cape Florida light.

In his formal Coast Survey report, F. H. Gerdes wrote, "From the upper falls to near its entrance into Key Biscayne Bay . . . water in the Glades was 6 feet 2.5 inches above low tide."

When in the early 1940s Miami author Marjory Stoneman Douglas was asked if she wanted to write a book about the Miami River for the American Rivers series, she asked, "What river?" The short length and little-known history of the Miami River suggested a children's book, *Freedom River*, but did not intrigue her as much as it did later authors. She was intent on exploring whether the vast and mysterious Everglades might, indeed, be a river of some consequence, worthy of national attention. It was a river to write about, while, she explained, "the little Miami River is no Mississippi." (Later, scientists would describe the mighty ocean river off Key Biscayne—the Gulf Stream—as flowing with the force of a thousand Mississippis.)

Dangerous Places and Safe Anchorage

Gerdes noted three dangerous places near Key Biscayne:

- Water-witch shoal, abreast of Key Biscayne, Quicksands, 3 or 4 ft. of water
- Sambos, Quicksand knolls, off Cape Florida, 3 or 4 ft. water
- Fowey Rocks (Soldier Key Reef), rocky ledge off Soldier Key; 2 or 3 ft. water

As this hard-working surveyor was engaged in the triangulation of the Florida Keys, his daily journals showed the careful detailing of a

In the pencil drawing, the tip of the island is shown from offshore; the lighthouse, with the keeper's cottage surrounded by a picket fence, is to the east; harbor with sailboat on the lee shows anchorage of Hilgard's Petrel. (F. H. Gerdes)

meticulous mind and hand. Sometimes he sketched pencil drawings, even across two pages or the end sheets of his notebooks.

In the mid-nineteenth century, F. H. Gerdes drew his own ship and described his favorite anchorage on the west side of the island, "off from Cape Florida Lighthouse close to the beach in 14 feet and perfectly protected by a sandbar stretching across." A half century later, a channel was dredged by Henry Flagler around Cape Florida and into the bay to bring materials to the mainland for the extension of his railroad. Thus began an unending process that destroyed the sandbanks and sandbars, including favorite anchorages.

Gerdes also drew the lighthouse and compound as seen from the deck of his ship. This drawing is an important graphic record that shows coconut trees (*Cocos nucifera*) at Cape Florida. By an artist's rule of thumb, they are at least sixty feet high. Gerdes may have been drawing the mature palms delivered as sprouts to lighthouse keeper John Dubose by Dr. Henry Perrine, for these trees would be survivors of the hurricane of 1835, the Indian attack, and the first acts of purposely clearing away island vegetation done earlier to set up the fort, then by the surveyors themselves.

Indian Hunting Grounds

The Coast Survey team used the Dubose house overlooking the bay on the Hunting Grounds as a station diagonally across from Cape Florida to the southwest. The Hunting Grounds with hammocks and springs has always been regarded as prize mainland. On its ridges, bones of mastodons and mammoths have been found. From archaeological investigations in the 1980s and 1990s, archeologists describe ancient species of horses, deer, llamas, dire wolf, saber cat, sloth, and big bears that once roamed the south Florida plains; condors circled overhead. For some years carbon dating placed human beings in north and

On the Indian hunting grounds on the mainland there is plenty of large game.
—JAMES A. HENSHALL, 1881

central Florida ten to twelve thousand years ago, which prompts at least one scholar to assert that the first Floridian was "a contemporary of the last of the large ice-age mammals." In 1986, Robert Carr's archaeological discoveries in areas along the extensive mainland ridge first brought to the surface new evidence in south Florida that the Hunting Grounds, which had offered some solid ground, fresh water, and food to the Tequesta Indians before the Europeans arrived, could have been a stopping place for even earlier bands of possibly cave-dwelling paleo-Indians.

The tract of land, later known as Cutler and now the site of the Charles Deering estate in custody of Dade County, contains valuable clues of environmental and historical significance to the global puzzle. The latest environmental marking came in 1992 when Hurricane Andrew, with winds clocked as high as 164 mph, and gusts projected to be up to 212 mph, roared ashore, pushing a 16-foot storm surge over the area and disturbing archaeological sites. From findings by archaeologists, geologists, and other scientific experts, we learn about our beginnings, and our future. The Serengeti Plain in Africa has been described as the cradle of civilization, although recent finds in China challenge the claim. Perhaps the Hunting Grounds is south Florida's Serengeti Plain.

Earliest House

In 1826, John Dubose and his sons built the first house at the site designated in documents as the Hunting Ground [Author's Note: Mapmakers and scholars variously refer to the mainland area that runs approximately from Cutler to Coconut Grove as the big and little Hunting Grounds.] Under the preemptive laws of the land, the Dubose children had title to the 160 acres which they held and cultivated until 1850.

In October 1826, William Pinkney wrote from Key West to Stephen Pleasonton, "I am informed by several who have landed at Cape Florida, that Mr. DuBose the Keeper does not live in the dwelling . . . he has built a house on the mainland several miles from the lighthouse . . . he has given the whole direction of the light . . . to a black woman." Pinkney was exaggerating; Dubose had not abandoned his post. John Dubose wrote to Dr. Henry Perrine in 1837, a year after the lighthouse attack:

> "My son, John Dubose, took up, in 1832, (under the pre-emption laws of the United States) 160 acres of land, called, in that country, the hunting-ground. He has improved it, and planted there until January, 1836, at which time the settlers all deserted their homes. This land is distant from the Cape Florida light-house, southwest, twelve miles."
> —*Published in the Congressional Record.*

Writing again in the same year to Perrine, he said, "My son (John D.) took under his charge some of your plants, viz: Sisal Hemp, the three species of Aloes, or Pulque, the Annatto plants, the Date, the paper Mulberry, and Turmeric, and planted them at the hunting-ground. I was

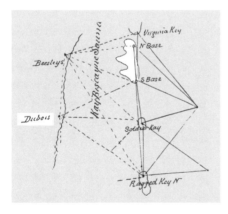

Triangulation to the "Dubois" (Dubose) house on Hunting Grounds. (National Archives)

there in May, 1835; they were growing well. Since then, that place has been in possession of the Indians. We have every reason to suppose they are still there."

Plant Introductions: Cape Florida and the Hunting Grounds

When Perrine was attempting to establish his credibility as the first person to introduce a particular mulberry into the United States, he wrote Dubose, who replied in a testimonial letter published in the Congressional Record: "With respect to the inquiry you make as to the person who first introduced the Morus multicaulis into East Florida, I think I am warranted in the assertion that the plants forwarded to me from New York (by your order) in May, 1833, were the *first that had been seen in East Florida.*"

He added, "At the time I received them, I was unacquainted with their nature and value [for the silk industry]. The eldest one, planted at the Cape Florida lighthouse, bore a few mulberries in November, 1835; and one planted in my garden on the main grew so rapidly, that I have often been obliged to cut all the limbs off, say six feet long; and as I did not know that they would grow, they were thrown away." But his son had an idea. On "about the 14th December, 1835, my son, as an experiment, cut off six small limbs, and stuck them in the ground. In twenty days from that time they had taken root, and had a new coat of leaves on them."

The Dubose land was not distant from the grant subsequently given to Perrine by the U.S. Congress for the first official tropical plant-introduction station. But in actuality, the only local introductions were those done by Dubose and his son Johnnie on the key and on the Hunting Grounds. Due to the Indian wars, the good doctor was destined never to cultivate his grant.

On January 3, 1836, Johnny Dubose closed up the house, checking out the property and the plants as he said farewell to the Hunting Grounds, heading for Cape Florida and evacuation of the entire bay area for points south. The Indians were returning with a vengeance to their ancestral grounds.

James Stays Behind

Recent findings by the author reveal that carpenter James Lawrence Dubose, another son of the first lighthouse keeper, and his family were in residence at the Hunting Grounds in 1843, and from 1846 to 1850. Private letters in the hands of his descendants confirm his occupancy of the family-held property, to which all the children held title. Their mother Margaret's brother-in-law, John Kershaw of South Carolina, had secured title to the 160-acre tract for them in the 1820s.

James was the last of the family to move to southeastern Texas onto lands that, although inland, seemed a bit reminiscent of the Hunting

Grounds, but less flat and definitely rolling. The house built for his father John, the retired lighthouse keeper (who left Florida after being a representative to the constitutional council from Key West), was at an oxbow along the banks of the blue waters of the Guadalupe River on property still maintained by the family. This house also was built by John and his sons Elias, Luis, and David (Key Biscayne's first native son).

James stayed in south Florida, sometimes working with his good friend George Lewis, the two of them having apprenticed in Mystic, Connecticut, to ship carpenters. Afterward, James built wooden houses in Key West, and then surprised most everyone by marrying Elizabeth Duke, who had grown up on the Miami River. Lizzie was the daughter of Reason Duke, the second lighthouse keeper on Key Biscayne. There are subsequent lighthouse romances in south Florida, but only one in which the grandchildren could boast of having had the first *and* second keepers of Cape Florida light as their own two grandfathers!

After their marriage on December 20, 1841, James and Lizzie divided their time between Key West, Key Biscayne, and the Hunting Grounds. From the Hunting Grounds, James wrote family in Texas:

> About 20 months after I was married, I was taken with the measles. . . . I was at the point of death. I was sick about 2 months, all the time Elizabeth watched by my side day and night. If it had not been for her I would have died. When I got up she was taken with the same. I worked . . . in Key West but my health got so bad I could not stand it so I came here to see if it would do me any good. I can say now I enjoy good health for the first time since you left here.

They must have moved into the old house built at least fifteen years earlier by his older brothers and his father. Apparently, the Indians who had occupied the Hunting Grounds, before and after attacking the lighthouse, had not burned it. A carpenter by trade, James would have renovated the house when he regained his health.

The house was the site picked by F. H. Gerdes for an important Coast Survey station. The mainland mark on the Dubose property, which he located twelve miles south of the Miami River between Shoal Point and Black Point, could easily be seen offshore as he began the triangulation of the region. He reported that along the mainland coast "some hammocks and fertile spots are found at several projecting points. Among the latter the hunting grounds occupy the first place. Here cultivation has very sparsely begun, though the produce of the soil, in sugar, rice, corn, limes, oranges, olives, &c., was very rich. On the Miami river are also some small plantations, that seemed, before the late Indian outbreak, to thrive well."

One of the great advantages of the Hunting Grounds was fresh water. It was long used by aborigines, and later passersby, including pirates and mariners who filled their casks here. The Duboses, as the first settlers, appreciated this natural resource on their excellent mainland property. This spring is clearly identified on early U.S. Coast Survey maps of Key Biscayne Bay.

The Hunting Grounds were the site where the second Dubose-Duke grandchild was born. James wrote on April 16, 1846, "I had almost forgotten to tell you that I have got a little Girl 3 months old. It is very large and very handsome. They say it looks like Mother so she must see it for I know you all will love the little fellows. O what would I have given if father could have seen them."

By 1849, James and Lizzie had three children: Little Jimmy Jr., Harriet, and Elias. James wrote to say he had completed an $800 contract on a house in Key West but had become sick again. The doctor advised him to go to Key Biscayne to recuperate. As soon as he could, thereafter, he prepared to join his family in Texas.

As for the disposition of the Hunting Grounds, "I intend to sell this place soon or leave here for good. I shall take a good look at Texas this winter and if I like it I'll never leave."

They left Florida in 1850.

Louis Agassiz (1807–1873)

To learn more about the reef, Alexander Bache of the U.S. Coast Survey invited his friend, the great zoologist and geologist Louis Agassiz, to come to Key Biscayne. Agassiz took up his work at the edge of the Gulf Stream some seventy-five years after Benjamin Franklin (Bache's great-grandfather) made the first credible observations of the stream, its temperature, and characteristics and, in 1769, produced a chart of the Gulf Stream. The Coast Survey in 1851 directed the ship *Bibb* to Florida with Agassiz aboard. Agassiz would examine the still-mysterious formation and science of the subtropical and only-known living coral reef off the North American continent. For ten weeks he wrote reports aboard the *W. A. Graham*, according to his logs in the National Archives.

Franklin, earlier, and then Bache and Agassiz used their enquiring minds and scientific bents to advance coastal knowledge and the field that would become oceanography. A hundred years later, to honor the contributions of Agassiz, a major marine laboratory established on Virginia Key would name its first building for him.

Agassiz wrote in detail of the reefs from Key Biscayne to the Marquesas, specifically referring to how and where coral grew in communities, pinpointing its nature and variety, examining geological formations, the building and dying process, patterns subsurface and above, aspects of wave and ocean-water movement, and of hurricanes and tides. He measured underwater depressions and heights off and on shore, removing much speculation and, in the process, discovering where it would be prudent to erect lasting lighthouses, beacons, and signals to safeguard ships sailing near the reef. "The northernmost keys, which converge toward the mainland are covered by silicious sands," he reported. "Their beaches are of like character, and slope towards the Atlantic, while their mud flats spread along the western shores. South of Cape Florida no more silicious sand is to be seen."

Soft flats lie off "Cape Biscayne," Agassiz continued, ". . . minute

By a thorough investigation of the reef we will be able to point out the exact & suitable positions for lighthouses and marks for the navigator, to show the currents & their general run, so that the necessary allowance may be made for the same; and in the course of time, when Government has furnished lights along the islands, with the aid of our current charts, I venture to say that one half of the deplorable shipwrecks, that now happen, will not take place. The seaman running up the Gulf against wind and currents will be able to see lights on every tack to the Northward. —ALEXANDER D. BACHE sand and mud shoals laid bare at low water . . . [where] one sinks ankle-deep in the dense coral growth" which includes an "endless variety of Gorgonias" (sea fans) and many Porites. He found sea urchins, sea cucumbers, hydrozoans, tunicates, and "a deep orange colored Starfish and Manicinas. . . . Such shoals are the best field for the collector," he wrote. Star corals, brain corals, sea fans, and other reef species were common on the flats off Key Biscayne into the 1950s. Much dredging, silting, and traffic have since destroyed these coral gardens.

Extracts of Agassiz's report were used by Bache in his own Superintendent's Report, but "for various reasons it was unpublished" in its entirety.

The two men continued to share findings, thoughts, and plans. Agassiz wrote Bache, "We need museums in which all the various relations which link together the different groups shall be exhibited at the glance, where the anatomical preparations illustrating this structure shall be placed side by side with perfect specimens showing their internal forms; where the remains of extinct forms shall fill the gaps existing between the living, where embryological specimens shall illustrate the succession of changes all the types undergo. . . . The country which shall build the first, will take the lead in the future progress of our science." Through his efforts, the Museum of Comparative Zoology, which has been called the forerunner of all American natural-history museums, was established at Harvard in 1859. By 1872, Agassiz had inspired many American cities to have a good museum, and had trained most of their curators. A summer school he established for teaching marine natural history evolved into the Marine Biological Laboratory at Woods Hole, Massachusetts, now a world renowned modern complex.

Agassiz was the first marine scientist to study the coral reef in Florida, describing and illustrating the underwater world from Key Biscayne to Key West. His works ushered in the beginnings of serious oceanographic investigation at the top of the reef.

Alexander Agassiz (1835–1910), who as a sixteen-year-old had accompanied his father on the never-to-be-forgotten reef-and-island explorations, took it upon himself at Harvard to publish, in 1881, the earlier important work on the great Florida coral reef. It was illustrated with "the beautiful drawings of corals . . . prominent Florida species," made into lithographs from his father's artwork. Like his father, Alexander explored Florida waters for the U.S. Coast Survey, sailing in 1877, 1878, and 1880 aboard the steamer *Blake*, the vessel also used by John Elliott Pillsbury for his 1884–1890 studies of the Gulf Stream current that prompted him to recommend navigators use the current to shorten the forty-five-mile crossing between the Bahamas and Florida by setting their course for Fowey Rocks instead of the customary route of sailing farther north to Jupiter.

Alexander visited the area again in 1893–94 to study coral formations. Many treasures are exhibited in the venerable Agassiz museum at Harvard University which houses a portion of the Florida collection

Louis Agassiz, famed zoologist and geologist. (Mathew B. Brady, American Portrait Museum)

as well as specimens from worldwide research and expeditions led by both Louis and Alexander in the nineteenth century.

Louise Hall Tharp, Agassiz biographer, wrote that "Everywhere he went, Agassiz continued to urge naturalists and laymen alike to send him specimens, live ones if possible. From Walden Pond, Henry David Thoreau sent fish, turtles, and a black snake. When Agassiz informed him joyfully that among the fish was an unnamed species, Thoreau was enchanted: "How wild it makes the pond and the township," he wrote in his journal, "to find a new fish in it!"

Agassiz and Bache are also to be credited for their contributions during the formative years of the Smithsonian Institution, where Bache served as a Regent.

A Hub of Activity

During the watches of several lighthouse keepers, including Reason Duke, Temple Pent, and Robert R. Fletcher, the island was a hub of activity. It was not just spongers and wreckers and locals who stopped by. There were members of the Coast Survey and other scientists who came to call or made the island their base. Keepers and their families were able to watch and learn how much new instrumentation worked as TOPOGs agilely took readings from thermometers, barometers, hydrometers, and so forth. During the time when the Coast Survey team set up camp, the Cape was transformed into a lively campground with the island population exploding to more than forty people.

When Duke's term ended, Temple Pent became the third lighthouse keeper. Appointed 1852, and then again as the seventh in 1866, Pent was a Cape Florida pilot in the early 1820s. A Bahamian known as a south Florida squatter, a pioneer, a wrecker, and turtler, he attempted to prove the earliest mainland donation grant which he applied for in 1817. He served as Territorial Senator and became known as Old Squire Pent. He took a paying position with the U.S. government as lighthouse keeper at the age of fifty-eight. Later, descendants in Coconut Grove sometimes found themselves living on streets named after family members.

Robert R. Fletcher, appointed 1853, the fourth lighthouse keeper, was a doctor and owned property on the Miami River where he built a house and store; upstream he operated a coontie starch mill, using power from the river rapids. He married Mary Margaritta Mabrity, whose father was the first keeper of the Key West light. After his death, her mother, Barbara Mabrity, became keeper. During her watch, the lighthouse collapsed in the hurricane of 1846; she survived, but fourteen persons who had taken refuge in the tower drowned.

Dr. Fletcher, county clerk from 1844 to 1846, represented Dade County in 1846 and 1847 and served in the Florida Constitutional Convention of 1865. The Coast Survey people were on hand during the Fletchers' term on Cape Florida, which ended when George Meade and his builders arrived with bricks and mortar to heighten the tower.

George Gordon Meade (1815–1872)

At mid-century, Lt. George Meade was charged with helping to shore up what critics called a deplorable lighthouse warning system. He did a preliminary survey of navigational needs along the keys before assuming the responsibility to design and build lighthouses on- and off-shore along the Florida reef, and he accepted the challenge to redesign the inadequate Cape Florida light. It was, however, in 1835, as a twenty-year-old that Meade came to his first Florida assignment by hitching a ride from the north, approved by the War Department, with one of his brothers-in-law, Alexander Dallas, commander of the U.S. *Constella-*

George G. Meade, later the Union General at Gettysburg, designed the plan for elevating the Cape Florida lighthouse, including installation of a Fresnel lantern to increase visibility. (Florida State Archives)

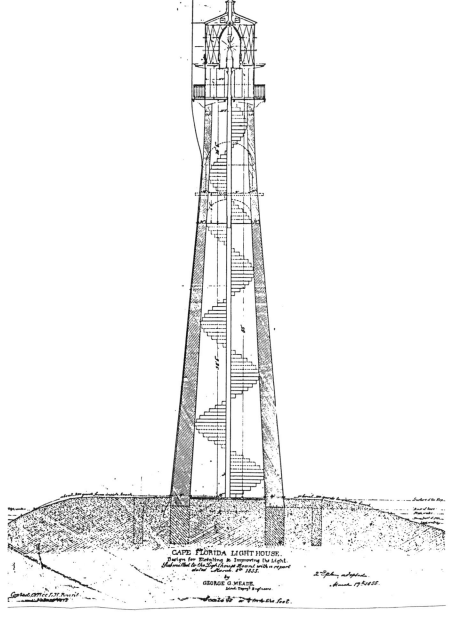

tion, flagship of the West Indies Squadron. They took a three-week cruise through the West Indies en route to Key West. They arrived just as the "possible Florida Theater of War" erupted into the Second Seminole War with the massacre of Maj. Francis L. Dade and his command in central Florida, the burning of plantations around St. Augustine, and followed by the Cooley family massacre in south Florida.

Too late to protect the victims, Dallas sailed a battalion of marines and other troops to Tampa "just as the Seminoles withdrew." Meade was among those sent to retrace the fatal steps of Major Dade. Later in the spring of 1836, the brevet lieutenant was given the assignment to escort by schooner, flatboat, and foot, from Tampa west to the Mississippi, a party of four hundred captured Indians (some of the 3,824 Indians and blacks who were "relocated" to Arkansas during the Seminole Wars). This duty occurred four months before the Indian attack on Cape Florida.

In 1852, when the Topographical Bureau of the Corps of Engineers established the U.S. Lighthouse Board with Lieutenant Meade as a member, he was attached to the Seventh District, which included Carolina, Georgia, and Florida, to prepare preliminary reports on coastal needs. He wrote clearly that on Key Biscayne, "The Cape Florida Light, marking as it does a prominent point on a most dangerous coast . . . [close to] currents and dangerous reefs . . . renders it of absolute importance that it should be increased to a first-class sea-coast light."

Before he arrived on Key Biscayne, long before he became famous as the great Civil War general, civil engineer Meade worked with another brother-in-law, Maj. Hartman Bache, in the northeast. He gained immeasurable respect for the work of senior topographic officers, or TOPOGs. They swarmed over woodlands and wetlands, illuminating the coastal geography and geology of the seaboard, "bringing to light all hidden dangers," as Meade wrote in his notebooks, "furnishing the evidence of the wants of navigation."

As a designer of lighthouses, he required "details of soundings, meteorological studies, and measurements of the tides in every season . . . force of wind, of high breaking waves, ocean currents, and general exposure" to plan a "durable structure . . . [and] to select a site."

Major contributions to scientific marine literature were made by Alexander Dallas Bache, Gerdes, Hilgard, Louis Agassiz, and Meade in Florida.

Meade selected specific foundations and locations along the coast. He designed brick towers, including ones at Key West and Jupiter Inlet. Ingeniously using the latest technology, he erected the earliest screw lighthouses at Carysfort Reef, Sand Key, and Sombrero Key located offshore on long metal legs screwed directly into the underwater reef.

On Cape Florida the site selection remained as before; his challenge was to rebuild the lighthouse so that it could be seen from the shipping lanes at least twenty miles at sea in all directions. Visibility was a problem. How many wrecks there had been over the years! Meade heard the complaints and fears of mariners as far north as Newfoundland, Boston, and Staten Island who were coming to believe that the

Cape Florida light was nothing more than a Lorelei, luring sailors to shipwreck. Yet it was the northernmost of the four most important lights that guided an enormous amount of shipping from the Gulf of Mexico through the Florida Straits. Captains told fearful tales of searching for a sight of the light and instead running right up on the reef as they looked for the warning. Meade decided to raise the tower thirty feet and replace the lantern with a grand French-designed Fresnel lens. Its powerful concentrated beam would be seen farther out in the Gulf Stream.

The greatly improved lighthouse lens had been developed by Augustin-Jean Fresnel in the 1820s, but some thirty years passed before one was installed at Cape Florida. It was no longer just talk that Stephen Pleasonton's objections to installing a Fresnel lens earlier were due to a deal he had made with contractor Winslow Lewis, who held a patent on those installed at dimly lit Cape Florida and other coastal lighthouses. Their inferiority was recognized, but the decision would have to wait until the Lighthouse Board took over in 1852, and Pleasonton's tenure ended. George Meade, a fighter of some prowess, landed with a powerful second-order Fresnel lens. It would be illuminated on March 18, 1856, as announced in a March 23rd notice.

The increased height of the tower raised both the new lantern and the hopes of passing captains. Yet the value and effectiveness of an *onshore* lighthouse as a navigational beacon at the top of the dreaded reef would continue to arouse controversy. Still, for nearly a quarter century, Meade's ninety-five-foot tower served bravely during the transition from sailing ships to great clippers to steamships that ultimately would need more sea room, as they began to navigate farther offshore.

The Last Lighthouse Keepers

The fifth lighthouse keeper, Charles S. Barron, a Virginian living on the mainland, was appointed in 1855 and oversaw some of Meade's building. The following year, he initiated the Fresnel lens, with its more powerful beam, its focal point a hundred feet above sea level, at a time when there was anticipation that the heightened Cape Florida light hereafter would steer maritime ships safely past the critical narrow passage offshore. Several months prior to his appointment, the "eccentric" Dr. Barron and his "self-sacrificing" wife, Wilhelmina, were described in some detail in a traveler's diary written in January and February 1855 (first published in *Tequesta* in 1983 with notes by Wright Langley and Arva Moore Parks). The diarist feared that the "life of seclusion" weighed heavily on Wilhelmina. Nonetheless, the Barrons set sail in May for an even-more-isolated life on the island bringing their belongings by boat across the bay from their house on top of Key Biscayne Bluff on the mainland, where their rocky property included gardens, hammocks, and the old Indian spring known as the Punch Bowl. Barron had watched the Coast Survey team at work on either side of the bay and come to some mistaken conclusions such as that the

---

NOTICE TO MARINERS.

LIGHT-HOUSE AT CAPE FLORIDA.

Notice is hereby given that the light-house tower at Cape Florida, has been elevated 26 feet and surmounted by an iron watch room and lantern, and furnished with a catadioptric apparatus of the 2d order, fixed, illuminating 315° of the horizon.

The focal plane of the apparatus is 100 feet above the mean sea level.

The tower and lantern are painted *white* (as before.)

The new light was exhibited for the first time on the night of the 18th inst., and will continue to be shown from sunset to sunrise till further notice.

By order of the Light-house Board:

GEO. G. MEADE,
Lt. Topographical Engineers.

KEY WEST, FLA., *March 23, 1856.*

Notice to Mariners, March 23, 1856, signed by Meade notes, "The tower and lantern are painted white (as before)." (National Archives)

"Everglades were formed by a submarine volcano." No matter his scientific judgments, he later moved to Key West and became a judge.

Barron assistants included Nicolas Adams, whose brother walked the coastal beaches from Lake Worth to Miami as a "barefoot mailman." John Christian, a Dane, was another assistant with previous experience at Carysfort Reef light near Key Largo. Their service was during the final period of the third and final Seminole War, which had little impact on Key Biscayne, although a Key West newspaper of November 1858 quoted Barron as reporting "Eighty Seminoles in Miami within two months." On the Miami River, Fort Dallas had been reactivated in the mid-1850s, prior to the close of the "Bowlegs War," as it was called.

Minorcan-born Simeon (Simon) Frow, the sixth lighthouse keeper, was appointed in 1859 and therefore on duty at the start of the Civil War. Following Abraham Lincoln's election, Florida seceded from the Union on January 11, 1861, seizing government property and many U.S. forts. In the view of the Confederacy, federal lighthouses, if allowed to operate, would guide Union patrols and endanger southern blockade runners. In August 1861, a trio of barefoot rebels invaded Cape Florida, mounted the tower, and audaciously destroyed the Fresnel lens.

Keeper Simeon Frow was shaken but unharmed. Splinters rained down on the platform and lantern pedestal as the gang of three shattered the great lens and removed the reflectors, plunging Cape Florida

President Abraham Lincoln posed with David Farragut (left behing Lincoln), who would become first U.S. Admiral, and with David D. Porter, Jr., who would become second. Farragut, whose father came from Minorca, was the protégé of Porter's father. The younger Porter warned of dangerous inadequacy of Cape Florida light. Also pictured, (at Lincoln's right) are William T. Sherman, George H. Thomas, Ulysses S. Grant, and Philip H. Sheridan. ("Council of War," National Portrait Gallery)

THE COUNCIL OF WAR.

into darkness. Cape Florida light, thereafter, for the duration of the war, was out of commission: Union blockaders lay offshore; in one incident, the crew of a federal ship sent a raiding party ashore for coconuts. In another instance, they rounded Cape Florida into the bay to discourage blockade runner George Lewis, whose Miami River house and mill were torched and burned to the ground.

Frow's descendants like to tell how he came to Florida as a stowaway on his father's shipping line out of Majorca, the largest of the Balearic Islands in the Mediterranean. He lived in St. Augustine in the first quarter of the century, then moved to Key West and married a Bahamian woman, Sarah Thrift, in 1839. A pilot and mariner, Frow and his family would play prominent roles in the bay area. His sons also kept the Cape Florida light and, in fact, when Fowey Rocks light was completed in 1878, Simeon and his sons moved offshore to operate it.

Unlike previous lighthouse keepers, in the 1870s the Frows had a friendly relationship with the Indians who now lived on the mainland in peace, although they never signed a peace treaty with the U.S. government. Daughter Catherine (Roberts) recalled, "When we went to Cape Florida, there was no one else around here but Indians. They were real nice, those Indians. They used to bring us venison." On Thanksgiving, the Seminoles delivered wild turkey and venison fresh from the Everglades to the keeper and his family and remained to enjoy the dinner. Once a Seminole paddled out at night and, without disturbing anyone, went into the lighthouse tower where he was found asleep in the morning, according to interviews published, a century later, by Bill Baggs, editor of *The Miami News*.

Simeon's son John, appointed 1868, was the eighth keeper. He and his father and brothers Joe and Charles and their wives spent an accu-

SAILING DIRECTIONS

APPROACHES TO THE INSIDE OF THE REEFS

1st or North Entrance. When Bear's Cut is open, steer in for the Cut W.S.W.¾W.(S.80°15'W.) until the Lt.Ho. bears S.S.W.¼W.(S.30°W.) then steer South (S.4°20'W.). This latter course leads down inside the Fowey Rocks with 20 feet least water.

2nd Entrance. When the Lt.Ho. bears W.S.W.¾W.(S.80°15'W.) steer in for it until Soldier Key (the first Key to the Southward from the Lt.Ho.) bears S.S.W.(S.26°50'W.) then steer South (S.4°20'W.) which course leads down inside the reef in 20 feet least water.

3rd Entrance. Bring Soldier Key to bear S.W.¼W.(S.52°18'W.) and steer for it until the Lt.Ho. bears N.W.¼N.(N.35°W.) or Fowey Rocks S.E.¼S.(S.35°E.) then steer South (S.4°20'W.). These courses, if accurately steered, lead inside Fowey Rks. with 20 feet water; but a vessel will be liable, from the set of the current or wind, to run over a spot of a single cast of the lead, with 17 feet water upon it.

ENTRANCE TO KEY BISCAYNE BAY

Having crossed inside the Reef by any of the above passages, steer South (S.4°20'W.) on the line indicated, until Soldier Key bears W.¼S.(West) or Fowey Rocks bear E.¼N.(East) or until on a line joining Soldier Key and Fowey Rocks then steer for Soldier Key. When ¾ of a mile from it, the Lt.Ho. will bear N. by W.(N.7°W.) a little Northerly; then steer North (N.4°20'E.). These courses will give nothing less than 9 feet at low water until up to the Bar lying just to the Southward of the Swash Channel, which has but 8 feet upon it at low water, and which should be crossed to the Eastward of its middle, as there is a 6 feet spot about midway between the banks on either side. To avoid this spot, a vessel when up with the Southern edge of the Bar should have the Light bearing N.N.W.¾W. (N.20°45'W.) cross the bar steering North. (N.4°20'E.). When the Lt.Ho. bears N.W. by N.(N.29°20'W.) the sand beach to the Westward of the Lt.Ho. will be in range with the Western point of trees on Key Biscayne, then steer on this range N.W.¼N.(N.37°45'W.) until the Lt.Ho. bears N.N.W.¼W.(N.21°30'W.) when run in by the eye between the banks on a N.W.¾W.(N.49°30'W.) course, giving the sand beach a small berth, and anchor

Sailing Directions, published in 1861, may have come in handy for Union blockaders since the lighthouse, dark throughout the Civil War, provided only a day
mark. (American Philosophical Society)

"Bay Buisquine." (Harpers Magazine, 1871, University of Miami, Archives and Special
Collections, Otto G. Richter Library)

mulated twenty years at Cape Florida and then several more years of duty at Fowey Rocks light.

Recalling the Frow's tenure, well-known pioneer Ralph M. Munroe, upon his first trip to Florida, wrote, "One day was spent on a sail to Cape Florida and a visit to the lighthouse and its keepers. These were the Frows, Old Johnny, Young Johnny, Brother Joe and their wives. Everything was in perfect order, as is customary with such establishments, and the surrounding grounds, including a fine garden, were also in good condition."

John bought a prime tract of land across from the island, 160 acres at $100, which would be subdivided many times and upon which much of Coconut Grove was built. Munroe purchased land from Frow, as did Charles and Isabella Peacock for the area's first inn or hotel. The large Frow family intermarried with many early settlers (the 1870 census lists eighty-six residents in Dade County, a sparsely settled area which included much of southeast Florida) and played an important role in the bay area.

Lighthouse Keepers

	Appointed	On duty*
1) John Dubose	1825	1825–36
2) Reason Duke	1846	1846–52
3) Temple Pent	1852	1852–53
4) Robert R. Fletcher	1853	1853–55
5) Charles S. Barron	1855	1855–59
6) Simeon Frow	1859	1859–65
7) Temple Pent	1866	1866–68
8) John Frow	1868	1868–78

*Records vary concerning the years of duty. Temporary keepers included William Cooley, January 1836; John W. Thompson and assistant Aaron Carter, July 1836.

Tides on Key Biscayne (published 1861)

Highest	3.0
Lowest	
Mean low	0.6
Spring tide	0.1
Neap tide	0.1
Mean rise and	
fall of tides	1.5
Mean duration	6 hrs

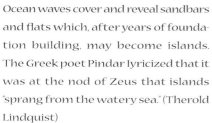

Ocean waves cover and reveal sandbars and flats which, after years of foundation building, may become islands. The Greek poet Pindar lyricized that it was at the nod of Zeus that islands "sprang from the watery sea." (Therold Lindquist)

Marine scientist's profile shows barrier island in evolutionary stages, from bottom to top, ocean to bay. (Harold R. Wanless)

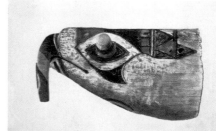

Ancient masks and sea turtle carvings discovered on Marco Island attest to artistic skills of south Florida's indigenous peoples. (Watercolors by expedition artist Wells Sawyer, 1890s, Smithsonian Institution)

Fornells Castle, perched on a cliff, overlooks the Mediterranean and the town of Fornells. Fornells means "oven" in Catalan. (Harvey Blank)

The island of Minorca, lying in the Mediterranean Sea, is a kind of sister island to Key Biscayne. Both are known as "The Island Paradise," with magnificent beaches and historic lighthouses. (Lluís Real, Imatges de Menorca)

Scipio Bowlegs, a black Seminole, sailed a large dugout canoe across swells of the Gulf Stream from Key Biscayne to freedom in the Bahamas. Artist James Hutchinson paints Bowlegs in traditional turban and tunic with silver gorget. (Evelyn and Nixon Smiley Collection)

Mary Ann Davis, the first American owner, bought title to Key Biscayne in her own name from an heir of the wife of Pedro Fornells. On July 9, 1827, three years and three days after receiving the original deed, a judge examined Mary Ann Davis "apart from her said husband" and declared she assumed title to Key Biscayne of her own free will, consent and right of dower. (Oil portrait, circa 1850s, after a tintype, discovered by the author in Galveston, Texas.) (Blank Collection)

John Dubose (1779–1845) The exquisite miniature, painted on ivory by Edward Greene Malbone, whose portraits of other Carolinian and Charleston aristocrats are primarily in museum collections, is treasured by the descendants as a likeness of great charm. We saw it in the home of one of the DuBoses (who spell the name with a capital B) in southeastern Texas where, to these present ranchers and business people, their Carolinian plantation past seems very distant. They can relate better to the days John Dubose spent opening the Florida frontier. (DuBose Collection)

The Elnathan Field House, as it is known in its historical designation in Monmouth County, New Jersey, was the northern home of one of Key Biscayne's earliest coconut planters in the 1880s. (Randal Gabrielan, Middletown Historical Society)

American artist Harry Fenn (1838–1911) depicted the Cape Florida Signal Station in operation. Signal flags fly on yardarms of the lighthouse when it was conscripted into service for the Spanish-American War. (Mariners' Museum)

Cape Florida Lighthouse, c. 1900, oil painting by American artist Boyer Gonzales, with ancient Tequesta burial mound in foreground and keeper's cottage along-side tower. (Davis Collection)

Long a plantation landmark admired by painters, sailors, and beach walkers, the two-story Dade County pine house with red barrel-tile roof stood in coconut groves overlooking the ocean and Gulf Stream. It was the original home of Hugh Matheson in Coconut Grove; when damaged in the 1926 hurricane, it was carefully dismantled and floated by boat across Biscayne Bay. Barged through the cross-island canal, its new location was behind low-lying dunes where it was restored. About a half century later, along with the barn and other structures, it was uncere-moniously knocked down by devel-opers. (O. E. von Fuhrer, 1960s, H. L. Jordan Collection)

Lighthouse and palms by Boyer Gonzales. (Rosenberg Library Collection)

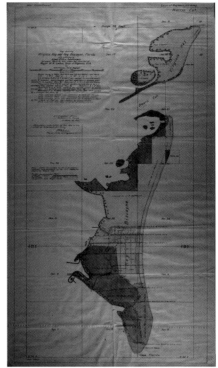

Presented by the Mathesons and Deering at a Congressional Hearing, this 1915 Army Corps of Engineers survey map of Key Biscayne and Virginia Key is accurate and detailed. Never before published, it was uncovered in 1989. (National Archives)

Palms. (Boyer Gonzales, Rosenberg Library Collection)

Kapok (Ceiba pentandra), witness to three-quarters of a century of change on the Key, silhouetted on Village Green. (Harvey Blank)

Coral Gables, The City Beautiful, was founded in 1921. For two decades, Key Biscayne was part of incorporated Coral Gables. (Watercolor by Martin Linsey)

Fast-growing Australian pine forest (1960s) sprang from seeds escaped from cultivation, to grow on filled land after natural ecological communities and native growth had been removed. (Blank Collection)

Hurricane waters cover island from ocean to bay, flooding land and homes after Betsy in 1965. Old cisterns on east side of Matheson barn stood but diesel gas tank, long submerged underground in bunker, popped out of the ground. (H. L. Jordan Collection)

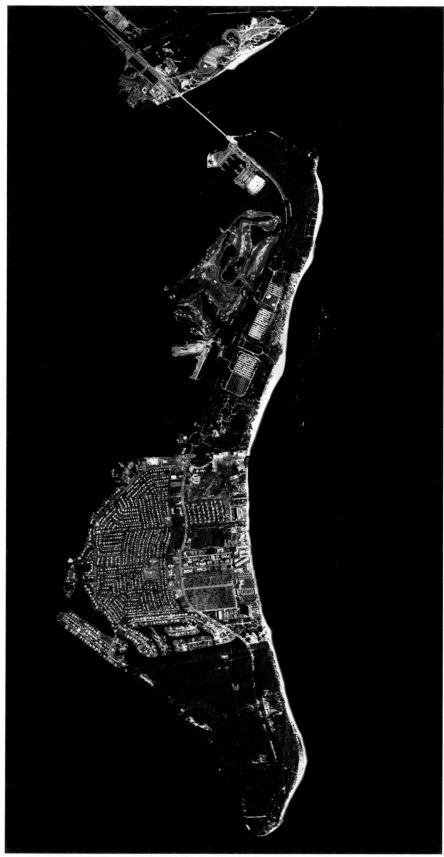

Satellite photographs from Bear Cut to Cape Florida made prior to the great storm of 1992. (National Oceanic and Atmospheric Administration)

State-of-the-art stadium, home of The Lipton Championships, with Miami skyline seen across Biscayne Bay. (Tennis Center at Crandon Park)

Osceola, the great resistance leader during the Seminole War, whose English name was William Powell, was unknowingly honored when the new high-span bridge to the Key was named the William Powell Bridge, after a county employee. (George Catlin, American Portrait Gallery)

First Florida weatherman was the pelican. (J. W. Hill, 1848, Blank Collection)

Fishing boat and nets on beach, c.1900. (Boyer Gonzales, Rosenberg Library Collection)

Green Turtle, most common species on ocean beach for many years, was depicted in the mid-1700 by American artist and naturalist, Mark Catesby. (Blank Collection)

Renourishment in 1987 helps protect severely eroded beach and threatened buildings along sand-starved Atlantic shore. (Blank Collection)

An historic lighthouse stands witness to natural beauty, belying coastal movements of sand and sea and the restless flow of human traffic, winds, and ever-changing tides. (Boyer Gonzales, Rosenberg Library)

Through the centuries, the mangrove and the alligator have been symbols of survival and renewal in the tropics. (Mark Catesby, 1754 lithograph, Blank Collection)

Fowey Rocks Light Supersedes Cape Florida Light, 1878

In 1748, the HMS *Fowey* was wrecked on the reef five miles off Cape Florida, giving its name to the dangerous coral rocks. One hundred thirty years later, the Fowey Rocks lighthouse, an offshore iron-pile light, was built there to supersede the Cape Florida light. Thus, not only did the rocks become a grave marker, but the tower stands as a lasting monument to the lost ship and its crew.

Fowey is the name of a fortified seaport town in Cornwall, known well to early Britons for its ships and for privateering extolled during the siege of Calais in 1346. It lies on the River Fowey, sometimes pronounced Foy.

Although few who pass the 111-foot-tall lighthouse that straddles the dangerous rocks have ever heard of the original place, all prefer to stay off the dreaded Fowey rocks and add no more history to the name.

Fowey light, visible for nearly sixteen nautical miles, is of the same genre as others down the reef introduced to Florida by George G. Meade in the early 1850s. Meade had assisted Maj. Hartman Bache in the building of the first-ever screw-pile lighthouse in the United States at Brandywine Shoal, Delaware Bay. It was his idea that this new English concept would solve the dilemma of erecting Florida lighthouses directly on the reefs without constructing artificial foundations.

Eastward of Soldier Key, and five and a half miles S.E. 1/2 S. from Cape Florida, is Fowey Rocks Lighthouse, on the northern extremity of the Florida reefs. It is an iron framework, with the lantern one hundred and ten feet above the sea, showing a fixed white light, visible in clear weather some sixteen miles. This light is situated at the northern entrance to Hawk Channel, leading between the line of Florida Keys and the outlying reefs, along the Florida Straits to Key West. The channel is from three to five miles wide and is about one hundred and forty miles from Virginia Key to Key West.

—JAMES ALEXANDER HENSHALL,

Last Onshore, First Offshore

The first lighthouse keepers of Fowey were father and son, Simeon and John Frow, lately living on shore at the keeper's house on Key Biscayne, then transferred offshore. John daily watched the building of the daddy-long-legs of a lighthouse, supervising from the very small island to the south, Soldier Key. Government supplies were transported by work boats to Fowey Rocks and, on raised platforms at different levels, living quarters were constructed "about thirty-eight feet above the water" with a circular stairway leading "from the dwelling to the lantern." When the keepers wanted to take a day off, to sail to meet friends or families on Soldier Key, Key Biscayne, or across the bay, they climbed down the scaffolding to a bobbing boat the lighthouse tender christened the *Geranium*. [Authors Note: The *Geranium* was later used as the rescue boat that saved many American crew members when the *Maine* exploded in Havana harbor, starting the Spanish-American War.]

It is not known how much the Frows knew about the Spanish Grant at Cape Florida, but they probably knew the owner had been born on the small island of Minorca. Simeon, the father, was also born on the island. In Catalan, the language of northeastern Spain (Barcelona) and the Balearics, the word *frau* (frow) means reef rock. How fitting for the father and son to serve as the last keepers of the Cape Florida lighthouse and the first keepers of the lighthouse on the reef rocks called Fowey.

Fowey light, superseding Cape Florida light, marks top of the Florida reef's dangerous coral rocks as light warns ships to keep to the east where the ocean bottom drops out and deep Gulf Stream waters race past. (Historical Association of Southern Florida)

"Lighting the entire horizon," on June 15, 1878 (notice signed May 9, 1878), the Frows took charge of the new station. On July 1, according to their log, they experienced heavy squalls and "one of the storm panes was violently struck and cracked by a large bird." The elder Frow and two assistants rode out the first hurricane at Fowey on September 7, reporting "Heavy hurricane blowing . . . unabatted" for three days with "plate glasses of lantern leaking badly." Later log entries reported "heavy seas breaking over reef" and rescue missions, sightings, visitors, and day-to-day duties and observations.

One assistant keeper was Robert H. Thompson, who earlier romanced and married Frow's daughter Julia in 1867. Another assistant was Jefferson B. Browne, later the author of a history of Key West and a member of the Florida Supreme Court.

Almost one hundred years after it was first lighted, Fowey Rocks light was given a face-lift when twentieth-century solar panels were installed. One can only imagine how the first keepers of the Cape Florida lighthouse would have marvelled at the replacement of the burning oil by sunlight! Who could have dreamed that daytime rays would light the mariner's passage through the dark hours of night?

Notice to Mariners, May 9, 1878. New light on Fowey Rock—Cape Florida Light Discontinued. (National Archives)

NOTICE TO MARINERS.

(No. 10, of 1878.)

UNITED STATES OF AMERICA—COAST OF FLORIDA.

New Light on Fowey Rocks, Florida Reefs—Cape Florida Light Discontinued.

Notice is hereby given that, on and after June 15, 1878, a *fixed white* light of the first order will be shown from the light-house recently erected on the Fowey Rocks, (northern extremity of Florida Reefs,) Florida.

The illuminating apparatus is to be catadioptric, lighting the entire horizon. The focal plane is 111 feet above the mean sea-level, and the light will therefore be visible in clear weather about 16 nautical miles.

The structure is placed in about 5 feet of water, and 150 feet south of Beacon P. It is an iron frame-work, in the form of a truncated pyramid, resting on a pile foundation. The keeper's dwelling is placed about 38 feet above the water, and a cylindrical stairway leads from the dwelling to the lantern. The entire structure is painted dark brown, except the keeper's dwelling and the stair-cylinder, which are painted white.

Approximate position of light-house, as taken from the Coast-Survey charts:

Latitude, N., 25° 35′ (22″.)

Longitude, W., 80° 05′ (50″.)

Magnetic bearings and distances of prominent objects: Cape Florida light-house, NW. ½ N., 5⅜ nautical miles; Carysfort Reef light-house, S. by W., 22⅝ nautical miles.

On and after the exhibition of this light, the light now shown from Cape Florida light-house will be discontinued.

By order of the Light-House Board:

JOSEPH HENRY,
Chairman.

Office Light-House Board,
Washington, D. C., May 9, 1878.

TEN

Through the Eyes of the Coconut

THE MOST PERFECT OF PLANTS

The coconut palm is a sacred tree of myth and legend, an emblem of fertility, a tree of creation; it is venerated throughout the Pacific rim and its islands. The romance of the South Seas suggests itself to those who see it as the symbolic tree of the tropics. In the Caribbean Islands and many places close to the equator, the coconut palm flourishes. But *Cocos nucifera* is not native to the Western Hemisphere. Remarkably, its watertight nut travels on ocean waves and currents; it traveled around the planet and came to root itself in shores distant from its Asiatic origins. Later shipwrecks, in which a vessel's holds were filled with nuts for commerce, accounted for some coconut trees in Florida, including the first ones to wash ashore and seed themselves at the spot thus designated as Palm Beach.

But before Palm Beach, there were coconuts in south Florida and the tropical zone. One of the earliest accounts was by a Jesuit in 1568 describing the Tequestas going to an island seven leagues from the present-day Miami River mouth to eat "coconut and palm grapes." If indeed they were eating coconuts and not coco plums (the translation is debated by plant experts), Key Biscayne could boast the first documentation in the Western Hemisphere of *Cocos nucifera*. Other palm species were identified by the many sixteenth- and seventeenth-century Spanish, French, English, and Dutch voyagers to the West Indies, Mexico, and South America; in fact, the palmetto palm was specifically cited many times as an aid to navigation.

The first planted and documented coconut trees were introduced to Cape Florida by Dr. Henry Perrine at the lighthouse compound where they were cared for by the first keeper and recorded in the *Congressional Record* as prospering in the 1830s. The first major cultivation on Key Biscayne began as "coconut planters" from New Jersey arrived in the early 1880s to create a subtropical palm-lined beach.

Coconut sprout. (Blank Collection)

The ongoing look of a tropical paradise began early and its tradition continued in spite of coconut blights and hurricanes. Planting and replanting of coconut trees kept the island resort palm-fringed and romantic. The coconut's many uses and life-sustaining products cause it to be described as "the most perfect of plants."

Traditional uses of the coconut palm are for food and drink: ripe and green nuts yield meat and liquid. The unripened nut contains a liquid not unlike a coconut-flavored soft drink; juice from the flower spathes is made into a toddy and can be fermented. Meat from the ripe coconut is eaten raw or grated, pressed, or squeezed to produce a sweet milk. In the islands, the soft meat is fed to babies. Coconut confections are a treat. Hearts of coconut palm are regarded as an exotic delicacy in the Western world where the palm "cabbage" from native palmettos is more common. Coconut oil is made from the dried meat, or copra. Every part of the tree has a use:

- coconut shell: cups, vessels, scoops, ladles, hanging orchid pots,
- husk: carved sculptures; inside coir fiber: doormats, ropes, brooms, brushes, cordage, orchid and garden beds
- fiber: clothes, toy dolls, moccasins, packaging, padding
- spathe: bowls, trays, floral displays, toy boats
- frond: thatch roofs, woven baskets, mats, fans, partitions, shelters, hats, masks, fish traps
- kernel: copra (dried): oil, soap, candles, coco butter, cosmetics
- trunk ("porcupine wood"): timber for building

Fringe Benefits: Osborn and Field, the Coconut Planters

In the early 1880s, two men from Middletown, New Jersey, hoped to turn sandbars into gold bars, sandspits into island resorts. They planted coconuts along a ninety-mile coastal strip from Key Biscayne to Jupiter. They were cashing in on the seventy-cents-per-acre offer made by the Internal Improvement Fund of Florida. There was revived interest in the incentives of the Great Swamplands Act of 1850 (which allowed huge blocks of swampland to be sold "for pennies" to investors who would help drain it).

The coconut planters came fast upon the heels of Hamilton Disston,

"The strength of the coconut stem (trunk) is marvelous. The old trees are very tall and have trunks so slender that it seems incredible that they can support the great crown leaves and, at the same time, the ponderous, but graceful, cluster of fruits. Yet they do, and, moreover, in a hurricane the trunks bend easily and bring the tops almost to the ground, whence they usually spring back to the perpendicular just as if nothing had happened."

—JOHN K. SMALL, 1929

As our skipper wished to obtain some cocoa-nuts, which grew abundantly on the [island] shore, and proposed to employ the time ... in catching turtle, he consented to bring up for a few hours (at Key Biscayne), advising us to keep a sharp look-out for Indians. . . . Standing into a small bay, lined on either side with mangroves and cabbage-palms, we came to anchor. At the outer point was a deserted lighthouse, which we agreed would serve as a guide to us should we have any difficulty finding our way back.

—WILLIAM H. G. KINGSTON, IN THE FLORIDA WILDS, 1880

the Philadelphian who, for twenty-five cents an acre, purchased four million acres in Florida, much of it in the Everglades (with plans to drain the whole lot).

While many developers and new property owners inland would be faced with dredging and filling in order to use their acreage, Ezra Asher Osborn (1823–1895) and Elnathan T. Field (1839–1919) went for the beaches. On Key Biscayne and to the north, they cleared brush upland of the dunes, removing salt-tolerant mangroves and palmettos, buttonwoods and sea grapes; they swept great gashes through the wetlands and woodlands to crisscross the island. They were the first to eliminate Indian mounds, level ridges and dunes, and pull up beach and other virgin vegetation in the name of improving the land. Public officials gave them incentive to proceed. The whole state would profit if they were successful in their enterprise.

More than three hundred thousand unhusked coconuts were planted in Florida in this carefully thought-out adventure-for-profit. Accounts vary, but the most definitive history of the coconut palm in Florida was recently discovered in the 1929 writings of John K. Small at the New York Botanical Garden. According to Small, seventy-six thousand coconuts were planted on Key Biscayne, the southernmost beach for the mass planting. Burlap bags of unhulled coconuts, purchased at a penny per nut, were imported by schooner from Trinidad, and workers, imported from New Jersey, studded the eastern seaboard with the sprouts.

The developers found backers for their scheme and Osborn, who was also a conveyancer, hired workers and organized operations to expedite the job. Field arranged for coconuts to be shipped in from the West Indies. They knew that after they "improved the land," they could develop it for other purposes at their leisure.

Among their early investors was John C. Collins, who would later come down to see for himself whether money would grow on trees. He stayed to become the father of Miami Beach by developing tracts of land primarily purchased from the senior partners (and by building a wooden bridge to the mainland). Collins, recalling that the venture began with a formula Osborn and Field presented to venture capitalists, wrote in 1913, "About a third of a century ago two men from the eastern part of New Jersey were informed that a well-grown coconut tree would produce a mature nut for each day of the year; hence by calculating the value of each nut, multiplying this by the number of trees per acre, and the product by the number of days in a year, they figured that the value per acre would exceed the value per acre of apples, pears or peaches grown in New Jersey."

No one challenged the numbers (which even today might convince an unwary trader of commodity futures) and besides, at pennies per acre, how could they go wrong? Predicting profits from coconut harvests and bumper crops of tourists, they envisioned a ninety-mile-long colonnade of palms along the balmy tropical beaches where winter was never known. For the first time, but not the last, the oceanfront, soon to be called the Gold Coast, was perceived for its fringe benefits.

Osborn's and Field's motley crew of tough New Jersey surfers and others recruited for coconut planting on beaches from Key Biscayne to Jupiter, Florida, group to pose for a pioneer photographer. (Ralph M. Munroe, Historical Association of Southern Florida)

Before leaving Monmouth County, Osborn and Field, like impresarios, laid out their plans. Landings along the coast would not be easy and, the way they happened, might well have been billed as Florida's first vaudeville-by-the-sea.

The cast included workers hired and rehearsed in New Jersey; their props included skiffs, houses, land-clearing and farm equipment, and tools and supplies shipped from New York on the Mallory Steamship Line. From Key West, where the ship docked before heading for New Orleans, they were transhipped by schooner back to Key Biscayne Bay where there were no wharfs. In fact, Key West had the last ones they would see for the entire engagement.

Their unique unloading operations were staged in water offshore from uninhabited beaches, which is why Osborn and Field had selected not farmers but seamen for the job. The men were trained in sea rescue off the Jersey coast and had shown their ability to handle themselves in dangerous offshore surf. During the next few years, they would continue to prove themselves in successive landings between Cape Florida and Jupiter Inlet. They did not hesitate to jump into the clear waters teeming with fish. Key Biscayne, with its offshore barrier sand ridges and bars, was usually calmer than farther up the coast.

In calm waters or rough, the landing proceeded in sure-fire order. Surf boats were rapidly launched and supplies tossed from the mother schooner into the bouncing skiffs as if the men were carrying out life-saving duties. They not only had provisions to off-load but stubborn mules as well. These they pushed off the decks into the water to swim ashore where the braying and hollering reached a crescendo as the mules shook off the water, kicked up their heels, and lay down for a roll in the sand. It was a noisy landing!

All their provisions and staples, supplies and gear were rowed in, floated in, or carried ashore by husky workers. They unloaded farm equipment, grubs, hoes, and machetes for clearing and jerking up the wild and native plants that grew so abundantly on dunes and on the low sand ridges. Sea oats and sea grapes grew seaward, low scrub and beach grasses behind, and cabbage palms and palmettoes on the ridge.

Always there were mangroves straddling the wetlands and guarding the breeding and roosting grounds of animals with fins and wings and some, like the raccoons and bears, with fur, or, like the lizards and snakes, with scales. Once the interfering brush and mangrove screens in this wild subtropical tangle were jerked up and cast aside, Osborn surveyed the land and Field prepared it for planting. Fifteen-foot roads intersected every quarter mile, and a three- to four-foot circle was cleared for each nut, allowing 110 to the acre.

Meanwhile, the schooner *Ada Doan* with her own crew set sail for the Indies. Orders were to pick up a load of unhulled nuts and deliver them posthaste back to Key Biscayne. Once the schooner was sighted on her return from Trinidad, the excitement grew as the captain sailed in on prevailing southeast winds toward Key Biscayne. Anchoring as close in as possible, the crew hurled burlap bags packed with green and brown nuts into the sea, hoping the tide would float them closer to shore, but the planters, as they would do all along the coast, fearlessly rowed out in their Seabright-built surf skiffs (which they had repaired after the sea-rescue service had condemned them in New Jersey) to recover the goods. Time was of the essence; they were concerned that the nuts must be bedded before they began to sprout. (Later, the foreman reported that only five percent did sprout before they were planted.)

But on Key Biscayne, the coconut planters' achievement was short-lived. Although they labored with great diligence along a hot four- to five-mile strip from the lonely, vacated lighthouse around Big Bend and north toward Bear Cut, they didn't realize that the island's hungry little rats and rabbits would find the coconut sprouts a rare delicacy. The marsh rabbit was particularly voracious; unlike the cottontail known in New Jersey, it had short ears, short legs, and could swim in either fresh- or saltwater whether it was carrying a coconut heart between its teeth or not. In any event, the marsh rabbit ended these early dreams of a coconut beach on Key Biscayne by nipping them in the bud.

According to correspondence in the 1920s from Commodore Ralph Munroe to botanist John K. Small, Field and Osborn planted, all told, "about 316,000 nuts . . . but the ravages of rats and rabbits, combined

The coconut planters' prefabricated houses, shipped with supplies more than a century ago, were the first houses to be erected seaward of the "coastal construction line" of the future. (Ralph M. Munroe, Historical Association of Southern Florida)

with poor soil in places, made a failure of the coconut business. The remaining trees so enhanced the value of the land that much was gotten back indirectly from the investment after all."

Fortunately, the Key Biscayne disaster did not reach the ears of government officials. On September 3, 1885, at the capitol in Tallahassee, the seal of the Florida State Land Office was affixed by the Trustees of the Internal Improvement Fund, with the governor's signature uppermost, on the conveyance to Osborn and Field of the deed, including sections and fractional sections in townships 54 and 55 which covered Key Biscayne, placing in the new owners' hands, for seventy cents an acre, the prize oceanfront "To Have and to Hold . . . forever."

Thirteen years later, it became apparent that the United States and Florida had overlooked the private holding of the Mary Ann Davis heirs on Cape Florida. The Executive Order setting aside Key Biscayne (and Virginia Key) as a military reservation also had been overlooked.

And so lawyers were called early to the island of Key Biscayne. Where others had found shifting sand, they found firm footing. Legal fights over public and private claims, deeds, titles, and land uses continue to this day on the sought-after barrier island.

Elnathan T. Field's Oak Hill Nurseries were well known in New Jersey, as evidenced by materials provided by Randall Gabrielan of the Middletown Historical Society. In the Wolman and Rose Atlas of 1878, Field's greenhouses are depicted in ornamental formal gardens with fashionable visitors. According to a local clipping of the same year, "A few evenings ago, quite a number of people gathered at the green houses of Mr. E. T. Field, Middletown, to look upon a blossom of the tropical night-blooming cereus [also called the moon goddess]. The peculiarity of this flower is that it blooms only at night and that for 'One night only'. . . . Mr. Field and his Florist . . . took great pains to give their friends a sight of this rare flower." Soon afterwards Field was drawn to the subtropics, acquiring a piece of the exotic Land of Flowers where salt-tolerant plants and wild beach dunes challenged his imagination.

Field's home was built "with a commanding view" from its observatory atop the 180-foot-high Oak Hill in Monmouth County, New Jersey.

Orderly New Jersey nursery owned by one of coconut planters contrasts with the wild scenery found along Florida's barrier beaches. (Middletown Historical Society)

GREENHOUSES at OAK HILL NURSERIES. E.T.FIELD, RED BANK. MON.Co. N.J.

"The water is furnished from an old Indian spring some distance off by hydraulic power." Its owner accumulated much Florida acreage in the 1880s. "E. T. Field and his family will leave here about the first of December for his cocoanut plantation in Florida, where he expects to spend the winter," according to the local paper in November 1885; until his death in February 1919, he tended and developed real estate between Cape Florida and Palm Beach, including founding Hypoluxa.

In fact, he was a lone voice protesting the proposed dredging of Government Cut through his Miami Beach property to make a direct entrance for the Port of Miami. When he refused to sell his land, the government condemned it. [Author's Note: Present-day Fisher Island and South Beach (SoBe) lie on either side of the Cut which was opened in 1905.]

Field and Osborn were the only "coconut prospectors" who owned and worked property on Key Biscayne. Other coconut investors from Red Bank, New Jersey, were Henry Lum, his son Charles, and Stillwell Grover (the latter related to the Osborns). Their interests were on "the beach opposite Miami" (present-day Miami Beach). Conversely, Field and Osborn held land on both barrier beaches. Lum's role in the extensive coastal planting has been exaggerated in previous accounts, although he may well have initiated the idea after a trip to south Florida in the 1870s. In any event, the men from Monmouth County, in or out of step with one another, investing in coconut futures, saw their return years later (after the syndicate was disbanded) not because the nuts sprouted but because land values shot up and, developed or not, they realized, as Munroe wrote to Small, "fabulous prices" for their beachfront tracts.

Ezra Osborn's wife, Sarah Corlies, accompanied him on Florida trips; his ventures into real estate carried on the tradition begun in her own family by forerunners from London, who in the 1640s had come to "this country for the purpose of speculating in lands in New Jersey." According to historical documents, including family papers, assembled by Gabrielan at Middletown, she and Ezra lived on the ancestral tract in a house built in 1814 which is located in the King's Highway Historic District (National Registry of Historic Places). Sarah's family homes include the Osborn-Taylor House, which is a landmark.

Osborn, whose father was a tanner with a shop in Middletown Village, was a civil engineer and laid out the Fair View Cemetery in 1855 (at a time when there was a movement to make beautiful parks for the deceased); it was a romantic plan finely laid out "in lots, walks and avenues, and well set with evergreens and deciduous trees." The barrier beaches of Florida were not so orderly.

In 1887 from New Jersey, Osborn wrote his young twenty-six-year-old foreman, Richard Carney, to ask, "Are there any bearing trees on Key Biscayne besides those [you reported were growing well] at the Lighthouse?" He and Field approved of putting wiring around the base of the trees to keep the rabbits from eating the terminal bud and killing the trees, according to correspondence held at the Historical Association of Southern Florida. Up the coast from Key Biscayne, "Rabbits are not eating any. It is supposed that wild cats there kill all the rabbits," Carney wrote. Osborn also wrote that he was "proposing to Mr. Field that we had better send to thee half a dozen barrels of different kinds of fertilizer to give a fair trial around the plants" that were growing along the beaches.

"Am in hopes the cold northers will not come along only now and then," he said, for Field was concerned they might affect the plants. In January 1886, the year before, temperatures had dipped precipitously with one reading of thirty-six degrees. (Later, Ralph Munroe reported this record from Long Key, the site of prosperous coconut planting in the keys.)

Part of the original group of seamen-turned-planters, Carney was a friend of Osborn's son, Frank, from Middletown days. "Frank will write thee the gossip," Ezra said, and then, sounding like a Quaker father, he added, "Look after the plants sharp and report to us thy judgement all around."

Later Dick Carney became a well-known captain in the bay area, running a small steamboat from Lake Worth to Coconut Grove. He joined pioneer Ralph Munroe in wrecking, reconnoitering, and other adventures.

It appears Carney never had to buy a house, but used one of the knock-down portables, sometimes called the first house on Miami Beach, although Henry Lum's son, Charles, actually built a two-story house there in 1886.

About the time the first houses were going up on the barrier beach to

A solitary monument. (Davis Family Album)

the north, Key Biscayne's oldest house, the empty keeper's cottage, burned down. Its shingled roof went up in flames, leaving only a brick shell, two chimneys, and memories.

John H. Duke, son of second lighthouse keeper Reason Duke, sailed past the solitary lighthouse and sent a letter to Texas to his old friend William Louis Dubose, one of the sons of first keeper John Dubose. The letter, from Santa Rosa County, Florida, was dated May 5, 1890:

> There is five lighthouses built on the outter edge of the reefs from Key Biscayne and K.W. most all the Islands from Miami to K.W. is fruit & vegetable gardens the wrecking business is all done a way with since so many lights is fixed on the coast.
>
> There is no one living on Key Biscayne Bay that you know, though the Miami countery is thickly settled mostly by Northern people raising Pineapples & vegetable, for the Northern markets. There is a man living at the Hunting grounds it is a fine place. The Island of Key Biscayne where you lived when the Indian War broke out & you remember all the settlers on the main land had to make there way to the Island for safety. That light is extinguished by the government some time ago an Iron open fraim Tower has ben built out on the reef seven miles from the Island. The old brick Tower stands there Solitary and a lone like it was a monument for some departed one.
>
> —*DuBose family papers*

ELEVEN

New Lease on Lighthouse

MUNROE AND HIS MERRY CREW

I n 1886, by an Act of Congress, the Secretary of the Treasury was given authority to lease the Cape Florida lighthouse. For the five years from 1888 to 1893, it was rented for the grand sum of $1, or twenty cent per annum, and used as headquarters by the Biscayne Bay Yacht Club. Hailed as the southernmost yacht club in the United States and, at ninety-five feet, the tallest in the world, it was on all the charts. Among the first founders was yacht designer Ralph Middleton Munroe (1851–1933), a South Florida booster who in the 1890s took charge of the island's Mary Ann Davis tract during the owner's absence.

(The Biscayne Bay Yacht Club later removed itself to the mainland where it is a Coconut Grove landmark; sixty years later, the new Key Biscayne Yacht Club was established on the island.)

Ralph Middleton Munroe: Call of the Tropics

Munroe credited the daughter of poet Ralph Waldo Emerson, neighbor of his grandfather in Concord, Massachusetts, with arousing his desire to come to the tropics. She gave him books to read, such as *Robinson Crusoe*. From the time "Robinson Crusoe hove his grappling hooks into the rigging of my imagination," he wrote, "the lure of coral sands and waving palms was complete."

Perhaps he would have gone to the South Seas except for meeting Ned Pent, the son of Temple Pent, who served as the third lighthouse keeper on Key Biscayne. Young Pent arrived on Staten Island aboard a steamer bursting with salvage collected during a winter season on the Florida reef, and the pilot was as full of stories and yarns as the ship's holds. Ned Pent was the pilot for the Coast Wrecking Company, fore-runners of Merritt and Chapman (for whom Munroe went salvaging years later). This salty fellow held the local New Yorkers spellbound at the dock spinning out true stories of pirates and wreckers, whom he personally knew well. Pent developed a friendship with Munroe and

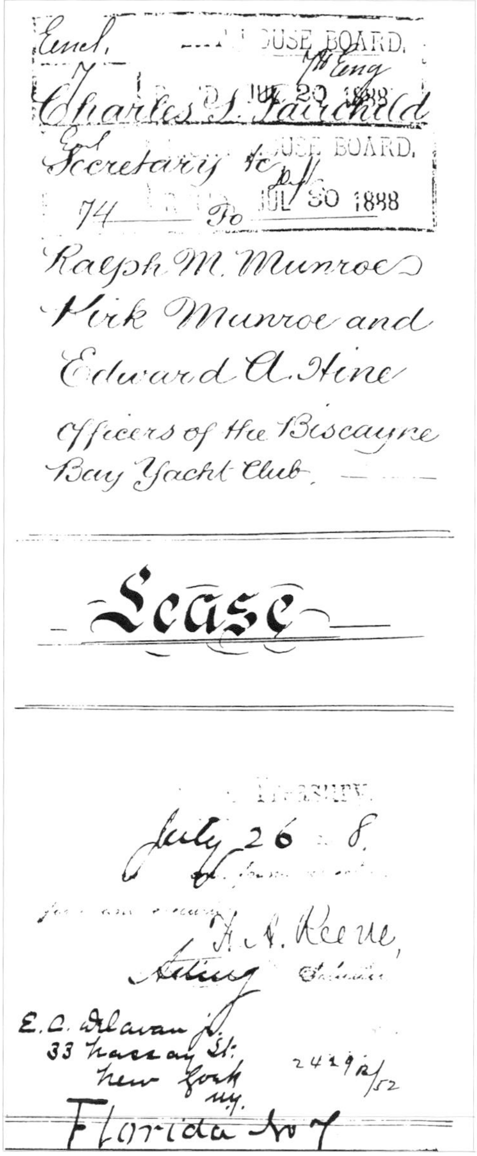

[Left document — handwritten lease cover:]

Encl.   ...OUSE BOARD.
                              1st Eng
Charles S. Fairchild   JUL 25 1888
Secretary to the   ...USE BOARD.
                              JUL 30 1888
74   Do
Ralph M. Munroe
Kirk Munroe and
Edward A. Hine
Officers of the Biscayne
Bay Yacht Club.

Lease

TREASURY.

July 26   8.

... H. A. Keene,
Acting   Solicitor

E. C. Delavan Jr.
33 Nassau St.
New York
N.Y.   2429/a/52

Florida No 7

[Right document — handwritten lease text:]

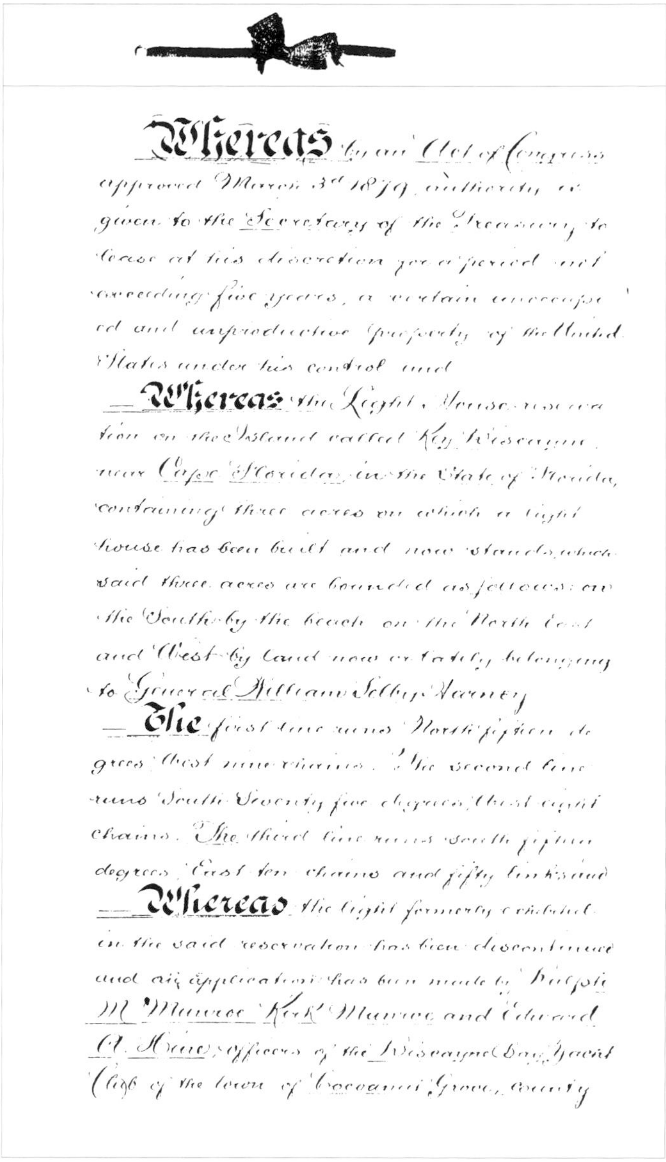

Whereas by an Act of Congress approved March 3d 1879, authority is given to the Secretary of the Treasury to lease at his discretion for a period not exceeding five years, a certain unoccupied and unproductive property of the United States under his control and

Whereas the Light House reservation on the Island called Key Biscayne near Cape Florida in the State of Florida, containing three acres on which a light house has been built and now stands, which said three acres are bounded as follows: on the South by the beach on the North East and West by land now or lately belonging to General William Selby Harney

The first line runs North fifteen degrees West nine chains. The second line runs South Seventy five degrees West eight chains. The third line runs south fifteen degrees East ten chains and fifty links and

Whereas the light formerly exhibited in the said reservation has been discontinued and an application has been made by Ralph M Munroe Kirk Munroe and Edward A Hine officers of the Biscayne Bay Yacht Club of the town of Cocoanut Grove, county

struck home as he illuminated Munroe's childhood visions of the tropics. South Florida was a lot closer than the South Pacific.

Munroe's first visit in 1877 coincided with the last year the Cape Florida lighthouse was in service. As he came up through the keys, he let his mind play with the "romantic yarns of pirates and wreckers" and "wandering spongers"; later he would contribute to the lore of south Florida by using ably, but not harming, its natural resources.

Munroe bought land from the Frows on the mainland where he built his house, the Barnacle, but he kept his spyglass trained on either end of the green-fringed island opposite his property, sailing to the key regularly, sleeping on its beaches, combing its shores from Bear Cut to Cape Florida.

Munroe also pointed his spyglass on the raised platform at Fowey Rocks, and sailed out each week to supply the keepers—among them a

Lease of 1888 with U.S. government for southernmost yacht club, founded by Ralph Munroe (who became the first commodore), American author Kirk Munroe (no relation to Ralph) and Edward A. Hine. (National Archives)

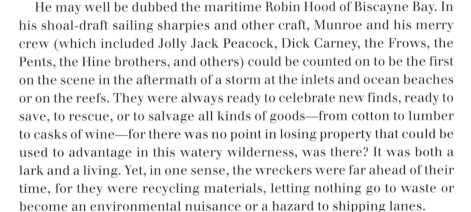

Lighthouse yacht club hailed nationally as the tallest clubhouse in the world. (Ralph M. Munroe, Historical Association of Southern Florida)

Earliest yacht club members, Commodore Ralph M. Munroe and Edward A. Hine (right), are joined by Richard Carney. (Ralph M. Munroe, Historical Association of Southern Florida)

Frow or two—with all manner of goods including regular reading matter. Undoubtedly, his lookouts, in turn, provided him with early notice of shipwrecks and salvage opportunities near Key Biscayne.

He may well be dubbed the maritime Robin Hood of Biscayne Bay. In his shoal-draft sailing sharpies and other craft, Munroe and his merry crew (which included Jolly Jack Peacock, Dick Carney, the Frows, the Pents, the Hine brothers, and others) could be counted on to be the first on the scene in the aftermath of a storm at the inlets and ocean beaches or on the reefs. They were always ready to celebrate new finds, ready to save, to rescue, or to salvage all kinds of goods—from cotton to lumber to casks of wine—for there was no point in losing property that could be used to advantage in this watery wilderness, was there? It was both a lark and a living. Yet, in one sense, the wreckers were far ahead of their time, for they were recycling materials, letting nothing go to waste or become an environmental nuisance or a hazard to shipping lanes.

Munroe's own home was built of salvaged lumber, twice used (earlier in the Frow homestead), and while much new material was ordered by Waters S. Davis, owner of Cape Florida, when he was building the house at the Cape, most of the lumber went through Robin Hood's own sawmill (which had a reputation for providing pioneer home builders with supplies salvaged from the sea). His most profitable wreck was the Norwegian tramp ship *Ingrid,* which went on the reef north of Fowey Rocks with eight hundred thousand feet of lumber. Munroe bid $1 and took the lot, "lightening and rafting off some three-fourths of the remaining cargo, and stacking it either at Coconut Grove or on Cape Florida."

At century's end, when Munroe was in his forties, he was hired to take charge of the Mary Ann Davis tract, to clear it and to prepare it for cultivation and the building of a private park and winter home there on the original land grant on Cape Florida. It occupied much of his time, and the actual clearing and building on the island gave a boost to the local economy. Davis records show that Jack Peacock, Dick Carney, and Israel Lafayette Jones were also on the payroll.

Munroe was economically and environmentally provident. Perhaps it was his Scottish blood—no matter that one of his ancestors was beheaded in the Tower of London! He could also be mischievous as in eventual negotiations in the sale of the Cape Florida tract—changing the whole destiny of Key Biscayne.

Sailor's Paradise

Munroe called the bay area "a sailor's paradise," especially for his beloved sharpies, a class of sailboats related to the raked-mast pinkies and bugeyes long used by Chesapeake Bay fishermen. Simple cat-ketch rigs, with holds for the catch or other cargo, centerboards, and a narrow beam for their length, distinguished these shoal-draft craft. Easily maneuverable and catching light breezes, with their centerboards raised, they could cross the flats like sailing rafts; then with their centerboards lowered, they could sail into deep waters.

Commodore Munroe designed and built at Coconut Grove many wooden sailing ships that sailed the bay and circumnavigated Key Biscayne. His sharpies were singularly useful in the shallow tropical waters, for they drew no more than eighteen inches with the centerboard up, and where other sailors dared not go at low tide, he could sail, or pole, even crossing the shallow Feather Bed Shoals on a changing tide, even sailing to Cape Sable on the *inside*, through back-bay country. A replica of one of his boats, the *Egret*, is now to be seen at the Barnacle, a state-owned park in Coconut Grove.

A sister ship of the *Egret* was designed in the 1950s by the Commodore's son, Wirth Munroe, and his grandson William for John D. Gill [Note: the author's first husband]. This boat, called the *Ibis*, was launched from the beach on Key Biscayne, and home port was Hurricane Harbor on the key. She carried on the Commodore's tradition, sailing the inside and outside waters from Cape Florida to Cape Sable to Key West, nosing into every inlet and every secret cove and island of the subtropical Florida wilderness, disturbing nothing, rounding Key West, sailing offshore, sailing with dolphin, flying with flying fish and birds, seldom going against the wind.

The Commodore designed the *Presto*, with a deep narrow bilge hull with centerboard, a forerunner of a new class to be used in both shallow waters and serious ocean sailing.

Sailing across becalmed bay, Kirk Munroe approaches Coconut Grove anchorage. Key Biscayne in background. (Ralph M. Munroe, Historical Association of Southern Florida)

Special Delivery to Cape Florida

Ralph Middleton Munroe sailed often to Key Biscayne, but he never missed a Tuesday evening, when he slept under the stars and awakened at dawn to sail out to the Gulf Stream to intercept the regular Mallory steamship run from New York to Galveston via Key West. He had an arrangement with the captain who brought him waterproof canvas-wrapped packets which were heaved overboard while the ship was underway. Attached to flotation sticks, the pouches delivered up-to-date newspapers and gazettes to the transplanted Yankee-turned-Florida pioneer. This was the area's first special-delivery service, and it was watertight.

TWELVE

Reclaiming Father's Lighthouse

WATERS SMITH DAVIS

By way of Galveston and Paris, Waters Smith Davis (1829–1914) sailed to Key Biscayne to reclaim Cape Florida in the early 1890s on the original Spanish Land Grant purchased by his mother Mary Ann nearly seventy years earlier. It was not just a sentimental journey. Waters Davis was engaged in shoring up his rights to defend the much-sought-after title, and he would hire a Jacksonville firm to advise him.

Mary Ann Davis died at her son's home in Texas in 1885, at the age of ninety-two, fit and clear-headed close to her death. She had outlived her husband, William Goodwin Davis, by some thirty years in Galveston; she had outlived her son, Edmund Jackson Davis, who was governor of Texas from 1870 to 1874 and died of pneumonia in Austin. Mary Ann Davis left her land in Texas and in Florida to her surviving heirs, including the governor's widow and children in Austin.

After preliminary investigation, Waters Davis learned that the Mary Ann Davis title, confirmed in 1824 by an Act of Congress, was not altogether secure. In fact, if he wanted to keep the tract, he would need to spend much time and money to defend it. Private correspondence reveals how in 1887 he purchased for a total of $600 all rights and interests of other heirs to formalize a new deed in his name in 1893. He sought the advice of a lawyer in Jacksonville after he received a letter from W. W. Dewhurst, Esq., of St. Augustine concerning a party claiming a part interest in the land. The man who had threatened to take half the property was none other than St. Augustine's distinguished former mayor, Venancio Sanchez, whom Davis's father had invited into partnership around 1840. Davis recollected the young merchant in territorial days who had gone to Cuba and purchased half the title to Key Biscayne from the oldest stepdaughter of Pedro Fornells. Sanchez was alive and well; he was affluent and adamant that he was not interested in being bought out. Waters Davis was not interested in

losing one acre or one inch of the property to this so-called noble Spaniard-cum-entrepreneur whose agents in 1841 had publicly called his father "a rascal and a liar," thereby having defamed his mother's integrity as well on the front pages of Florida newspapers.

In 1896, having spent nearly a decade of his retirement absorbed in all manner of Key Biscayne activities, Waters Davis gave a deposition in Galveston (where he was an important citizen) in which he stated that all taxes were paid on the Mary Ann Davis tract, declaring he had "erected buildings and put the land in cultivation, several houses and large fields, other improvements, erection of jetties for the protection of the land from erosion by the sea at a cost of many thousands of dollars." He was establishing a case to show that he alone had every right to keep this land, which his family had taken "actual possession of" in the 1820s, even though the title might be legally disputed.

There were other disputes: the lots sold to the former Army Col. William Harney resurfaced; so did the conflict with the coconut planters, Osborn and Field, who had been permitted by error of the U.S. government and the state of Florida to purchase "public land" that was already privately owned. Davis asked for and received quitclaims, and wrote Field that he hoped to "soon get out of the hands of the legal fraternity."

But Davis was not so fortunate with the venerable Venancio Sanchez, Esq., who lived to the age of ninety and was not about to bend to anyone. When Davis requested a patent from the U.S. government, Sanchez filed a protest. Although the patent had already been signed by President Grover Cleveland in April 1896, Sanchez effectively blocked its delivery. For two years, Davis waited. Had his father's old adversary won their long dispute? After agony and maneuvering in 1898, the protest was overruled by the Surveyor General, the Land Commissioner, and the Secretary of the Interior. It was a victory for Davis.

Reclaiming father's lighthouse.
(E. O. Gross)

Sanchez died the following year and Davis considered the threat to litigation had become history.

But it was not a closed case. Some two decades after Davis's death, the heirs of Venancio Sanchez resumed the fight for what they considered their legal claim. Ultimately, it took a Supreme Court ruling to clear the title.

After affably settling his conflict with Field for the title to Key Biscayne land, Davis wrote him, "I have largely increased my pineapple farm on the Cape this year having planted about 60,000 slips. I had planted about 15,000 the previous year." Davis was following in Henry Perrine's footsteps (Perrine, in 1838, had written the Secretary of State that a letter from John Dubose confirmed that the *Bromelia pitas*, "brethren to the edible pine-apple" still "continue propagating in the vicinity of Cape Florida"). Davis continues, "I have also set out about 200 palms with other trees and in addition two or three hundred cocoanuts—nearly all of which are doing well. I have built a neat and roomy cottage there and propose to spend some time on the Island this winter with some of my family, and I hope to have the pleasure of meeting you there."

To clear the trees and brush and land, Davis hired Israel Lafayette Jones from the Peacock Inn in Coconut Grove. Davis built a house for him on the bay side of the island, where he and his Bahamian bride, Moselle, lived, becoming the first nongovernmental residential caretakers since the Minorcans ninety years earlier had protected their land grant on Cape Florida.

Planting and cultivation were under way in 1893–94 on six acres cleared and prepared by caretaker Jones. He set out a total of seventy-five thousand pineapple slips for Davis, who hoped to grow a tropical cash crop of the native American bromeliad. On the mainland, Ralph Munroe had earlier built a pineapple-canning factory and was eager to market the Davis harvest. In spring Davis wrote from Galveston to Munroe suggesting he clear more acreage to set out bananas: "possibly an acre . . . is too much if you think so plant only 1/2 acre in them and reserve the balance for other tropical plants which I can send down next winter." In private papers preserved by his heirs, Davis laid down his plans for Cape Florida.

Additionally, the same year, he planted five hundred palms; in 1895 he had nearly a mile-long "Avenue of Coconuts" running north from the lighthouse, planted from three to five hundred feet from the ocean edge. He landscaped with coconut rows along the bay, some crossing the island, running by the house, creating a lane from the lighthouse to the bay. A few coconut and date palm descendants survive to this day.

On an 1898 map, drawn by Lt. Col. A. N. Damrell of the Army Corps of Engineers who must have walked the property with Commodore Munroe and perhaps with Davis, there is a "Partial List of Varieties of Trees growing in Waters S. Davis Park." The list begins with the Australian pine, probably the first casuarina purposely introduced to Key Biscayne (which eventually, after the later dredging, filling, and drastic clearing, took over the land to become a forest to the detriment of native and other plants). The list included banana, bamboo, co-

Texas Governor Edmund Jackson Davis (1827–1883), Waters's brother, established military rule during his autocratic reconstruction term. Born in St. Augustine the same year his mother's title to Key Biscayne was confirmed by the U.S. Congress, Davis became a volatile lawyer, judge and Union general. He championed freed blacks, gave out 9,500 political plums, established a system of free schools, and founded Texas A&M University. He passed a carpet-bag constitution, and enraged citizenry to become known as "the most hated governor of Texas." (Southeast Texas Institute)

Son of governor, West Point's Britton Davis visited family at cape. Following his military assignment to escort Geronimo to the west, he wrote an admirable book, *The Truth about Geronimo.* (Blank Collection)

conut, coffee, guava, orange, lemon (probably lime), frangipani, mulberry, rubber trees, pear, plum, papaya, and date, fishtail, and royal palms.

The fields ran back of the house to a barn with a hay loft. Davis kept a horse and a cart which were used by the farm hands. The cart was cleaned up when the grandchildren visited for rides along the coconut avenues and over the flat, wide beaches. There was a storage house for fruit-packing boxes and other farm tools and implements. Farther from the house, Jones planted large vegetable gardens, where he grew plenty of tomatoes and some Indian corn. On the lighthouse reservation there was an old orchard.

Davis, wiser than most about barrier-island living, instructed that the house be built 120 feet from the high-water mark, six hundred feet from the keeper's dwelling, and raised ten feet above the ground, so that the first floor would be safe if water rose in a storm. He paid attention to every detail, carefully giving exact instructions to Munroe who agreed to take charge of building. Overlooking nothing, Davis sent

Work cart drawn by work horse becomes a carriage for Sarah Huckins Davis, her daughter Mary, and friend from Galveston, Texas, who have shed elegant garb for casual dresses and sun bonnets. (W. S. Davis)

Idyllic tropical hideaway, Cape House commanded a magnificent view of bay, keys, and ocean. A commodious two-story raised cottage with five bedrooms, verandas on three sides, detached cook house, and servants quarters behind, it stood 600 feet west of keeper's cottage and lighthouse. Built in the 1890s, it was the teamwork of designer Ralph Munroe of Coconut Grove and civil engineer (and cartographer) E. A. Hensoldt of Galveston, Texas, with much input from Waters S. Davis. (E. O. Gross, Larroca/Davis Collection)

Key Biscayne

London-born Charles Peacock of Coconut Grove, the area's first hotelier and jack-of-all-trades, helped build Cape House. (W. S. Davis)

orders through the mails to Ralph Munroe, Charles Peacock, and Richard Carney who helped build the Cape House. He shipped them materials and goods from many ports including Galveston, Chicago, and New York. "If the well water will not do to drink and it is necessary to have a cistern, I can have one made here and forward [it]," he wrote in June 1893; a follow-up letter told precisely how many feet he expected the faucet to be installed from the pump in the kitchen, and so forth.

Cape Florida's extensive landscaping and cultivation were carefully laid out. Davis left little to chance; he sent to the cape not only tropical plants and trees that were not immediately available locally, but also fertilizer. Many acres were cleared, although most of the tract was kept in its natural state. Freshwater ponds, bogs, and buttonwood, and mangrove swamps were not disturbed and, except on the southern tip of the island, he left native vegetation including large palmettos and shady poisonwood trees. Nor did he level ancient Tequesta mounds, which survived until 1950 when modern land clearers unceremoniously bulldozed them along with the ancient mangrove and palmetto forests. A treasured seagrape tree served as the photographic backdrop.

Group in hammock are Uncle Alfred Munroe, author Kirk Munroe, Sarah H. and Waters S. Davis, with Mary Davis visible in the branches. (Davis Family Album)

Buying Back the Lighthouse

In May 1893, Waters S. Davis wrote to Rear Admiral James A. Green, U.S.N., chairman of the Lighthouse Board in Washington, D.C., "As the Government has abandoned the Light House and a fire having destroyed the keeper's house and other out buildings and as the Gov't apparently has no further use for the property, I write to ask on what terms I can have the tract reconveyed to me."

However, it was not until 1903 that Davis bought back "Father's lighthouse" from the U.S. Treasury for a bid of $400. In 1898, after renovation of the light tower for the Spanish-American War, a drawing that mapped the south end of Key Biscayne declared, "Waters S. Davis has been appointed sole custodian for the lighthouse property by the Honorable Secretary of the Treasury."

Locals and others gathered for outings on the Key: family and friends arrived each winter from Galveston, New York, Chicago, and elsewhere to vacation with the Davises in their spacious two-story winter bungalow on their warm subtropical island that could have been in the South Pacific. It was an idyllic setting, and there was always a gardener and caretaker for the lush subtropical grounds in the midst of wild scenery. There were groves and lanes of coconut palms inland and along the beaches, and the fronds rustled in the trade winds, accompanied by lapping waves; the whirr of wings and bird chatter, hoots, and cries filled the air. Acres of mangrove swamps and virgin forests attracted and sheltered a wide range of wildlife, and every tide brought in surprises. Shelling and beachcombing beckoned. Thousands of egrets, ibis, herons, and roseate spoonbills roosted and fed on the island, and

A large gathering on a sunny day at Davis house on the cape. (Ralph M. Munroe, Historical Association of Southern Florida)

birdwatching could not have been better from the veranda of Cape House. Sunrise and sunset were tropical extravaganzas. Nights under the stars and moon were romantic.

Besides, Waters and his wife Sarah had the best view *and* the tallest building in town. An observation room unparalleled in the entire area—the lantern room of the lighthouse—offered a panoramic view. They could see far north up the coastal beaches, northwest to the Miami River and deep into the Everglades, west over Coconut Grove, and southwest over Cutler Ridge (the Hunting Grounds) and Turkey Point. To the south they could see across lower Biscayne Bay over coral flats and Bache Shoals to Soldier and Elliott keys. To the east was the Atlantic Ocean, a sparkling palette of greens, violets, and lighter blues. Four miles offshore, the Gulf Stream, a deep indigo-blue band, stretched to the horizon. Beyond lay the Bahama Islands, forty to fifty miles away.

For their grown children, Waters II, Sarah, Emmeline, and Mary, and their grandchildren, there was ongoing excitement when a school of dolphins played offshore, a school of tarpon flashed, or a giant stingray leapt high as if it would be airborne. The view was never static, always changing.

The family and their guests enjoyed the sense of being totally removed from the pressures and urgency of city life and commerce. Although they were content on their island, nearby change was in the air.

Henry Flagler, the Standard Oil magnate, was riding the rails down the eastern seaboard from New York to St. Augustine, the end of the line. Then, seeing the possibilities of luring visitors farther south, he built his own railroad from St. Augustine up to the St. Johns River and then south to Palm Beach, with grand hotels at several stops in between. Residents of the bay area saw some possibilities of their own. To bring the railroad to Miami, several landowners, among them Julia Tuttle and William Brickell, who owned much on the mainland, gave him prime property (in present-day downtown Miami) so that he could build his railroad depot and open up a resort and port.

Waters Davis, who had not only watched but been instrumental in strengthening the major port at Galveston, where he brought in the Gulf and Santa Fe Railroad, had already made his millions. He was retired and not about to join the greeters. Still, he shared with Coconut Grove friends, who regularly sailed out to the cape to commiserate about Flagler's invasion, the old stories his mother and father had told him about their own dreams some seventy years earlier.

He told them how his determined mother, Mary Ann, and his overpowering father (who had been Deputy Marshall of St. Augustine with duties from the St. Johns River to Cape Florida) had schemed up the idea of a port of entry on Cape Florida, drawn up a town plan, and sold lots. The lighthouse was the focal point of the plan; the town circled around it as if it were a monument of a central plaza. Waters told how Father had even written the President of the United States in January 1843 urging that he himself be appointed lighthouse keeper when the tower was rebuilt—because then he could be on hand to supervise the

Three generations, grandmother Sarah, her daughter Sarah, and grandson Harry Hawley, Jr., stand before lighthouse, with mangroves and ocean in distance. Path is cleared to plant coconut-lined trail to lighthouse. Waters's wife, Sarah Huckins Davis, was the daughter of Reverend James Huckins, one of the founders of Baylor University, tracing ancestry back to John Alden and Priscilla Mullens. (Blank Collection)

building of the port town on Cape Florida which would command and protect mainland traffic and settlers.

Father would have rushed to give Flagler wharf space on Key Biscayne and sell him prime water frontage. Waters Davis was not interested in carrying on his father's dreams; it was enough that Father, William Goodwin Davis, would go down in history as south Florida's first developer.

Waters and Sarah watched, probably with some annoyance and some amusement, as dredges came into Biscayne Bay to deepen the entranceway off Cape Florida, then to dig "Flagler's channels" the length of the bay to the river to bring in work boats and supplies. Eventually the sand suckers would disturb the entire area, and from their bird's-eye view in the tower watch room, the Davises could watch the results of the work as the crystal-clear waters of their tropical-fish aquarium-in-the-bay were muddied by spoil and silt.

But before too long, Flagler had made a new decision: he would abandon the Cape Florida entry to the bay and make his own direct short cut from the ocean to the mainland, creating a port, and he would ask the U.S. Congress to pay for it.

Waters Davis was relieved. Father's dream was finished, and now it must be laid to rest. Key Biscayne could lie in the lee of history, and perhaps it would remain undeveloped and unspoiled.

The Davises continued to come to the island until 1913. It had become their refuge in the aftermath of the disastrous Galveston storm in 1900 which "almost swept Galveston off the face of the earth." More than six thousand people had been killed and thirty-seven thousand structures destroyed. It was called the greatest natural disaster in American history. (This designation would remain until 1992 when Hurricane Andrew devastated south Florida.)

After the 1900 Galveston storm, Waters discovered the original headstones missing from the Mary Ann Davis family plot. To the eye of a hurricane, no place is sacred. On a barrier island, a cemetery has little chance of living up to its Latin meaning: *coemeterion*, a sleeping place. Fortunately, after the Texas storm when the cemetery in the center of the island was wrecked, the Episcopal church records were found, and the graves were given substantial new headstones of grey granite.

In a less well-known cemetery, on an exposed barrier island on the Atlantic, soldiers were buried with military honors during the Seminole Wars. There were neither relatives nor a permanent population to keep vigil over the burial ground on Key Biscayne. As hurricanes and erosion destroyed the southern edge of the low-lying island, washing out some 450 feet at "South Point" between the 1840s and 1870s, the cemetery at Cape Florida was swept into the sea. This is the site of Key Biscayne's offshore graveyard, where brightly colored corals replace fresh flowers as reminders of those war casualties of long ago.

In the aftermath of the Texas storm of 1900, the entire island city of Galveston was raised ten feet above sea level, the houses jacked up and elevated by mandate as dredges pumped fourteen million cubic yards

Wirth Munroe, in his sailor suit, played with Davis children on Key Biscayne, sailing over with his parents, Ralph and Jessie Munroe, and older sister, Patty. (W. S. Davis)

of sand from the Gulf of Mexico. Three Davis houses were raised. (After Davis's experience, Munroe decided to raise his Coconut Grove home, the Barnacle, and put in a ground floor. Cape House was originally elevated ten feet in anticipation of rising waters.) After the Galveston hurricane, the little foliage that survived the winds was destroyed by saltwater and wet sand pumped in during the grade lifting. The Davises began to come more often to the cape, for they now especially appreciated the lush vegetation and undisturbed wilderness. They visited places of interest in Florida, making many friends, taking many photographs. While researching this book, long-lost albums, discovered in Galveston, Dallas, and Cape Cod, revealed yellowed photographs taken before and after 1900. Commodore Munroe was taking magnificent photographs of south Florida, and his glass negatives were preserved; one imagines he gave the Davis amateurs some tips. The quality of the Davis pictures varies, but the record is unmatched.

The *Fornella* of Key Biscayne, designed by Ralph Munroe for Davis, was the first motorized water taxi on the bay. She heralded a new form of transportation to the offshore island, which had been first visited by Indian dugout canoes and, thereafter for many centuries, visited almost exclusively by sailing ships. She was named in honor of Pedro Fornells, first title holder to Cape Florida.

Aboard the *Fornella*, a thirty-six-foot cruiser with centerboard and auxiliary sails, the Davises visited many points of interest in the area, including the Punch Bowl, which was located on the mainland on Key Biscayne Bluffs (now known as Silver Bluff, south of the present-day toll gate to Rickenbacker Causeway). The Punch Bowl was described well by James Alexander Henshall, a visitor in 1881, as "a large spring in the hamak of Mr. [William] Brickell, and near the shore of the bay. In times gone by the buccaneers, pirates and wreckers of the Florida Keys and Spanish Main . . . fill[ed] their water casks from its great, rocky bowl. Of course the usual stories of buried treasures near the haunts of pirates obtain, and many and vain have been the searchings in the vicinity of the Punch Bowl."

The Davises went to the source of the Miami River and discovered that from its mouth to its head (east to west), it stretches less than five miles, about the same length as Key Biscayne (north to south). The Falls, another natural attraction visited by the Davises, with camera in hand, previously had been described by Henshall: "A few miles up the Miami there is quite a rapids, called The Falls, which will well repay a visit, being a lovely and most romantic spot." They sailed to other points of interest he described. "At the head of the bay, Snake and Arch creeks empty. Spanning the latter is a natural stone bridge or arch of coralline rock, under which boats may pass."

They learned about local history on their day sails. Arch Creek Natural Bridge stood witness to the routing of Seminoles by Col. William Harney, who had bought the first two lots of the 1839 town planned for Key Biscayne by Mary Ann and William G. Davis. At the south end of the arch bridge stood Luis the Breed's stone house and mill. Luis, who was part Indian and part Cuban, was the link between the Indians and their Cuban source of supplies. During a bitter battle, Harney and his troops drove out the Indians, demolished the house and mill, and killed Luis.

Later, Vincent Gilpin, co-author of *The Commodore's Story* and sometimes collaborator with Ralph M. Munroe, wrote that natural features were the local "points of interest considered worth picturing in 1887 . . . the works of man being represented only by a few primitive houses and small sailboats. . . . The Everglades . . . an unexplored wilderness, jealously guarded against white intrusion by the Seminoles . . . keenly mindful of repeated evictions enforced on them by unscrupulous white settlers. The Hunting Grounds at Cutler . . . the haunt of deer and bear and panther.

"Indian Creek . . . a desolate lagoon, haunt of wild duck and crocodile, a dozen or more of the latter often being visible at once. The Miami River . . . a mangrove bordered stream, with four or five small buildings on its whole length."

The Davises did not take the commercial boat rides up and down the bay that thrilled early sightseers who arrived by railroad after April 1896, but John Sewell, the third mayor of Miami, recalled in *Miami Memoirs*, "A trip to Cape Florida Lighthouse was one of the popular trips of the day."

Among family and friends of the Davises was the well-respected artist Boyer Gonzales (1867–1934). He stayed at Cape House as the guest of his brother, Julian Caverly Gonzales, and sister-in-law Emmeline Coit Davis, at whose wedding he was best man. Like his good friend and mentor Winslow Homer, Boyer painted tropical land- and seascapes. Boyer and Julian (and their descendants) traced their roots through their paternal grandmother's family in Valladolid (in Old Castile) back to Ponce de León. Julian's and Emmeline's children spent time at Cape Florida, as did the other Davis grandchildren before 1913, exactly four hundred years after their ancestor discovered the island of Key Biscayne.

Edith Boyer Gonzales, Davis grandchild, poses behind a fan palm in front of mangroves at Cape Florida 400 years after her supposed ancestor Juan Ponce de León discovered the island. (W. S. Davis)

Astronomical Names

Without being aware that the first astronomical and magnetic observations in the area were made in 1849 and 1850 from the lighthouse by J. E. Hilgard during the U.S. Coast Survey, headquartered at Cape Florida, an amateur but extremely astute young woman turned her telescope on the skies above Cape House about fifty years later.

Her name was Mary Huckins Davis and she was the granddaughter of Mary Ann and William Goodwin Davis. Her parents called her their resident astronomer. In Paris they bought her a fine telescope which she carried with her and used to watch the movement of the stars over Key Biscayne. She set it up on the wide veranda and sometimes carried it down to the beach for a 360-degree view—north, south, east, and west—undiminished by lights or obstructions of any kind.

Sometimes the Milky Way was a star-spangled banner ablaze in the firmament; other times the points of one or another constellation—Orion, Sirius, Cassiopeia, Aries—stood out against the clear blackness overhead. The east-to-west path of the planets crossed over Cape House, and with the aid of the telescope, she could see clearly the red fire of Mars and the brilliance of Venus, among others.

Portrait of Israel Lafayette Jones, first Davis caretaker. (Ralph M. Munroe, Historical Association of Southern Florida)

The USS Maine and the Spanish-American War both blew up in 1898, madly exciting Key West and its naval vessels, its crowding Cuban refugees and their conspiratorial Junta.

—MARJORY STONEMAN DOUGLAS,
THE LONG FRONTIER

Undoubtedly, Mary shared this telescope (now a prized possession of her great-grandniece Sally Larroca) with others, including members of the Munroe family, when they visited the island.

Ralph Munroe used his own telescope (now used by his grandson Bill) on the mainland to watch the comings and goings at the Cape; in fact, he kept an eye on all the action along the bay, training his telescope from the boathouse on everything that moved. He must have liked this young lady who kept her eyes open and her elders on their toes.

Mary was at home anywhere in the world, for, like navigators of old, she knew where she was by the position of the stars; she became an exceptional help in navigating Florida waters. She is remembered in the Biscayne Bay area, however, not for naming stars but for naming two newborn boys. They were the sons of Moselle Jones, of whom she was very fond because Moselle and her husband, Israel, were a part of the life at Cape House. Israel was the caretaker and Moselle helped with everything. They lived in their own planked house on the bay side close to the big house.

According to Munroe in *The Commodore's Story,* when their sons were born, "Moselle appealed to Miss Mary Davis for suggestions of great men to name them for. Miss Davis could think of no more admirable heroes than King Arthur and Sir Launcelot, and so they were named. To Moselle the title was an integral part of the name, and they were always addressed by both together; I can still hear her musical hail from the doorway: 'Oh you, King Arthur! Come to dinnah!'" Mary's photo album shows a picture on Key Biscayne of the baby, captioned "King Arthur." He and his brother are believed to be the first black Americans born on the key.

Spanish-American War: Cape Florida AXHV

The excitement of the Cuban war of independence from Spain spread north from Key West to Key Biscayne, where the lighthouse (not yet in Waters S. Davis's possession) was reactivated as a U.S. Signal Station. The Signal Station proudly displayed its newly designated International Code letters AXHV. One of thirty-six stations along six thousand miles of coastline from Maine to Texas, Station Number Four at Cape Florida was considered important because, after all, it guarded the vulnerable Florida seaboard, and everyone knew that only ninety miles of water separated Key West and Havana. High-spirited headlines fueled rumors that the Spanish fleet was poised to attack the U.S. coast.

Before the United States declared war, enthusiasts in Florida rallied round the Tampa-based Cuban revolutionary party in exile, founded there in 1892 by Cuba's great poet and writer, the liberation leader Jose Marti (1853–1895). There was support from Key West to Tampa, where many of Marti's countrymen had settled. Smugglers of arms and ammunition, called filibusterers, were running private small craft in and out of international and Florida waters using the old harbors, inlets, and bays of picaroons and pirates, and, in fact, repeating in reverse the

Jones moved his family to Porgy Key, where W. S. Davis later photographed them. Jones had learned to plant pineapples at Cape Florida, where they were not a success, but they flourished on the coral-rock soil of the upper Florida Keys. Pineapples are native to America . (W. S. Davis)

tradition of smuggling begun by Cuban "fishermen" who had supplied Indians with powder and guns to fight the Americans.

The smugglers who were caught were tried in south Florida courts and judged by sympathetic jurors, so that they returned again and again to the keys and the high seas, a pattern not unknown today. In any event, the Floridians were ready to go to war when the *Maine* was blown up and sank in Havana harbor.

Later it became evident that there was little danger to the United States, but there was public alarm. When in the spring of 1898 Capt. John R. Bartlett, U.S.N., was put in command of the Signal Service, he acted swiftly. His orders were to allay the public fear. In a 1901 *Century* magazine article, Bartlett recalls he assigned four quartermasters to each station and equipped his men with telescopes and field glasses "to watch for the Spanish fleet." He was amazed at the excitement generated; he had set up telephone and telegraph lines and nightly he was besieged by sightings of "mysterious vessels" offshore; he confessed later that if he were awakened by such a call, "I generally turned over and dismissed the officer with the remark: "Sea serpent again. Keep these reports until morning."" He and the military in charge never expected the Spanish fleet to attack.

Realizing the unlikelihood of any threat, Ralph Munroe continued piloting boats past the Cape Florida entrance into the bay and, in fact, in his book *The Commodore's Story*, he wrote, "That spring the Davises stayed late on Cape Florida and for some time the Munroes lived with them there, thus being right on the spot." He was amused when his sidekick Dick Carney mistook a charter ship offshore for a Spanish ship. And when there was a subsequent rumor, before the arrival of the

A good friend, Bessie Royston from Galveston, behind Jessie Munroe with Ed Hine, Ralph Munroe and host Waters S. Davis (in pith helmet) on front steps of Cape House. (Davis Family Album)

troops on the mainland prompting the newly incorporated city officials of Miami to wire "frantically for coastal defense guns," Munroe began to call "the whole thing a little short of silly . . . everybody in Miami was hastily packing up to leave, and the Munroes and Davises stayed on at Cape Florida, having a lovely time."

U.S. troops were sent to protect the national interests. Across from the island at the mouth of the Miami River, Henry Flagler's new Royal Palm Hotel opened its doors to welcome officers of the U.S. Army. Outside, eight thousand soldiers put up tents to make camp in an area cleared for this purpose by Flagler's men. Here the troops waited for orders to sail to Cuba for the invasion. The call did not come. Instead the command was given at Tampa, on the west side of the state, where Theodore Roosevelt and his Rough Riders, among others, boarded the ship to lead the invasion that would win national adulation for Roosevelt and freedom from Spain for Florida's close neighbor, the island of Cuba.

Viewed from the lighthouse, there was much activity as the men serving on the island practiced their routines, keeping watch over the waters and the Gulf Stream passage, running up signal flags and admiring them as they flapped in the breeze, read by occasional passing pilots and captains.

The first enemy ship captured from Spain brought everyone to the beaches. It sailed past Cape Florida and up the newly dredged "Flagler Channel" to the Florida East Coast dock on the Miami River. There was a lot of amazement as "the first Spanish prisoners brought to American soil were landed. . . . The whole city went to the dock to see the Spanish general and his soldiers transferred to the train, and the Spaniards did quite a business selling their money, trinkets, and even buttons on their uniforms to Miami citizens for souvenirs," wrote John Sewell in his memoirs.

When the U.S. troops, who had waited in vain, finally left Miami for the north, they did not go by sail but by rail; they left without passing the historic Cape Florida lighthouse, a maritime landmark that over the years had witnessed almost all the significant arrivals and departures in the area. The island's historic position at the crossroads of history was changing, even as the lighthouse, like the troops, was once again mustered out of service.

With and without the signal flags flying, the tower would always remain a colorful landmark on the southernmost barrier island of the United States.

Some say the Spanish-American War established the United States as a world power. Certainly it gave Key Biscayne a new place in history, noticed by hardly anyone, except perhaps an occasional reader of *The International Code of Signals for the Use of All Nations*. Issued by His Majesty's Board of Trade in 1901, it lists worldwide code letters including AXHV, those used on Cape Florida.

Each station was provided a ninety-foot mast with yard which in many cases was set up in the ground like a flagpole beside the house or platform used as headquarters. On Key Biscayne, it was rigged from the top of the tower. International signal flags were to signal warnings to

White tower looms over private reconstruction work by Davis of keeper's cottage and compound, following occupation by U.S. armed forces during Spanish-American War. Photo dated September 11, 1900. (National Archives)

passing vessels of the merchant marine to advise "the proximity of the enemy."

According to reports, wire netting was requisitioned to protect station crews from mosquitoes, but the chief regretted there was no such protection from rattlesnakes that threatened crews along the Florida coast. At some sites "there is a rattlesnake for every foot of land on the island. The crew at one station sent me the skin of a rattlesnake which measured seven feet in length," wrote the captain at the Navy yard.

Although "daily exercises and drills" were mandatory, and "outside communication forbidden," it appears that the rigidity of the assignment and strict adherence to orders may not have been followed at all times at Cape Florida.

By 1898, the first weather station in the Miami area (forerunner of the National Hurricane Center) was working on Cape Florida; the district director in Jacksonville was a friend of the Davis family. Israel Lafayette Jones, who was living year-round as estate caretaker, would become the Wind Signal Keeper in 1897. After the turn of the century, tides were regularly measured and published for Cape Florida and the Miami River mouth for some years.

"The Pelicans . . . can judge with certainty of the changes of the weather . . . the best of all prognosticators of the weather are the Wild Goose, the Gannet, the Lestris, and the (Brown) Pelican," wrote John James Audubon. He continued, "The Brown Pelicans are as well aware of the time of each return of the tide as the most watchful pilots. Though but a short time before they have been sound asleep, yet without bell or warning, they suddenly open their eyelids, and all leave their roosts the instant when the waters, which have themselves reposed for a while, resume their motion."

Matheson's Island

THE COCONUT PLANTATION

Joyous, ebullient, full of zest ... he loved to share both his pleasures and high spirits with others.
—WILLIAM LYON PHELPS, AMERICAN POET, PROFESSOR AT YALE UNIVERSITY

W. J. Matheson, casual in his coconut grower's hat, buys property north of Cape Florida tract and transforms it into a tropical garden paradise. (Matheson Family Collection ©Finlay B. Matheson)

In his run to the top of corporate America, William John Matheson (1856–1930) moved with alacrity from the chemistry bench to the boardroom, making unusually sound decisions whether he was about to found a new corporation, fund a research program, negotiate with the president of the United States, or buy a tract of land 5,680 feet north of a certain coconut tree close to the Cape Florida lighthouse.

It was during the first decade of the century that this exuberant industrialist and man of many skills and interests began buying the available high land and wetlands on Key Biscayne until he held seventeen hundred acres, more or less, running east to the ocean, west to the bay, north to Bear Cut, and south to the Cape Florida boundary line.

Born in Elkhorn, Wisconsin, he was the son of Anna Meigs Lighthall and Finlay Matheson, who had come to America from Scotland. When in 1865 his father was hired by a sugar grower in British Guiana, the family moved to equatorial Georgetown on the Essequibo River. Their older son, William, was fascinated by the tropical jungles and wildlife, which he would remember as a childhood dream of paradise. However, he and his brother were quickly shipped off to school in Scotland. En route their ship was struck by a fearful November hurricane.

On Christmas day, 1865, the Georgetown *Gazette* reported, "We very much regret to learn that the ship *Strathleven*, which left this port for London on the 3rd of September last, sprung a leak on the 4th of November on the bank of Newfoundland, and was totally lost. Intelligence had arrived from Falmouth that the crew had safely arrived there in the *Marmion*. At the time of her loss there were three passengers on board, viz., Dr. Walker and Masters Hugh and William Matheson. Previous to the loss to the vessel, Captain Hannington and a cabin boy were washed off the quarter-deck, and have not been since heard of. Dr. Walker died on the 14th of November, ten days after the wreck. We are happy to be able to state that the other two passengers, the Masters Matheson, have reached London in safety."

After their rescue, the boys finally made it to Glasgow, exposed at a tender age to the deadly force of storms bred in the tropics.

It is a wonder that W. J. Matheson ever returned to the tropics, but he

did, and he invested much love and many of his resources in south
Florida. In 1926, the eye of a brutal storm swept across Key Biscayne
and Miami, devastating the area and undoing much of what he had accomplished in the first quarter of the century. Yet he supported rebuilding, a tribute to his ever-resilient spirit.

During his time in Scotland, W. J. was fascinated to learn about an
eighteen-year-old research student of the Royal College of Chemistry,
working in his homemade laboratory in his garden in 1856 (the same
year that Matheson was born) who had made the breakthrough discovery that ushered in the development of synthetic aniline dyes. The
work by William Henry Perkin, who was eventually knighted by the
Queen, revolutionized the textile industry and then affected almost
every other manufactured product in the world.

Matheson, too, was a precocious young man. Having grasped the
importance of the ongoing investigative research into coal tar (one of
the by-products of the expanding gas industry), he was one of the first
Americans to comprehend that the textile industry, which previously
had depended on vegetable dyes, such as that from the indigo plant and
logwood, would now march hand in hand with the chemical houses
that manufactured synthetic dyes. The earliest advances were not in
England, but in Germany, where giants like Leopold Cassella & Company broke new ground. In 1880, as their agent, he formed William J.
Matheson & Company, as importer and distributor of Cassella products,
and from then on was always a step ahead of the fast-paced aniline
industry.

Matheson's ability to combine his scientific and business acumen
was a distinct advantage; he was the founder of the National Aniline
and Chemical Company and later the Allied Chemical and Dye Corporation. Over successive years, he was considered "the guiding spirit,"
creating and maintaining the leadership and "technical organization by
which the textile industry of America was kept in the advance guard of
progressive manufacturing nations."

In 1881 he married Harriet Torrey of East Aurora, New York, and
they had three children: two sons, Hugh Merritt, followed by Malcolm,
and a daughter, Anna (Nan). They lived near Huntington, Long Island,
at Lloyd Neck in a grand old estate known as Fort Hill. Although later
separated from his wife, W. J. was always close to the children.

Sometimes as younger children they would board their father's
steam yacht, *Laverock* (Scottish for *lark*), and ride with him from the
Oyster Bay dock down Long Island Sound to the downtown pier not far
from his Manhattan office near Broad and Wall streets. But the cruise
they most looked forward to was traveling down the East Coast to
Florida during the winter season. First, they went to Ormond Beach;
later, when Hugh was boarding at the winter quarters of the Adiron-
dack School (forerunner of Ransom-Everglades School) in Coconut
Grove, they discovered Biscayne Bay.

W. J. was relieved to say farewell to his boardroom colleagues who
gathered each winter at Henry Flagler's fashionable watering hole in
Ormond Beach, where Henry Ford, Barney Oldfield, and also Eddie
Rickenbacker raced the first fast automobiles upon the broad, hard-

Harriet Matheson and the children,
young Malcolm, Hugh, and Anna. (Jean
Preston Guyton Collection)

packed beaches, between scheduled and unscheduled affairs in the railroad hotel. Matheson preferred wind power. He enjoyed sailing into the bay past the Cape Florida tower, past the charming Davis house with its wide verandas suggesting casual island living, and he admired the beautiful groves of coconut and date palms along the sandy shores.

W. J. bought property on the mainland in 1902 and built a winter home in Coconut Grove overlooking the bay, with Key Biscayne in the distance. He became enchanted by the island that was always in view.

In 1908, the first of a series of deeds conveyed to W. J. described tracts on Key Biscayne from ocean to bay that he bought from Ezra Osborn's widow, who, thirty years earlier, had sailed with her husband to the island where his crews of New Jersey surfers had planted seventy-six thousand coconuts. W. J. then accumulated land from the boundary line of the Davis property north to Bear Cut, over seventeen hundred acres.

Much of this land he left in its natural state. The rest of the tracts he cultivated, making important plant introductions and assessments that helped bring this country's tropical agriculture out of its infancy. In the process, the sand island was transformed by flowering and fruiting plants and trees and magnificent palms of many kinds. Areas of native growth of palmetto, sea grape, poisonwood, and scrub were cleared for coconut plantings that would cover some eight hundred acres.

Midway across the island, back from the "coastal ridge," Matheson pumped in bay bottom to fill in swampland. He purposely did not disturb the mangrove forests or hammocks on the north and northwest of the island, but left these wetlands as a preserve for native flora and

View from air shows early plantation plantings, buildings, and roads. Barn was headquarters. (Matheson Family Collection ©Finlay B. Matheson)

fauna (except for the first mosquito drainage ditches in Dade County). That was his way, which is further demonstrated in other lands he owned.

On Mashta Point, he built a great house, where the family entertained, some say in the style of F. Scott Fitzgerald, others say with more elegance and less Gatsby. They did not live there but brought their guests by boats, or welcomed them from their own private yachts. Except for Mashta House, the island structures were designed for business.

Quite by accident, the man in charge was Hugh Merritt Matheson (1886–1952), W. J.'s oldest son. He graduated from Yale University with a degree in science, which he pretended not to take seriously, although both he and his father always had laboratories in their homes and in their gardens (inspired, perhaps, by Sir William Henry Perkin, whom W. J. had admired while a student).

After graduation, Hugh did not come directly to Florida, for he began work in one of his father's companies. When Hugh became ill with lead poisoning, an occupational hazard in his father's business, W. J. moved rapidly to save his son from the ravages of the Madhatter's Disease, well known to tanners and dyers. Medical experts declared the prognosis was good—if he spent his life outdoors. One of the outcomes of his illness was that he fell in love with his nurse, Liguori Hardy, and married her. But that was only one of the outcomes. The other was that, because he had doctors' orders to work outdoors, his father urged him to manage the Key Biscayne holding, which he already had under cultivation.

Key Biscayne became the antidote to his illness. Hugh Matheson was a lucky young man: his father had given him the Fountain of Youth.

Father and son breathed easier, and Hugh began to enjoy his gift. Under his direct guidance, much clearing, planting, and building took place as the focus grew beyond the earlier limited planting of lime trees begun in 1910. There would be experimental planting and testing of varieties of fruit trees, coconuts, ornamentals, and exotic flora to increase knowledge of tropical plants, assess their commercial feasibility, and determine their salt tolerance, cold tolerance, and disease susceptibility. But it never became so tedious that Hugh didn't have fun.

From the mainland headquarters on the Miami River, where there were warehouses and wharves and a regular twice-a-day boat run to the key, they operated an almost self-sufficient island plantation. Settlements housed and fed workers; there were packing houses and docks, commissaries and a school, a big barn and outbuildings, canals and wells, irrigation and windmills. After mechanization, there was a generator; trucks took the place of a wagon, two jennies and a jack of the "jackass express," which hauled mail, ice, and groceries. In the fields, mulching took the place of burning.

There were sanctuaries for native wildlife and special provisions for endangered species (one of Hugh's interests), such as the almost extinct flamingo reintroduced to Key Biscayne from the Bahamas, and Galapagos turtles watched over by Hugh for the New York Zoological

A Corsician Citron tree, from the Mediterranean region, grew well on Key Biscayne. Hugh Matheson, in front of tree, holds one of the "Ugli-fruit" for cameraman David Fairchild (Fairchild Tropical Garden Collection)

Chopped up roots of palmettos cleared from the fields served as mulching for the plants and as road surface. (Gleason Waite Romer, Florida Collection, Miami Public Library)

Society. Locals were wrong if they thought the island was merely a rich man's playground or bauble.

From Malays to Maypans

The significance of Matheson coconut and other cultivation on Key Biscayne may be little noted elsewhere, but one great naturalist and plant explorer kept records. The eminent David Fairchild recounts that "the work of introducing tropical plants into Florida was begun in 1898," but until 1921, the Office of Plant Introduction of the U.S. Department of Agriculture, which he headed, "busied itself with avocado and mango varieties . . . because no one in Florida was interested in testing a collection" of coconuts. But there were more than eighty-six known varieties of the coconut palm, "one of the very great plant foods in the world," and it was time that the work of collecting and experimenting started.

W. J. Matheson stepped forward. By 1920, he already had a head start of thirty-six thousand coconut trees, mostly Jamaican Talls, growing on his plantation on Key Biscayne, and he was delighted to take on a new role in the scientific development of tropical agriculture in America. He opened his "unusual facilities for the testing of all kinds of foreign plants . . . which first demonstrated their ability to grow on the sandy soil of his Key," wrote Fairchild.

Tropical plant introduction and experimentation were conducted for every seed variety. They were catalogued, and collections were nurtured and propagated in "large and airy" lath houses. Groves were carefully bordered and laid out with close attention to detail from preparation to bedding to spacing and irrigation. Nothing was left to chance, and much was learned about plants suited to seacoast conditions.

"The first important introduction of a coconut variety was in 1921," wrote Fairchild, "when the late W. J. Matheson financed the bringing in of the Malay Dwarf coconut from the Federated Malay States and established them on his Key Biscayne plantation. This was a joint enterprise with the Department of Agriculture, and its success gave Mr. Matheson much satisfaction. They can now be seen from Crandon Park, their gorgeous gold fruits decorating the whole landscape."

Most other Florida coconut growers planted palms shipped from the West Indies, as planters had done since the 1800s; they were not inter-

Screened sheds house the Golden Malay coconut, first introduced to the United States on Key Biscayne. Department of Agriculture forwarded sprouts to Matheson. David Fairchild photographed a colleague on inspection during quarantine. Note flourishing banana specimens on the left, and, in the background to the right, a native "Dade County pine" and introduced Australian pines. (David Fairchild)

ested in research but in immediate production and profits. It wasn't until the 1970s that the significance of Matheson's introduction of the Malay palm a half century earlier was appreciated, although few knew the history of how the trees had come to grow in Florida. In parts of the Caribbean basin and in subtropical Florida, a devastating blight wiped out eighty percent of the Jamaican Talls and attacked and killed more than thirty other varieties of palms on the East Coast. Commercial growers and private owners tried desperately to save their trees, using every means including spraying and inoculation, but to no avail. Then, looking for survivors, scientists announced that the Malay Dwarf was one of the few coconut palms growing in Florida that had the ability to fight lethal yellowing and the "coconut blight." The other that seemed to have immunity was the Panama Tall palm.

U.S. Department of Agriculture scientists, who earlier had developed the tangelo, a hybrid of the orange and tangerine, now turned their talents to the coconut palm. Working in Homestead at the Plant Introduction Station, through which so many foreign plants had come into this country, they successfully grew a hybrid coconut palm by crossbreeding the Malay Dwarf and the Panama Tall—an odd couple by any rule. They named it the Maypan, and it can reach eighty or more feet in height. But like most hybrids, the Maypan cannot reproduce unless it is hand pollinated.

The three types of Malay Dwarf (golden, yellow, and green), which surprisingly reach a height of from forty to sixty feet, became the coconut palms of choice, recommended in Florida to replace the Jamaican Talls. Replanting coconut palms killed by the blight, and in 1992 by Hurricane Andrew, has become a priority and commitment in south Florida landscaping, where there is renewed awareness of their ornamental and environmental value.

Key Biscayners can be proud that the hardy, disease resistent Malay first put down its North American roots on their tiny island.

A Candy of Copra

Copra (Malaysian: *Koppara*): The dried kernel or meat of the coconut from which oil is expressed.

It takes one thousand to thirteen hundred coconuts (each nut yielding about a half pound of meat) to make one candy of copra, as the measure goes in Sri Lanka (formerly the British colony of Ceylon). Four candies equal a ton. In 1933, the worldwide market had dropped. That year, from the island of Ceylon, sixty-five hundred tons of copra were exported at £8 (about US$40 in 1933) per ton, and expressed oil at £22 per ton, having dropped from £55 per ton in 1925.

If the Key Biscayne coconut plantation, which was "at least twice as big as any other one grove in this country," had chosen to market one thousand nuts a week to world markets, by Ceylonese measure, at £8 per ton of coconut meat, they would have earned less than £100 in 1933—which may be why they didn't bother.

Although the Mathesons extracted oil experimentally, and the nuts "contained as much oil and in some cases more than South American nuts" (as high as one quart from twelve nuts), when it was analyzed in the northern market, it was said to "correspond to a very high grade of Cochin oil, and delivered in New York City on the basis of the present market, was worth ten cents per pound in barrels."

Certainly the Mathesons kept on top of the commodities markets in Chicago, London—and Ceylon. However they figured, financial futures were not in a candy of copra, no matter how sweet the coconut meat on Key Biscayne.

But as Hugh wrote to John K. Small, "The coconut grove on Key Biscayne . . . produces more seed nuts for Florida planting than any other single grove, and is of untold value for its ornamental, exotic, and landscape properties; even if it never produced coconuts in a commercial way, it might be considered profitable."

Makapuno

The Mathesons were making a contribution to the culture of coconuts in the United States; the Malaysian introduction was the first of many joint ventures and, following W. J.'s death, Fairchild wrote that "Hugh inherited, along with the plantation on Key Biscayne, his father's interest in coconuts" and he continued to support, introduce, and cultivate important varieties. One was, in 1938, the amazing "ice cream" coconut from the South Pacific, noted for its taste, protein, and ability to germinate. Fairchild wrote an enthusiastic paper on the introduction of the Makapuno coconut of the Philippines into the U.S.A.

Key Biscayne coconuts were mailed home by tourists as Florida souvenirs, better than postcards. Thousands of perfect nuts were loaded from the husking shed on Hacienda Harbor (next to the present-day Key Biscayne Yacht Club) and shipped to Matheson's Miami River headquarters for distribution. During the 1920s boom, the supply just kept up with demand and "a very fair profit realized."

The first mature Makapuno coconut, "the ice cream coconut" introduced from the Philippines, is sampled by David Fairchild and Hugh Matheson, 1939. (Fairchild Tropical Garden Collection)

In 1933, during the Great Depression, Hugh Matheson donated fifteen hundred nuts, which were distributed from the Miami city curb market to the unemployed.

Fruit Compote

Fruit from tropical and subtropical zones in both the Eastern and Western Hemispheres was planted and tested and tasted. There were early introductions of different varieties of mango, banana, avocado (alligator pear), passion-fruit; there was breadfruit, carambola (star fruit), tamarind, mulberry, sapodilla (dillie), and almond. Ficus or fig trees were placed at the corners of cultivated fields as boundary markers.

Limes were the first trees planted by the Mathesons in 1909 and 1910, but after ten years they "realized that the lime grove would not be a commercial success." After 1919, the fruit of the lime trees was left to be eaten by those who lived on the key, who squeezed the fruit for juice

In the lath houses of the island's first plantation nursery (on site of present Village Green) thrived many ornamental plants, including varieties of crotons, bromeliads, orchids and, of course, palms, among them the Kentia, thousands of which went direct from Key Biscayne to northern florists and hotels such as the Palm Court at the Plaza, the Waldorf Astoria in New York, and the Palmer House in Chicago. (Gleason Waite Romer, Florida Collection, Miami Public Library)

and flavorings, used it on fish and greens, pickled it, made it into relishes and jams and, of course, pies. Lime juice with salt can be kept without refrigeration, as Bahamian and Florida Conch families have done for generations. The powerful mix, know as Old Sour, is used to "cook" raw fish and raw conch without fire.

Some plants considered by Floridians to be native have been naturalized. They include the key lime (*Citrus aurantifolia*) from Southern Asia. It grows in the Florida Keys today and throughout much of southern Florida. Like the orange and grapefruit, it was brought by Spanish and Portuguese explorers in the sixteenth century (earlier Arabs had carried it to North Africa and the Mediterranean).

Palms and Ponds

The *Congressional Record* quotes Dr. Henry Perrine asserting that the date palm was "introduced by me into tropical Florida," and in a letter to him, John Dubose confirms that, indeed, in the 1830s he had planted the African date sent by Perrine to Key Biscayne. Seventy years later at Cape Florida, Waters Davis landscaped with date palms; they were growing well when young Patty Munroe visited the island and "Daddy would take his machete and slice off a bunch and toss it in the boat for a picnic on the way home."

In humid south Florida, the dates never produced well enough to become a commercial crop, but the Mathesons maintained the handsome salt-tolerant date trees from Africa and Egypt for landscaping. They also planted other palms including more than a mile-long Royal Palm avenue that ran from the ocean to the bay. Where the land was low or boggy, mosquito breeding was discouraged by excavating shallow freshwater ponds and stocking them with fish. Native plants such as sawgrass (*Cladium jamaiense*), willow (*Salix amphibia*), and pond apple (*Annana glabra*) grew wild alongside the ponds that were landscaped with water lilies and bamboolike grasses; giant bamboo planted on the banks grew into enormous stands, along with pandanus and a variety of native and exotic ferns. Mud turtles, frogs, lizards, snakes, and rodents were common.

William Evan Thomas, who moved to Key Biscayne with his father, one of W. J.'s superintendents, in December 1914, described a small spring on the west side of the island, close to present-day "No-Name Harbor," south of the Matheson boundary. It was perhaps twenty-five feet in diameter and surrounded by a sandy area. "The spring was deep in the mangroves and the pool . . . as clear as crystal. . . . The Indians must have known about this spring." Here he saw many birds, including South American orioles.

Historically, with its fresh water and proximity to the Carribean, Key Biscayne has been an important junction on the Eastern flyway for birds migrating between North and South America, and a stopover for the winter season. Winged travelers found additional attractions on the island during the early twentieth century when tropical trees and plants augmented the native sea grapes, plums, and berries of historic habitats. Tropical mango, papayas, bananas, and cherries gave the island a fruity fragrance difficult to match. Swarms of butterflies and other flying insects offered cuisine-on-the-wing to insectivores. Exotic and native nectar flowed. The profusion of delicious seeds and fruits of coconuts and other palms, African tulips, night-blooming jasmine, and citrus made the island a destination for migrating birds who joined year-round inhabitants of the south temperate zone in this inviting habitat. And when the birds resumed their journey, they presumably distributed many seeds from Key Biscayne to distant lands.

The Florida Audubon Society was founded in 1900, and a state bill passed forbidding the killing of egrets and other birds for plumes, then fashionable on elegant millinery. In 1905, Guy M. Bradley was hired as a warden to defend Florida Bay rookeries, but he was shot and killed by unscrupulous plume hunters. His shocking murder prompted the passage of a national law that ultimately would destroy the U.S. market in plumes.

At the founding of the Coconut Grove Audubon Society (forerunner of Tropical Audubon Society) on April 16, 1915, Key Biscayne landholder W. J. Matheson and Charles Deering (owner of the Hunting Grounds site at Cutler, and brother of James who purchased Cape Florida) became its first lifetime members. Matheson invited members to bird-watch on Key Biscayne uplands and shorelines. Island caretakers protected the safe passage of thousands of resident and migratory songbirds, shorebirds, and other common and uncommon species.

It was not unusual to see enormous flocks flying overhead or skimming the water. Naturalist David Fairchild identified and recorded in his vestpocket notebooks seeing ten thousand herons and three thousand white ibis on a day boat trip to Shark River in December 1929, also not an unlikely count for Key Biscayne.

Definition of the Tropics

Henry Perrine wrote to the Secretary of Treasury in 1833 that tropical plants, including the coconut, banana, and a hundred other plants, "are flourishing at Cape Florida, [demonstrating that] the torrid zone extends north of the Tropic of Cancer into Southern Florida." He credited the tropical climate and uniformity of temperature in south Florida in part to "the hot ocean river running northwest-wardly along its shore." Cape Florida as part of the tropics has been described by other authors:

- *A tropical complexion . . . increases as you approach Cape Florida.*—John C. Williams, traveler and generalist, 1837
- *We visited Cape Florida and saw what I think is the most beautiful plantation of coconuts in the United States. It reminds one of the South Sea islands.*—David Fairchild, Notebooks, 1918
- *The Equatorial waters move from the south along the Florida coast to temper its climate and confuse the seasons . . . seasons intermingle . . . botanically, winter is eliminated, thus a land where spring meets autumn [and] floras of temperate regions and of the tropics not only meet, but commingle.*—John K. Small, 1920s
- *Cape Florida in the early days, had a pretty clump [of coconut trees] around the lightkeeper's dwelling. These were quite old trees and as there were none visible on the beaches north of this point, until later years, passengers on passing vessels were always called upon to take their first look at the tropics and their vegetation.*—Ralph M. Munroe to John K. Small, 1926
- *Where the coconut (Cocos nucifera) produces viable seed, there are the tropics.*—Thomas Barbour, That Vanishing Eden, 1944

W.J.'s Heating System

There have been many days when the natural heating plant which passes your shore would have been welcome to us.
—LETTER TO W. J. MATHESON FROM CHARLES DAVENPORT, SECRETARY OF THE COLD SPRING HARBOR LABORATORY, JANUARY 1929

From the beginning, skeptics had doubted that coconuts could be grown successfully at twenty-five degrees north of the equator. In 1929, the *Journal of the New York Botanical Garden #30* published: "Advice given to Commodore W. J. Matheson by experts from Kew Garden, London, and Washington, D.C., was that coconuts would not grow at a point more than fifteen degrees north or south of the equator; to which Commodore Matheson replied he had a hot water heating system in the close proximity of the Gulf Stream along the eastern shore of Key Biscayne." Recent studies by NOAA scientists corroborate that the "hot ocean river" runs closer to shore at Key Biscayne than at any other point but one along the U.S. East Coast.

Fresh Water

There is good water on it (Biskayno Island).
—BERNARD ROMANS, 1775

Not only did the island have the Gulf Stream as a built-in heating system, but it had a freshwater lens between two and three feet below the surface of the ground. "The water table seems to be just right for the proper development of trees," Hugh reported. To offset periods of drought, however, and until the roots of the nuts and sprouts were long enough to reach through the hardpan to fresh water, water sometimes had to be brought to the key.

During a dry fall in 1928, Bill Thomas, employed as a worker, recalled that a large tank of water was hauled across the fields by tractor. Where cultivation was on a filled tract of land, "I got the job of running the hose. . . . We put about a barrel of water on each tree."

The importance of irrigation, upon which the production of so many crops is dependent, was well appreciated by W. J., who had visited the sites of many early civilizations where aqueducts and other structures had been used to divert water to dry fields and valleys. One of the earliest efforts was in Minorca, where ancient people had built irrigation systems as sophisticated as those in Egypt.

W. J. knew that his own maternal grandfather, the inventive engineer William Abram Lighthall (1805–1881), drawing from his experience designing and building steamboat engines, set up in 1852 "on the banks of the San Joaquin River, the first steam irrigation plant ever devised and operated in California." From that time forward, important crops have come to market from California's water-dependent valleys.

There is, by some freak of nature, a fresh water layer over the salt water table.
—STEPHEN TRUMBULL, 1945, GARDEN EDITOR, *THE MIAMI HERALD*

The fresh-water table fluctuates with the tide, both daily and seasonally, and also with the seasonal rains.
—HUGH MATHESON

Watering the fields. (Gleason Waite Romer, Florida Collection, Miami Public Library)

Matheson Water Services

Water for irrigation of plants, as well as for cooking, bathing, and washing, was pumped from the ground, and rain water was caught in cisterns and supplemented by drinking water brought in by boat. It was distributed in green glass jugs wrapped in twine, and the water came

A water-wheel pumps from the Key Biscayne artesian well dug by Mathesons near barn. Great geyser gushed 30 feet in air. Water was drawn from Biscayne Aquifer. W. J. declared it no fountain of youth, but the alligator in residence must have shivered in the overflow pond created for its habitat. (Gleason Waite Romer, Florida Collection, Miami Public Library)

from wells on the Matheson mainland property. In fact, the Mathesons established the Coconut Grove Public Utilities Company in 1916, which supplied water service to residents of Coconut Grove; later they laid a pipeline to the plantation village.

The Mathesons knew the importance of fresh water and experimented with alternative power sources for pumps. On Key Biscayne, they used windmills and dug wells, including one deep artesian well. Their water tower was close to the barn, but storage tanks were rolled on wheels to the fields to water the sprouts.

Desalinization

We have found no laboratory notes showing that the Mathesons experimented with converting saltwater into fresh water, although we suspect they investigated methods of desalinization.

During the 1920s, Alexander Graham Bell, David Fairchild's father-in-law, tested his ideas on desalinization while he was visiting in Coconut Grove. On the same trip, he used W. J. Matheson's canal as a testing basin for the prototype of the world's first hydrofoil boat (which he later built in Nova Scotia). It is possible they discussed W. J.'s grandfather's pioneering work in the mid-1850s. W. J. had written a paper about his grandfather, W. A. Lighthall, who invented the surface condenser, "which enabled steam vessels to cross the ocean with a constant supply of fresh water in their boilers (condensed from salt water), thus saving fuel and avoiding usual boiler corrosion." It was used during the Civil War when "as each seacoast fort was taken by Federal troops, the Government installed Mr. Lighthall's condenser, thus furnishing pure drinking water for the soldiers." Contaminated water had been a serious problem, so his services saved many thousands of lives on the Yankee side.

While some islands and coastal areas today have desalinization plants, Key Biscayne relies solely on water piped from the mainland.

Sea Salt

While W. J.'s grandfather's condenser was converting fresh water from saltwater for the Yankees, Floridians were operating coastal salt works. The Southern economy was dependent on the production of salt, mandated by the hot climate to preserve meat and fish, and the Confederacy used about six million bushels of salt a year. Rebel salt works became prime blockade targets and a focus for Union raids. The most important operations were steam salt works with capacities from one hundred fifty to ten times that number of bushels per day. Additionally, there were coastal operations firing up wood-burning kilns to boil salt kettles (often converted sugar kettles) in which seawater was boiled down to a porridge, then spread on oak planks in the sun until the salt crystallized.

The earliest mention of salt making on Key Biscayne was in 1825 when Morgan Davis, an applicant for the Cape Florida lighthouse-keeper's post, represented himself as a maker of musical instruments who intended to keep the light and start up the manufacture of salt on the little island. He was not appointed.

Canals

From the bay into the midsection of the island, W. J. built the Hacienda Canal and Basin. This private canal used the technique of the Glades Indians, the area's first engineers, who bulkheaded water routes with palmetto logs, which did not attract marine borers. It was the plantation's working canal from which materials, goods, and products could be delivered or shipped between the mainland and the plantation center. Work boats and barges on regularly scheduled boat runs plied between their Miami River headquarters and the key. A large thatched-roofed pavilion was close to the entrance where well-maintained wharves, packing sheds, and a thatched husking house for coconuts were located.

A cross-island canal, 185 feet wide, was built close to the boundary line of Cape Florida. Through this canal, yachtsman had a shortcut from ocean to bay and an oceanside pier where they could tie up.

The natural haven long known as Hurricane Harbor was enlarged by Matheson on the bay side; inside Harbor Point were docks at a wooden manufactory where, among other natural products, Hacienda Honey, "nectar of the gods," was processed. The Matheson beehives were located on the east side of present Harbor Point, where beekeepers had charge of the Honey House and extracted the liquid from the comb. The bees collected nectar from blossoming coconut palm, logwood, and lime and other citrus, known by apiarists and gourmets to be superior sources of honey. "Hacienda Honey" was bottled and labeled on the island, sold in tourist shops in downtown Miami, and sent to select northern markets. The bees were also attracted to blossoms of the

Long pier into ocean for docking marked eastside opening of cross island canal (later called the Pines Canal); when seaside entrance silted, a bridge was built to span canal. The large bath house accomodated beach guests. (Gleason Waite Romer, Florida Collection, Miami Public Library)

A favorite landing for private yachts: Key Biscayne parties "signalized the height of the season and were marked by the assembling at the estate of the elite of the winter social colony...and many of the noted yachts [owned by Mellon, Vanderbilt, James, Carnegie, Field, Armour, Billings, Curtis, Fisher]," wrote one 1920's society editor. (Sarah Preston Carleton Collection)

native palmettos, the black mangrove ("the honey mangrove"), and the less common white mangrove on the west side of the island where prized stands grew, the remnants bulldozed in the late 1980s to make way for the International Tennis Center.

On Mashta Point, the water entrance to the magnificent Mashta House, which some called the island's pleasure dome, was through the opening to an inviting palm-lined, ring-shaped lagoon. The turquoise water basin was called the Atoll. Yachts docked along seawalls.

Island Music: Mashta House

They came by boat to Mashta House where W. J. kept a staff to prepare for their arrival from across the bay. Food and entertainment were lavish, tasteful, and the setting unmatched in the world. Sometimes there were fifteen guests; more often fifty. They were from out of town or from Coconut Grove, family and friends arriving for the incomparable sunsets when the late afternoon sky became an artist's palate before the setting sun, a giant fireball, dropped into the darkening Everglades to the west.

During the romantic parties on Mashta Island, the bay waters added their harmony to the sounds of music floating across the tropical nights. Lulu Mae Matheson, virtuoso pianist and composer, always responded to cries of "Maestra! Maestra!" With pleasure and an easy grace, the beautiful young woman sat at the piano, arranged her party frock across her knees, and waited until the roomful of friends and relatives were still. Then her dexterous fingers played along the ivory keyboard with the skill of Euterpe, the Muse of music.

Music was an integral part of Mae's life and so were Mashta House and her cousin, W. J. Matheson. At his invitation, she had moved, in her late twenties, from Wisconsin to Florida. A music lover himself and separated from his wife, Harriet, W. J. bought two grand pianos, one for his Coconut Grove home, the other for Mashta. Both became known as Mae's pianos; she was W. J.'s hostess and performer at his parties.

One of Mae's best friends was Marjory Stoneman Douglas. Both had graduated from Wellesley, although in different years. Mae made sure that Marjory was invited to parties during the Roaring Twenties. Marjory, seated next to Mae on the piano bench to turn the pages of the music, always remembered Mae's graceful fingers, how easily she played concerts, formal or informal. Mae composed and performed a piece called "Mashta."

At Mashta House with its golden wall, its Moorish arches, its elegant imported tiles, its exotic atmosphere, the nights were magical as singing voices joined Mae's music, drifting on balmy tropic breezes from Key Biscayne toward the mainland. Moonlight glittered over the water; stars and planets stood out like diamonds against the black sky. Dancing in the moonlit ballroom over travertine marble, one could feel like Vernon or Irene Castle, the illusion of perfection was so complete.

Life was idyllic. Mae's music lingered in the memory long after the party was over and the guests had boarded the elegant houseboats to go back to town, landing at the Matheson's Coconut Grove dock, to be escorted off by the crew and to stroll across the rolling lawn to the waiting motorcars.

After the hurricane of 1926, the Mashta House piano had to be carefully refinished, inside and out. It "almost went out the window," W. J.'s son Hugh wrote his father after the storm.

The storm may have been traumatic for Mae but it was not the worst thing to happen that year. It was a short time later that Marjory remembers sitting beside her friend and noticing that something seemed very wrong. "Have you hurt your hand?" she asked. Mae shook her head and kept on playing. Then, withdrawing her hands from the keyboard, she began to rub her fingers. They were stiff, she said, and they hurt more and more every day. W. J. took her to doctors for careful examinations and for second and third opinions. He was on the boards of important companies and hospitals. He knew everyone, but no one could help his young cousin. Mae, in her thirties, was the victim of arthritis in her fingers. Marjory remembers how valiantly she fought the crippling disease. She played when it was painful for her to touch a key, much less to play the trills for which she was famous among her admirers. Perhaps no greater tragedy can strike a pianist. Gradually Mae lost the agility and the grace that gave her such joy. Eventually she stopped playing completely.

Charming Lulu Mae Matheson, W. J.'s favorite cousin, cast a romantic note over Mashta House and its guests. (Jean Wood Guytan Collection)

Night Songs

Music was part of plantation life on Key Biscayne. In the early years, the work day ended at dusk. The people were dependent on fires, candle, or lantern light after the sun set in the west. A full moon was welcome, especially in the days before the generator.

That's when haunting music filled the night. The Bahamians and other black workers in their own settlement gathered close to the barn and Nassau Street; they came outside to catch the breeze, lean against coconut trees, sit on the dormitory steps or house stoops, and sing. They sang the old Bahamian island songs, spirituals learned from slave ancestors who crisscrossed the Gulf Stream after first coming in irons across the sea.

Down closer to the ocean "in the white settlement," there was a

The big barn stood on present-day Crandon Boulevard opposite Village Green. (Gleason Waite Romer, Florida Collection, Miami Public Library)

Close to big barn, wooden houses line Nassau Street, homes for Bahamian families in 1920s. (Gleason Waite Romer, Florida Collection, Miami Public Library)

different music. Many nights there was banjo playing around beach fires; voices rose in a mixture of music and rounds as grownups and children entertained themselves. When the wind stiffened, the clickety-click of thousands of palm fronds sounded like castanets accompanying the singers and dancers. When Arthur J. Clarke was superintendent of the plantation in the 1920s, he lived there with his family; he was the resident trombonist and his concert hall was the out-of-doors, although he was glad to join with any visiting musicians. He did not regard the Matheson captains as competition with their air-driven boat horns.

But someone then, as later on, always sounded, or played, a conch horn during nighttime revelries. When the last superintendent in the 1930s and 1940s, Clayton Sheldon, and his family lived there, he collected from the beach all kinds of conch and whelk shells, which he made into horns. He lined them up on the front-porch ledge according to whether they were bass or treble. Then when he had sufficient spirits in him, he became a one-man conch band. His concerts usually began around 3 A.M. and lasted until his lip gave out. [After his retirement, these nighttime musicals continued to the amazement of his nearest neighbors, the author and her family, who rented a cottage from the Mathesons from 1951–1965, when plantation operations were mostly at an end.]

There were forty-two workers in 1915; ten black families in 1920, which increased to sixty. Single workers lived in a bachelor dormitory (later relocated and named the Calusa Playhouse Music and Drama Club). Community and patch gardens provided pineapples, sugarcane, tomatoes, pigeon peas, beans, squash, melons, and corn. There were communal outdoor grills, and local buttonwood was prized for making charcoal; women baked bread in wood-burning ovens. Much was shared, including fish catches, turtle steaks and eggs, conch, crawfish, marine and land crabs, frog legs, opossums, raccoons, some fowl and other birds, and rattlesnake (only after the head was buried, and after the rattles were traded in at the commissary for a few cents cash). They collected oysters that grew on mangroves and picked papaya ripe from

Superintendent's Dade County pine house. (Mitchell Collection)

trees. Coconuts were part of daily food and drink, and staples were available at the commissary.

The white community, including families of the superintendent and his supervisors, several boat captains, the beekeeper, the mechanic, and the nursery keeper, was close to the ocean. In some years, the schoolmistress roomed with the superintendent's family; one school-master had his own house [Note: This same house became the author's cottage in 1952, and is the oldest house remaining on the island. In 1995, it was designated a historic property.]

At the dunes, Mrs. Arthur J. Clark and her son, James Linnaeus. (Mitchell Collection)

1926 Hurricane

W. J. was not in Florida when the devastating hurricane of 1926 struck Key Biscayne and Miami. The storm hit Miami with little warning near midnight on September 17 and battered the area for twelve hours. On September 25, Hugh wrote a letter to his father describing the events and damage. The toll in Dade County was not yet known, but later it was reported that on the mainland 113 people had died, 854 were hospitalized, and many more injured.

On the exposed and isolated barrier island, there was no warning for the small community of around fifty people who later would tell of their terror. There was no time for preparations when the eye headed for them and the storm surge roared in from the ocean, whipped into a great and terrifying froth such as none of them had beheld before. The "white settlement" was grouped along the beach where monster waves crashed ashore as the winds and water rose. They waded in waist-high water, carrying their children on their shoulders to the highest ground, gathering in one or two cottages which, miraculously, remained standing in spite of blown-out windows, crashing ceilings, and much damage. The "Negro settlement" was closer to the center of the island by the big barn; as the howling winds, rising water, and driving rain rammed inland, the men in the long, trembling dormitory clung to the rafters to keep from being swept away; later it was believed that their weight is what kept the roof from blowing off. Other black workers and their families sought refuge in the second-story loft of the barn and watched in disbelief as the ocean water poured through the center of the building "from sea to sea." They described it like a river rushing through a gorge carrying trees and parts of houses and equipment, sweeping them away. It was high tide on Key Biscayne from ocean to bay; the island was awash. In both settlements most of the structures were demolished, effectively demonstrating that the eye of the hurricane is, and always will be, color blind. The word hurricane is a Carib word, derived from the Taino *hurakán* (later translated into Spanish as *huracán*). In certain parts of the world it is equated to a tempest, ty-phoon, or cyclone.

Hugh wrote his father:

Immediately after the blow, I tried to reach Key Biscayne, but there were no boats left that would run in Coconut Grove. I came to Miami and got a police order from the Chief of Police to take any boat that

The 1926 storm surge and erosion toppled worker's seaside cottage. (Matheson Family Collection ©Finlay B. Matheson)

would run in Miami, that they would commandeer the boat for me, and give me police protection in case the owner would not grant the use of same. After looking around the only boat I could find was William Curry's. [Author's Note: The Curry family included two former assistant keepers at Fowey Rocks light.] Of course all draw-bridges were closed and [it] . . . would not go under the railroad draw without taking the top off . . . so we ripped the top off. . . . I found that on Key Biscayne the water had covered the island from one end to the other, probably at least three feet deep. There were only two white houses intact, the roads were absolutely blocked by fallen coconut trees so that a person had to climb over them every inch of the way across. All the white people were in one house and Mrs. Gordon, the bee man's wife, was cooking and taking care of all of them.

Almost all the large coconut trees were on the roads, were uprooted, and some of them broken off. There was no fresh water supply owing to the fact that the houses, in being ripped away from the cisterns, broke the pipes and allowed the water to fall out. In some cases, on the ocean front, the salt water got in over the top of the cisterns. We brought back to the mainland some of the women and children, and have since housed them in various parts of town in good shape. I had some of them with me the first night or two.

The situation at Key Biscayne now is well in hand. We have the crane and tractors on the roads, replanting the uprooted coconut trees and cutting away the ones broken down. We will have all the coconuts replanted at the division road in about two days more.

. . . Mashta [House] was in about the most exposed position of any place. . . . The water rose to a height of about three or three and a half feet on the main floor and the seas battered in the shutters and windows and swept right through the living room, dining room, etc. The amount of damage to the furnishings is very great. However, all the rugs were rolled up, but of course have been soaked with sea weed and salt water. The piano was upset and nearly swept out of the north window. The furnishings on the upper floors were badly damaged by water, as most of the window casings and shutters were blown in. Curiously enough, most of the coconut trees around the atoll stood, as also did the coconut and pithecolobium in the raised lawn on the west. Half of this lawn, however, was washed out. The gas plant and electric light plant were under water and put out of condition. As I said before, no fresh water supply is on the Key—not even the ground water which has been ruined on account of salt water being so deep all over the bay.

. . . The *Coconut*, by curious coincidence, was left on the ways and came through safe. Although we had no warning of the storm, and in fact the evening before the storm broke, I telephoned the weather bureau and they told me there was no danger of a severe storm but we might have a wind velocity of forty miles per hour. In spite of this fact my barometer acted rather queerly and I refused to take the *Coconut* off the ways although Fogal, the man owning the ways, and the two men aboard, were very anxious to get the boat to Coconut Grove. Your cook, Peter Johnson, and the engineer, saved the *Coconut* by filling the bilge block and allowing the water to come in up to the generator, then plugging same up and running boat motors half speed ahead to keep on the ways. The greatest danger was in her being smashed up by other floating barges and houseboats. Luckily she was untouched.

Hugh wrote of his father's bayside home in Coconut Grove that "the whole front . . . is a tangled mass of broken down trees, barges, launches, dredging equipment and debris . . . the damage is great."

The office on Second Avenue and the Miami River, where plantation business was conducted, was hard hit: "The water rose around the office grounds about five feet and . . . ruined a great many things in the file room. . . . The windows were blown out of my office and the rain swept through both floors. It left us with about eight inches of black mire on the lower floors. The packing house roof was completely demolished and part of the concrete walls were blown in. Everything was soaked and ruined in the packing house. The boat house had the roof taken off."

At Key Biscayne, "The *A. A. Kemp* [work boat] broke loose and came up over the top of the cement wall and wandered through mangrove bushes to the top of the packing house desk. Floated off again and was finally secured with a half inch line by one of the negroes. We had also two large barges in the basin that meandered around a bit and finally settled in the basin practically uninjured."

In Miami, "city water has been turned on and . . . they have electric lights in some places. The situation at Key Biscayne is well in hand and we are getting drinking water and food to them and patching up some of the wrecked houses for living quarters . . . and I believe we will be able to save thousands of trees. It is absolutely necessary to buy more equipment to save these trees, all of which material I am obtaining as fast as possible."

—Hurricane Letter, 1926 © Finley B. Matheson

I am terribly pinched for time in directing the outside work, or would write you further.

—Hugh Matheson to his father, from private papers of the Matheson family

After the Storm

On the undeveloped half of the hurricane-devastated island, nature proceeded with its own natural schedule of restoration. In the cultivated areas, the Matheson workers labored from sunrise to sunset to replant and rebuild what the fury of the storm had flooded, shredded, uprooted, and broken asunder.

Although ocean-side cottages, the ocean pier, and the bay-side docks were wrecked or swept to sea, the beaches and shoreline, dune vegetation, mangrove forests, and hammocks grew back at their own pace both at Cape Florida and on Matheson tracts where the ecosystems had not been critically weakened or destroyed by human engineering. The labors of Hercules went into not only the replanting of the coconuts, but also the renurturing of hundreds of elegant and rare tree specimens from Africa, Asia, and other tropical sites. The lath house and nursery were given special care by gardeners, and tropical-plant experts who had been following the experiments waited anxiously for word on the progress of the plants, whether bamboos, bombax, the sacred baobab, the African tulip trees, the Zaccgaeus grown from a cutting from the original tree in the Holy Land, or the Norfolk pines. How had they survived? In some cases, it took many years to reestablish the growth.

With time and nurture, the island plant life, and with it the wildlife,

Hurricane House built to give refuge to plantation community in the event of future hurricanes. (Blank Collection)

recovered. The island across from Miami and accessible only by boat, became an even more beautiful tropical paradise.

A Sense of Humus

"Mr. [W. J.] Matheson loved tropical trees and planted many of them and encouraged others to do so when Miami was still a village," wrote David Fairchild. "The experimental planting he and his son Hugh made around their residences in Coconut Grove and on their extensive holdings on Key Biscayne (about which a book could be written) were at the time the most extensive private experiments in plant introduction undertaken here. Mr. Matheson never tired of telling his friends of the behavior of his Malay coconuts, the banyan and sausage tree and baobab and many other species. Some of these he brought in personally and others I had the pleasure of helping introduce, for he put his facilities at our disposal when our Government funds were too meager to allow us to make more than very small trial plantings anywhere."

Many area trees, including the Golden Malay coconut, had their start in Key Biscayne soil, "generally a loose, calcareous sand with no rock but a small amount of humus," reported Hugh Matheson. The trees were then deck loaded on work boats, shipped across the bay, and transplanted on the mainland by plantation crews.

But it was not always so serious a business, because the Matheson sense of humor was equal to their sense of humus. To illustrate this point, according to old friends, there was "the night the forest moved from Key Biscayne."

One evening Hugh Matheson heard a friend, with whom he was having a sundown drink at Biscayne Bay Yacht Club, bemoaning the fact that his new "dream home" had been ruined because the builder destroyed all the tropical growth around it, so that it stood bare and exposed in the clearing. As other friends consoled him, Matheson roared over to Key Biscayne where he rallied workers to dig up and deck load several boats with full-grown palm and shade trees which they moved to the mainland. With their own heavy-duty equipment, they lumbered through the dark streets of Miami until they reached the "dream home" where, under cover of night, they planted their instant forest, so that the house was hidden from view. Returning to the Club, Hugh found that his friend had consumed many drinks and, as the story is told, when he set off for home, is it any wonder he couldn't find it?

Natural Habitats

On the mainland W. J. Matheson protected a virgin hammock for several decades where he did not permit timbering, dredging, paving, or building. This land of dense growth, slightly elevated above the marshy areas along the bay, is known as Matheson Hammock. He opened a number of trails through his jungles, personally leading visitors to show them the unexpected wildlife and beauty deep in a native Florida hammock, sharing the discovery of elegant wild orchids, blooming on the arms of giant oaks fringed with ferns and moss. Gumbo-limbo, co-coplum, mahogany, and wild cinnamon were alive with birds and butterflies. W. J. also led visitors through Key Biscayne nature trails. It was on the key that David Fairchild caught sight of a brilliant orange blossom and reported seeing his "first ever geiger tree blooming." He wrote, "A book could be written about Matheson's island."

On Key Biscayne W. J. left undisturbed several miles of shoreline vegetation and ancient mangrove forest that shielded hardwood native hammocks. The Plantation workers' children, including Helen Clark Mitchell and Bill Thomas, remember walking along planks through the native forest and how sometimes they would leave the open spaces of the wide beaches and oceanside to slip into the mysterious, dark interior. Not only could they play Indian games, but they discovered "baskets and conch shell lockets left at old Indian campsites." Climbing in and out of the aerial roots of mangroves, they looked in dark holes and crevices for Black Caesar's hidden treasure. Usually they found old glass bottles, wooden barrel staves, and unidentified bones.

Native orchids, Spanish moss, and other bromeliads decked tropical trees. They hung from the branches of white mangrove as well as giant buttonwood (estimated to be at least four to five hundred years old by island nurseryman Bill Cleveland in 1963). In the hammocks grew large gumbo-limbo, pigeon plum, mastic, poisonwood, and strangler fig, which often choked its frequent host, the cabbage palm. Birdie McAllister in 1938 wrote in the first systematic study of existing flora of Key Biscayne (submitted as a master's thesis at Duke University) that in the bushlands or thickets "two members of the palm family are the dominant species, saw palmetto (*Serona repens*) and cabbage palms (*Sabal palmetto*)." Earlier, Matheson wrote to Small, "The native growth found on the key was practically all saw-palmettos of enormous size, mixed with other growth, such as sea-grapes, cabbage-trees and poisonwood."

In mid-1920s photographs, towering "native pines" (*Pinus elliotti, densa*) are evident on the plantation. All of the workers' cottages and most of the out-buildings, including the barn, were built of Dade County pine, an exceptionally hard wood that grew on high ground for many years on the island. McAllister, recording its decline, wrote, "the pine has practically disappeared due to three forces: man, fire, and storm" on Key Biscayne.

Mangroves: The Walking Trees

The dominant native tree on the sand island was the mangrove. James Grant Forbes in the 1820s noted that the island presented "a mass of mangroves." Legend has it that the ancient Indians of Florida called it the "walking tree." It expands the edges of an island as it puts out long-legged roots, and it seems to be ever dancing as the tides rise and fall.

Louis Agassiz found these long-legged plants "both peculiar and interesting." In his report on the Florida Keys, he wrote:

The mangroves are among the most important geological agents in this region; but for them the loose sand and mud would remain an ever-shifting ground of movable particles. . . . [N]ew plants attain a length of some six inches before they drop from the old tree . . . at high tide . . . into the water, and are swept about and scattered by its movements. Like brownish-green sticks, fusiform in shape . . . they suggest the idea that a ship-load of cigars has been wrecked upon the reef, and swept inland by the tides. Presently these fusiform bodies are stranded along the edge of some mud flat, touching ground at last with their heavier loaded end. Their hold is at first very loose, but made to turn, by the rising and falling tides, like a rod upon a pivot, they soon work their way into the soft mud and plant themselves firmly. Immediately the long, rapidly growing roots begin to shoot out and soon form a close screen, giving stability to all the loose materials about them and holding the mud and sand in place.

Mangrove roots were in effect the first pilings driven into Key Biscayne: they shored up the island rather than invading it. Entire islands are built up by mangroves, as are the lee sides of barrier islands. If these mangrove pilings are torn out by people, there is no longer a natural stabilizer to prevent erosion. If a shore is sea-walled, the mangrove seeds will float away with the ebbing tide.

Mangrove roots as natural pilings have long been recognized for their strength and durability. The U.S. government found an innovative use for their wood when the Coast Survey team was putting up navigational markers that ensure safe passage along the Florida reef. F. H. Gerdes recommended discontinuing the use of imported steel, which corroded in saltwater. He explained, "The reef consists of a very soft lime rock into which, with steel spikes and crowbars, holes are made." He recommended instead using the wood of the mangrove tree which grows in saltwater flats. "Mangrove poles are exceedingly heavy, on which the worms or water have no effect," he wrote "They settle down and became completely cemented to the rock."

Mangroves. (Laurence Donovan)

One hundred years later, rods taken from a rocky outcrop, noted by Gerdes on the northeast coast of Key Biscayne, showed that he had a good basis for his idea. An unusual reef formation with "intricate latticed network of horizonal and vertical rods . . . similar in size and shape to the root structure of the living black mangrove" was first described by J. E. Hoffmeister for the Geological Society of America in 1965. Radiocarbon dating indicated these fossilized mangrove roots were from one to two thousand years old. The "petrified forest" with its own microhabitats is one of the few ancient features of the key to survive and be protected.

The living mangrove (black, red, white, with buttonwood) is known throughout the tropical and subtropical world as the island protector. It stretches island borders with every forward or sideways step. It possesses the power to counter erosion and is reputed to be the tideland's warrior-of-the-woods, standing fast against tidal and storm bores. It is a protected breeding habitat for many species of fishes and shellfishes, and marine biologists describe its incredible ecosystem as the basis of the aquatic food chain of marine estuaries that rise and fall with the changing tides.

Once upon an island, the mangrove and maritime forests of Key Biscayne were notable. The wildlife was abundant.

In an 1880 account, William H. G. Kingston related in *In the Florida Wilds* the amazement of two boys upon discovering at low tide that the stiltlike spindly roots of the mangrove trees were completely covered with thick clusters of oysters.

"Sure, do them shell-fish grow on the trees?" exclaimed Tim. "Though I've been the world round, never did I see such curious fruit."

Captain Crump explained how young oysters attach to any hard object.

Tim, jumping into the boat, rowed off, and soon brought back several branches of oysters, which he thought would serve us for breakfast. We found them, however, very bitter to our taste.

The skipper told us they were called 'coon oysters' as the raccoons are very fond of them. . . . While we were watching the shore, sure enough a raccoon came down, and seizing several oysters which hung just below the surface, picked them off the branch, and shaking them violently backwards and forwards, ran back with his prize to a convenient spot on the beach, where, with his teeth and claws, he opened the shells, and speedily devoured the contents. Presently we saw him dart into the water, and return with a handful of shrimps . . . and he again immediately sat himself down to devour them, giving each of them a pinch as he placed them by his side.

In Key Biscayne's dwindling mangrove forest, little wading bears, as the Germans called the masked raccoons in Europe, are found less and less enjoying nature's hors d'oeuvres of shrimp, fiddler crabs, or the oysters named in their honor.

Into the twentieth century, there was a diversity of wildlife on Key Biscayne. Animals and humans lived compatibly side by side on much of the island. This harmony would largely continue even when the Mathesons developed their plantation.

Key Biscay affords venison, and sometimes bear, likewise raccoons and doves.
—BERNARD ROMANS, 1770s
The Key abounds with wild-cats, bears, and other 'varmints' although we were only attacked by mosquitoes.
—CHARLES RICHARD DODGE, LATE 1800s

In the 1920s, when it became necessary to protect the coconut sprouts from predators such as marsh hares and rats, Hugh Matheson wrote that they were experimenting with methods of control, but "Poisoning has not been resorted to on account of the danger of killing other animals and birds." Lucky for the fauna on Key Biscayne that both W. J. and Hugh were experts on the use and abuse of chemicals.

Later, other developers and residents would generously use poisons, pesticides, and fertilizers on lawns, golf courses, and other developed land without regard for the animal population of the woodlands and wetlands.

Although legend may have the Florida panther roaming Key Biscayne, only an unexpected archaeological find will verify that the Everglades cat stalked the island. One early traveler said there were deer, but he did not detail whether he referred to the small key deer (currently protected on Big Pine Key) or white-tailed deer. Fossilized deer bones found by archaeologists in 1993 excavations verify such reports. Alligator or crocodile fossils are other recent finds.

Florida black bears roamed the island feasting on tasty white buds of cabbage palms and mangrove honey, eating turtle eggs, and possibly cuffing fish with their paws along the shore. At least they waded in the flats and left tracks in 1927 when surveyor Ronald M. Harper wrote in *The 18th Annual Report of the Florida State Geological Service*, "our bear (*Euarcatos floridanus*, originally described from Key Biscayne, one of the sand islands opposite Miami) ranges Northward to the Northern limits of the State." Few today believe that little black bears migrated down the coastal strand and swam between the islands. How do the doubters account for the way in which Bear Cut was named? Yet it is a historic place name which Roland E. Chardon dates back to 1733, and it appears thereafter on British surveyors' maps from 1765.

Bobcats and alligators have vanished, but still living on the island in lessening numbers are raccoons, opossums, marsh hares, and rats. In the Everglades, these animals and also deer can sometimes be seen swimming across creeks and "from island to island in the mangrove wilderness." And so it once was on a small scale on Key Biscayne.

Florida black bear lived in swamps, raided sea-turtle nests along the ocean beach, and left its name to Bear(s) Cut. On the threatened list, the bear still roams in remote areas of North Florida. (Laurence Donovan)

Everglades Overview: Courtesy W. J.'s Seaplane

A nation behaves well if the natural resources and assets which one generation turns over to another generation are increased and not impaired in value.
—THEODORE ROOSEVELT (1858–1919), PRESIDENT OF THE UNITED STATES, AND FRIEND OF W. J. MATHESON

The man who spearheaded the movement to make the Everglades a national park was a landscape architect, Ernest Coe, encouraged by David Fairchild and others including W. J. Matheson. Coe was a true visionary, determined, he wrote, to "perpetually protect . . . the primeval fastness of tropical South Florida."

In December 1929, he had seen only the fringes of the vast region from the ground and sea level, when W. J. Matheson took it upon himself to give him an overview. Coe wrote to friends at Royal Palm Hammock, "I was down your way . . . in fact, passed by, or rather over your very door, at about two-thousand feet in the air which, of course, precluded stopping. Commodore W. J. Matheson invited me to take an air

"Father of Everglades National Park,"
Ernest F. Coe visits with Ted Smallwood
at the general store in Chokoloskee, at
the western entrance to the park. (Ted
Smallwood Store, Inc.)

trip with him it being my first trip over this proposed National Park Region . . . [this] marvelous spectacle . . . probably cannot be duplicated, in many of its unique and outstanding features, anywhere else in the world."

His vision enlarged, he would lobby state and national leaders with others to raise support so that, in 1947, Everglades National Park was dedicated by President Harry S. Truman. It would be recognized as part of the International Network of Biosphere Reserves by UNESCO in 1976 and be designated a World Heritage Site in 1979.

The eloquent author of the classic book *Everglades: River of Grass*, Marjory Stoneman Douglas (born in 1890) was an admirer of the early work done by Coe, Fairchild, Matheson, and others to preserve the great water wilderness. She founded the grass-roots organization Friends of the Everglades, dedicated to the protection and restoration of this delicately balanced ecological system, the Everglades, which is the water-dependent environmental heritage of Florida. The Indians called the Everglades *Pa-haw-okee*, or grassy water. The survival of animals and people in the region depends on this "river of grass."

Interwoven Threads

Threads of cotton, coconut, and other fibres run through our story. They begin with the native people who wove grasses, vines, and palm fronds in the Everglades and along the coastal strands and islands. They were picked up by Columbus, who, on his second voyage in 1493, was welcomed by out-islanders who presented him with skeins of cotton and finished woven goods.

Shipwrecked sailors and missionaries in the sixteenth and seventeenth centuries describe clothing, baskets, fish nets, and shelter made of fibers woven by the native people.

An errant strand almost entered the pattern in the year 1773 in the Everglades across from "Biscaino Island," where a six-thousand-acre English land grant to Lord Dartmouth, surveyed by William Gerard De Brahm, was named the Cape Florida Society Settlement; the plan was to settle Swiss and French Protestants (Huguenots), who would raise crops that included cotton, indigo, flax, and hemp. But it never happened.

A definite connection, Pedro Fornells, the first Royal Spanish Land Grant holder on Key Biscayne, had come as a youngster to Florida with other immigrant Minorcans to work on the Turnbull plantation growing indigo and making dyes shipped in kegs to cotton mills in England.

The agave plant, used to make sisal, was introduced to the island by Henry Perrine in 1832, and John Dubose tended it close to the lighthouse. Earlier in 1827, the same lighthouse keeper was reprimanded for the sake of a cotton bale that washed ashore at Cape Florida. Instead of sending it down to Key West by revenue cutter, he bartered it for sacks of badly needed coffee. This became Key Biscayne's infamous cotton scandal.

Across the bay on the Miami River, Richard Fitzpatrick brought slaves and, encouraged by the commerical success of cotton planters in northern Florida, made an effort to extend the plantation system to southern Florida. He placed one hundred acres of sugarcane under cultivation and planted other crops, but the Seminole Wars disrupted his plans.

Before the lighthouse was built and shortly after it was burned, fugitive slaves, some from cotton plantations in north Florida and the Old South, embarked from Key Biscayne's shores for freedom to the Bahama Islands.

In the early 1880s, Ralph M. Munroe and his merry band of wreckers learned that an English steamer, the *Tregurno*, on a regular run from Galveston to Liverpool, had "struck a reef on the Bahamas Bank and jettisoned 2,300 bales of cotton which floated here." He wrote, "we rolled twenty-two bales of cotton above high water on Key Biscayne and duly marked it, which netted us several hundred dollars for a few hours work."

Waters S. Davis of the firm Sommerfield and Davis, or one of his colleagues, may well have filled the hold of the *Tregurno* when she was loaded with cotton bales at the Port of Galveston. His mercantile business included "a jute and cotton bagging industry and a rope manufactory." He sent cotton seed meal from Texas to Cape Florida to fertilize pineapples and enrich the soil.

W. J. Matheson had an interest in cotton when he bought his part of the island, for his companies were the largest American dye manufacturers, known worldwide, working with the textile industry. When Matheson introduced plants, like Perrine before him, he included logwood (*Haematoxylon campechianum*), a tree that yielded a dye, hematoxylin much sought after during colonial days for export between the New World and the continent. He imported his logwood from the Bahamas, but it had once grown wild in the Florida Keys and was timbered very early, according to John Lee Williams, who described it in the mid-1830s. The other plant dye, indigo now manufactured synthetically from coal tar, produces the ubiquitous blue cotton overalls and blue jeans. Whether Matheson knew anything about Turnbull's production of indigo or not, we do not know, but the thread runs through the history of our island.

The display of silk and cotton floss from the bursting pods of *Bombacaceae* trees introduced from South America and Africa (sacred trees in their native lands) pleased islanders and visitors. The earliest, planted in 1915 by the Mathesons, was the Baobab (*Adansonia digitata*), known in Africa for its bark that furnished fiber for "ropes strong enough to hold an elephant," reported David Fairchild. Nearby, in the present-day Village Green, were planted two Kapok (*Ceiba pentandra*). These grand trees produce the kapok of commerce, used for life vests, buoys and other flotation devices. The future is unknown for these significant natural monuments. The tallest at eighty feet was designated in 1995 as the Florida Champion Kapok by the Florida Division of Forestry. The Baobab was recorded as the second largest of that species on the Florida Champion Tree Registry.

The thread continues when the Davis heirs sold Cape House to International Harvester co-owner and heir James Deering, whose pioneering company revolutionized reapers, binders, and harvesting equipment that included sisal rope and cordage.

From the air Mashta House seems to float like Cleopatra's barge. Coconut palms on the point encircle the Atoll to Matheson's magnificent pleasure dome that was used for entertainment of friends and family during the 1920s and 1930s. Guests arrived by private yachts, often in late afternoon for unrivaled views of tropical sunsets. W. J. built this Moorish-style home on the west side of Key Biscayne after a sail up the Nile and an around-the-world cruise with his friend the Anaconda magnate, Arthur Curtiss James. He imported the architectural style and many materials to Mashta Point. Mashta is a word meaning "resting place," selected as a name by W. J.'s daughter, Nan — Matheson Family Collection ©Finlay B. Matheson

FOURTEEN

Deering's Hideaway

A DREAM UNREALIZED

James Deering. (John Singer Sargent, Vizcaya Museum and Gardens)

James Deering (1859–1925), the retired vice president and director of the International Harvester Company, had not always wanted to own a piece of a private island, but when he heard that the southern tip of Key Biscayne was available, he was pleased. He was already engaged in preparing a 180-acre site on the mainland, property he had acquired from the pioneer Brickell family (who had operated the first Indian Trading Post on the Miami River), which would be a palatial home unlike any in America. He would call it Villa Vizcaya, and work would begin in 1914 when he would boost the local economy by employing some thousand workers, including stone-cutters and artisans, many imported from Europe. Deering, who maintained residences in Chicago and Neuilly, a suburb of Paris, knew that his seventy-two-room imposing estate, modeled after an Italian villa and furnished with rare works of art that he and his friend, associate architect Paul Chalfin, collected in their worldwide travels, would be a formal showplace overlooking Biscayne Bay. Yet the island across the bay that he saw every day attracted him as well.

When Waters S. Davis decided a year before his death to sell the Cape Florida tract, he arranged for Ralph Munroe to be his local representative in the sale. Munroe was in the cat-bird seat, a position he must have relished, for few real-estate brokers have had such power over the destiny of the island. Many in the area then, and to this day, wonder why he did not sell it to W. J. Matheson, who had already bought the northern two-thirds of the island, with Munroe as agent. Matheson was motivated and qualified. There was great surprise when Deering became the purchaser. What had happened?

Some light was finally shed on this question in 1990 when the locked vault at Vizcaya was opened to us, and we read the first paragraph of a letter written by James Deering to F. L. McGinnis:

> When I negotiated for the Cape Florida land Commodore Matheson was also negotiating for it, each working without the other's knowledge. He offered $20,000, the price I paid, before I did, and was really

entitled to the property. Commodore Munroe, however, decided to sell it to me.

When I expressed my regret to Mr. Matheson that I should have interfered with him, he replied that it did not matter, as his anxiety was really to keep the property out of the hands of people who would exploit it, cut down the trees, and so forth.

The sale to Deering took a surprising turn. Up to this time, Matheson had adamantly refused to develop his land for other than agricultural purposes. Deering, however, soon changed his expressed intentions not to disturb the property. In 1914, less than a year after he bought Cape Florida, Deering wrote: "I should like to oblige Mr. Matheson in the matter of getting rid of the mosquitoes," but the cost suggested to him that Cape Florida's "future lies in sale for making homes . . . improving the land for a possible future development."

So he asked, "What is the cheapest way in which mosquitoes can be exterminated? How can this be done with the greatest permanent good to the property? What would be the reasonable method of handling the property with a view to its development some day or other, incidentally getting rid of mosquitoes?"

James Deering set out to solve the mosquito problem, to control "two species, the one breeding in salt mud, the other in stagnant rain water." Robert L. Stewart's engineers and surveyors in Cocoanut (sic) Grove recommended "filling mangrove swamps above tide flow for the one, and getting rid of water holding plants (palmettos &c) for the other." Mather & Son, Miami engineers and contractors, known for installing "water supply and irrigating plants in Dade County," including for W. J. Matheson, suggested "beginning at the Cape end . . . working north, clearing off everything you don't want, laying bare swamp holes . . . after [which] dredging could be set at work."

Cape Florida's palm-lined avenue, originally planted by Davis, led to lighthouse and eastside "Paradise Beach" from westside "Sound Beach" at dock. (Vizcaya Museum and Gardens)

Obviously, the land was not going to be left in its natural state, and the costs would be substantial. Before long, Deering's plans for the cape changed radically. Deering would call in New York experts for the serious work ahead.

Previously overlooked papers at Vizcaya reveal that he decided to develop Cape Florida as an island resort without equal in the United States. And his friend Paul Chalfin, who had helped build and decorate "the grandest house in America," the $10- million Villa Vizcaya across the bay from the cape, could not have been happier. Chalfin specialized in fantasy extravaganzas. Now he could design their tropical island.

Contrary to Munroe's belief that Deering would leave the cape alone, the millionaire from Chicago planned an internationally marketable resort, a precursor of planned island destinations. Chalfin wrote on March 18, 1916, that the "eventual development of Cape Florida . . . seems to me already admirably conceived. [Like you] I also had thought of the Pacific in contemplating these improvements and even of the Philippines, but a little more of Borneo and of Siam. You know Philippine buildings and many savage huts are altogether without color, whereas in Borneo, and as you approach the coast of Annam you get Chinese influence, which gives red, green and gold . . . do you not feel that color would be very agreeable over there?"

Deering agreed. He wanted to make Cape Florida "appear as tho' it were a place under the Equator . . . [that is] completely tropical . . . [like those of] the South Sea Islanders we have seen in picture books."

Instead of relying on locals like Ralph Munroe, who had helped Davis implement his improvements, Deering wrote to John K. Small, of the New York Botanical Gardens, "in the matter of making Cape Florida tropical." He had easy access to Dr. Small, whose Florida research, travels, and explorations were financed by James Deering's brother, Charles. [Author's Note: James received Small's plan, but it has not been found to date.]

For "reclaiming . . . the swamps for the use of land for winter homes," Frank E. Pratt of New York City drew up a blueprint, dividing the land by dredged canals, so every home would be waterfront and each have "access by boat and a safe harbor." Residents would move down a central eighty-foot-wide canal to ocean or bay. He wrote:

> Not including your reservation on the south end. . . . This land, when ready to sell, will have cost you about as follows [bulkheads and so forth would be additional]:

Purchase of land, 388 acres @ $50	$ 19,400.00
Filling 168 acres of swamp @ 322.60	54,196.80
Clearing " " " " @ 50	8,400.00
Planting Palms along Canals and Wind-Breaking Trees along property lines	3,000.00
Supervision & Engineering	5,000.00
Total	$ 89,996.80

This for 388 acres or $231.89 per acre.

It appears to me that there is here [on the cape] an opportunity for him to make a beautiful and very interesting development at the same time more than recovering the cost of the swamp lands.

If Mr. W. J. Matheson would devote his swamps to the same class of development, they would make one of the grandest spots in Florida.

—Frank E. Pratt (Deering's New York engineer), letter to Paul Chalfin, 1917

Lighthouse Restoration and Legal Hassle

In the winter of 1914, James Deering did substantial work "protecting the shore from the attack of the waves," initially bringing in crushed rock, cement, lumber, tools and equipment from Miami. Workers constructed six loose-rock, four grouted-rock, and three concrete jetties. The latter ran seventy-five, one hundred, and sixty-five feet and were three to four feet wide.

Deering consultants who submitted plans to combat shore erosion believed that the "main south-west jetty is the one best suitable for the making of land" and wished to carry it out on the flats about a quarter of a mile "to serve as a very efficient protection for the land already there and the lighthouse." They had little regard for the previous attempts at building jetties when less structured work with "coral rock" brought from the mainland and keys had been initiated and carried out for Waters S. Davis by Ralph Munroe, who felt an urgent need to save the beach from continuing erosion and who despised sea walls.

When Deering acquired the property from Davis (who had been appointed "sole custodian" of the lighthouse when he purchased it from the U.S. Treasury in 1903), it was "with the express agreement that he restore the lighthouse."

How Can He Think He Owns a United States Lighthouse?

So that he might restore the tower to "the original design," Deering wrote Washington to ask for government specifications and guidelines of his lighthouse. He was met with astonishment. His letter was circulated and an interoffice memo of March 17, 1915, asked, "How can he be the owner?"

It sounded very funny until the government officials learned that the letter writer was not a crazy man but a well-respected American businessman, one of the scions of the International Harvester Company. Legal discovery began in earnest. Evidence surfaced that an Act of Congress and two Executive Orders, fifty years apart, reserved the land for government use for the lighthouse and military purposes. They further found that the other owner of property on the island that was across the bay from the young city of Miami was the internationally respected dye manufacturer, William J. Matheson.

The federal government was tracing its claim back to the early years of Florida statehood when members of the U.S. Board of Engineers, among them young Lt. Col. Robert E. Lee, visited and recommended the land be reserved in an 1847 order signed by President James Polk. Fifty years later, in 1897, it was validated by a second Presidential Order. Between those dates there had been important exchanges of public and private titles.

It wasn't just that the U.S. government demanded to know how a private citizen laid claim to the lighthouse; Deering's ownership and Matheson's adjoining property were challenged.

On the island, work and planning came to a screeching halt. Although they were not great friends, Deering and Matheson joined forces to fight the federal government's claim to Key Biscayne and to search private and public documents, vowing to fight for their rightful ownership. They had already "made improvements" of more than $200,000 (equivalent of $2 million or more in 1990 dollars). (Deering at this time was building his mainland house, the $10 million Villa Vizcaya.) Their money, their reputations, and the future of the island were at stake. If they had to go to the president of the United States, they would do so.

The U.S. government marched forward, disputing the private ownership of Key Biscayne. Basing its case on previous executive orders and Acts of Congress, the government declared the island was reserved for lighthouse and military purposes only. Challenging private-sector titles and rights, reciting official decrees, the government brought forth much evidence that threatened the claims of W. J. Matheson and James Deering.

Deering and Matheson were men not only of power and wealth, but also of great perseverance. They hired a law firm to defend their titles, and their strategy was unusual. Far from being combative, backed up by the strength of his clients' connections, Frederick M. Hudson, their attorney, smoothly worked back corridors. Before it was over, the Secretary of War, the Secretary of the Interior, the Secretary of Commerce, and the Commissioner of the General Land Office came around—as did President Woodrow Wilson and the U.S. Congress. Hudson argued his clients' position as "innocent purchasers," having "no actual knowledge of the reservations . . . or of the *State's defective title* to the said lands." [Author's Italics].

He did not make public issue of information he uncovered in his own search of records: that two branches of the U.S. government had become lost in their own labyrinth of records. One department stood by the Executive Orders and Acts of Congress retaining Key Biscayne as a military reservation—not knowing that another department had conveyed lands to the state of Florida under the provisions of the 1850s Act of Congress concerning swamp and overflowed land. Moreover, the island had been made by Presidential Order a lighthouse reservation, and sold in parcels thereafter to private parties (Osborn and Field). Hudson was careful, moreover, when he reminded them that upon the outbreak of the Spanish-American War, a second Executive Order was signed wherein Key Biscayne and Virginia Key were declared military reservations.

Hudson had his petitioners ask that "the patent issued by the United States to the State of Florida be recognized and valid and binding."

When he met with members of the 64th Congress in July 1916, he stated clearly, "The patent was manifestly issued in ignorance of the existence of the reservation." Apparently, he said, "both the State authorities and Federal authorities had overlooked that reservation." And he pointed out, as he sought validation of the patent that would give clear title to his clients, that "Executive Order takes a precedence over the Government patent."

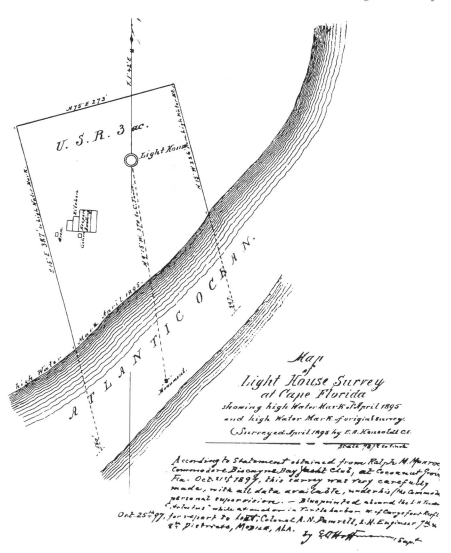

Map by E. A. Hensoldt in 1895 shows high and low water lines; note Bache monument is clearly visible at low tide. (National Archives)

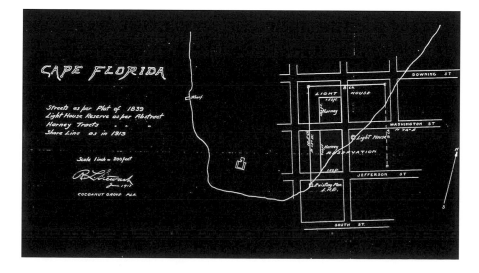

A comparison between the 1839 and 1913 shorelines shows the immense erosion which brought the edge of sea perilously close to the lighthouse and Cape House. (Vizcaya Museum and Gardens)

The waves were lapping at the base [and] the lighthouse might have fallen at any moment.

—JAMES DEERING, MAY 27, 1918

The 64th Congress agreed, thereby validating private ownership to Key Biscayne property held by Deering and Matheson.

Convinced his title was secure, Deering prepared to restore the lighthouse. He thought the tower restoration had mostly to do with fine points. "The bricks of the lighthouse must be reappointed," he said, and matched to those used before; he wanted the stairs and ironwork properly restored, not remodeled.

But when foundations of the lighthouse were investigated in 1918, he was shocked to learn from the engineer that the base was a mere four feet deep. He wrote his friend Paul Chalfin that the waves were lapping away a part of the foundation. "In other words," he wrote, "the lighthouse might have fallen at any moment."

Deering records sandbagging immediately and rushing to make the "foundations secure, as a duty both to myself and to the public."

He discovered that his jetties were not sufficient to prevent the sea from undermining the tower further. Studying charts comparing the 1851 high-water mark to the 1915 survey line, he learned that more than a quarter mile of beach had been lost. He put in additional breakwaters, and, before he was done, he had built sixteen major jetties (some one hundred feet out into the water), believing he could slow down wave and storm action that had worn away much of the cape.

Rebuilding the Lighthouse Foundation: 1918–1919

Deering's engineer, Frank E. Pratt, hoped to carry the tower foundation to bedrock, assuming that Key Biscayne sand was surface deep, unaware that Key Biscayne is little more than a sand pile in the sea.

Waves were lapping at the base of the tower. The engineer in charge rejected the proposal to build a seawall along the beach to protect the threatened tower. He said it not only would "totally destroy the beach for bathing or beauty," but if "built to withstand any storm, would be terribly expensive."

"I think it will be very simple to carry this foundation to rock by pilings which will cost a fraction of the sea wall," he said. Members of the firm of New York civil engineers had a surprise coming to them. As others before and after discovered, Key Biscayne was no Gibraltar, no Minorca, no Manhattan. It had no hard bedrock. Latter-day builders bored and cored to sixty and one hundred feet, driving pilings into layers of shelly sandstone with some skepticism and a prayer.

Pratt, whose men had taken soundings down sixteen feet (drawing false assumptions that a solid base lay not far below) had to design a reinforced concrete foundation of some ingenuity and great strength that was capable of holding up the tower. They consulted federal authorities, and records show a shipment of "330 steel shells for Cape Florida lighthouse underpinnings, direction of U.S. Government. Urgent."

Deering ordered engineers to build a maximum-security concrete foundation with steel casing that cost in excess of $10,000. Work was completed in February 1919. [Restoration engineers examining it in 1988 were surprised at its excellent condition and superior design.]

The test of the efforts of Deering's engineers came seven years later when the lighthouse stood up to the eye of the dreadful 1926 hurricane. Again it stood firm in 1992 when Andrew roared across the cape. The Cape Florida lighthouse remains in a precarious location anchored, so to speak, on an island of shifting sands.

Painting the Lighthouse

Cost of painting the lighthouse was $385, according to Deering records. The lighthouse exterior was left unpainted for some time after it was originally built in 1825, and the first keeper complained to Washington that it had not been whitewashed. George Meade had the bricks painted white (as before) after he heightened and completed the tower in 1856. A turn-of-the-century painting by Boyer Gonzales shows a white lighthouse; for many years during the twentieth century, the lighthouse was not whitewashed, so that descriptions of this period call it a "red brick tower." By the end of the twentieth century, however, the state of Florida and Dade Heritage Trust restoration plans of the Meade tower mandate that the red bricks be whitewashed.

Deering and Sanchez Litigation

When in 1920 James Deering was slapped with a lawsuit, the prospects of creating an exotic resort on Key Biscayne were put on hold. Once again he had to fight for his title, this time with the heirs of Venancio Sanchez, who had instituted action in District Court for "their undivided one-half interest" in the Cape Florida tract.

Deering and his attorneys were stunned, having no knowledge of the Sanchez claim. Had Davis known about it? Of course he had, but, at the turn of the century, he had thought it settled.

The notice of *Lis Pendens* involved "the Grant . . . to Pedro Fornells on the 18th day of January A.D. 1805." How far back did the claim go?

Trouble had been brewing even before the 1843 title was dated. Evidence was in the *Florida Herald* and *Southern Democrat.* In the Public Notice in May of 1841, when Venancio Sanchez's attorney R. D. Fontane had pronounced William G. Davis a scoundrel, he added, "I am determined to try the title of Mary Ann Davis in a court of Justice."

And so groundwork was laid for future litigation when Venancio Sanchez of St. Augustine had sailed to Cuba to purchase—from a daughter of Fornells' widow—the controversial half-rights to the Cape Florida property. She contended that her half brother, who sold to Mary Ann Davis, had no right to sell their shared inheritance in the Spanish Land Grant.

It was a long-drawn-out legal battle between the heirs of Sanchez and Deering with complex arguments including those related to revisiting "the Treaty between the United States and Spain," the implications of Territorial decisions, the 1820s Congressional acts, statehood, the Riparian Act of 1856, the Swamp Act, executive orders, surveys, and so forth. Arguments and hearings followed the whole way up through the court system until it finally was appealed to the highest court in the land. As Deering fought to prove validity of his title, he became disillusioned with his dream island.

It took the Supreme Court of the United States to bring the dispute to an end. It can never be said that Key Biscayne, one of Florida's earliest pieces of fought-over and sought-after real estate, did not receive its fair share of attention from the judicial, legislative, and executive branches of government. The decision came under the jurisdiction of Chief Justice William Howard Taft, who had never been to the southernmost barrier island, but had visited Key West (from which he sailed on a battleship to inspect the Panama Canal, which was under construction during his presidency), and the ruling was in favor of James Deering. The title was upheld by the Supreme Court decision. The Cape Florida case finally closed in 1926, too late for its owner to enjoy. James Deering died in 1925 aboard ship as he was making an ocean voyage from France. He would leave his magnificent mainland house, Villa Vizcaya, to the children of his brother, Charles Deering.

For many years, the fate of Cape Florida would be undecided.

FIFTEEN

Redrawing Property Lines

Immediately after Deering's death, there was talk that W. J. Matheson would move swiftly to buy out the Deering interest on Cape Florida so that at last he would own the entire island, but those who were speculating were not privy to the information that W. J. was negotiating to sell more than half of his own holdings comprising the northern half of the island. During the 1920s, the Florida land boom saw tidal waves of development sweep over the peninsula; often the front lines were fully submerged lands to be converted into artificial islands or wetlands to be dredged and filled into waterfront property; artificial islands like those called the Venetian Islands, pumped up from bay bottom off Miami Beach, became a boom-time rage.

A syndicate of developers was formed to suck up artificial islands on the coral banks just south of Cape Florida; these particular plans were effectively stopped by Ralph Munroe and others who warned of the dangers of blocking the bay's "safety valve" against disastrous hurricane tides and reverse bores. But one island builder persisted, turning his attention to Key Biscayne.

In a little-known maneuver, "Matheson Island" became a target of developer D. P. Davis (no relation to previous Cape Florida landholders). This self-made millionaire entered into a contract February 25, 1926, with W. J. Matheson. It stipulated that Davis "among other things, agreed to develop and re-sell" the north and midsections of Key Biscayne. This area, about fifty percent of which was submerged lands with riparian rights, extended from ocean to bay. It encompassed almost half the present-day village of Key Biscayne, north to Bear Cut, and all that is now Crandon Park.

Davis had much boom-time experience in island development, having turned $10,000 in mud flats into a reported $18 million worth of island lots near Tampa (Davis Islands) and, by filling salt marshes on the barrier island off St. Augustine, creating 375 homesites (Davis Shores), which are connected to the mainland by a bridge.

The island of Key Biscayne could only be reached by water, but Davis

Boom-time Florida-island developer D. P. Davis, in knickers, made bid for Key Biscayne in 1920s. (Florida State Archives)

could envision the distance across the bay spanned by a bridge. No wonder he made his bid for Key Biscayne at a time when the city of Coral Gables was preparing to incorporate and to include Key Biscayne. As he well knew, municipal bonds would be issued, as they had been in other areas where he had projects and where bonds were issued as financial vehicles to underwrite new cities and infrastructures, including bridges to offshore subdivisions.

When Coral Gables incorporated the island of Key Biscayne in its original charter, it saw its number of municipal bondholders increasing and its tax base broadening along with its geographic boundaries. Observers believe that the first proposed bridge attaching Key Biscayne to the mainland was part of the package. Then what Miami Beach was becoming to the city of Miami, magnificent Key Biscayne would be to Coral Gables. The new "City Beautiful" would have its own offshore tiara and uncontested tropical resort-in-the-making.

But D. P. Davis did not close the deal so quickly. It is probable, with all his statewide wheeling, that he had not read the U.S. announcement in the newspapers regarding the pending auction of random lots on Key Biscayne in the spring of 1926. It pertained to property at the north end of the island but the advertisement described the entire Key:

> Key Biscayne lies about 8 miles southeast of Miami, Florida, and is reached only by boat. No regular transportation schedule to Key Biscayne is maintained, but during the tourist season pleasure boats land daily near the old lighthouse on Cape Florida on the south end of Key Biscayne.
>
> The area of this abandoned military reservation is potentially valuable, for these lands are admirably suited to the growing of tropical fruits, and future possibilities exist in the subdivision and development of this area into winter home sites and resorts for wealthy tourists from the northern States.

The land to be sold at the Miami courthouse comprised 6.84 acres, close to Bear Cut, plats of land (known as the Tampa patents) that had not been sold to the previous owners, Osborn and Field, and were still in the public domain. By an order of President Calvin Coolidge, these lots were still caught up in the red tape of land once claimed by the government for military purposes. Once appraised for $1.25 an acre, now they were being offered for around $1,000 an acre. Boom-time fever brought bidders to the courtroom.

The Mathesons, who thought they owned the whole northern end of the island, had already invested heavily in much of the Key Biscayne land, except that covered by "mangrove and buttonwood timber." They had a million-dollar sale pending and they could not afford to let the random lots, which included ocean frontage, go to a higher bidder, even if they had to pay ten times the government's current appraisal.

"There was lively bidding for each of the tracts," Washington crowed with delight as auction results were announced: "The highest price probably ever paid the Government for an acre of land was recorded when a bidder offered $15,000 for a tract of ocean land on Key Biscayne.

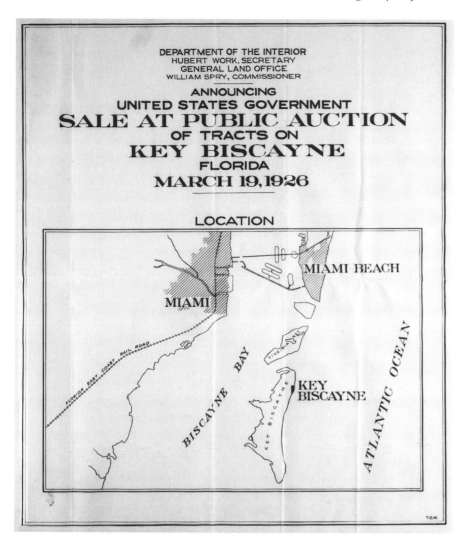

DEPARTMENT OF THE INTERIOR
HUBERT WORK, SECRETARY
GENERAL LAND OFFICE
WILLIAM SPRY, COMMISSIONER

ANNOUNCING
UNITED STATES GOVERNMENT
SALE AT PUBLIC AUCTION
OF TRACTS ON
KEY BISCAYNE
FLORIDA
MARCH 19, 1926

LOCATION

Sale at Public Auction by Federal Orders, 1926. (National Archives)

The lots were sold separately, they were purchased by one individual, who was the highest bidder on each tract."

The Mathesons paid $58,055 for land they thought they already owned. But their honor and their money were at stake. They could afford to take the gamble; the Key Biscayne property was only a small fraction of W.J.'s vast holdings. The Mathesons believed the title was now perfected, and the D. P. Davis contract could be closed at leisure. But before it was consummated, the forces of nature intervened. The disastrous hurricane of 1926 roared through South Florida, drenching and destroying property, people, and their dreams.

With the property on Key Biscayne under contract to D. P. Davis Properties, it is no wonder that the Mathesons hurried to clean up and restore their unmatched subtropical site. So much of their botanical planting and, in fact, half of their coconut palms had been wiped out by the storm.

Hugh wrote his father that he was purchasing new equipment and was proceeding as rapidly as possible in his hurricane clearing and replanting. It was a costly year for the Mathesons, between the auction and the storm.

The irony was that the prospective buyer, D. P. Davis, went into deep financial distress. He declared bankruptcy, turned his holdings over to a syndicate, and abruptly sailed for Europe on the steamship *Majestic.* He mysteriously disappeared en route, lost at sea—an accident or suicide. In late 1927, the properties were returned to Matheson and a quitclaim deed issued.

As for the relationship of Key Biscayne with the fledgling city of Coral Gables, it continued at arm's length, and there was no underwriting of a bridge to the island or any more imminent land development for a number of years.

W. J.'s Legacy

Aboard his yacht *Seaforth* an hour offshore from Cape Florida, returning from a fishing trip and cruise with guests to the Bahamas, W. J. Matheson died of a heart attack in 1930. He had had a deep sense of place and of home and wanted his children to have the security that comes with having holdings of their own, and to manage them and grow to love the land they held. Some land, including tracts on Key Biscayne, he had given to them during his lifetime. The rest, divided upon his death, included their winter home, historic Fort Hill (now on the National Registry) on Long Island, New York. Part of the estate near Huntington was given to The Nature Conservancy: known as Matheson Meadows, ancient oaks and woodlands remain in their natural state for public enjoyment.

In south Florida, as one of his legacies, just prior to his death, W. J. gave to the county eighty acres of virgin hammock land (now the five-hundred-acre Matheson Hammock) on the mainland across the bay from the lighthouse. Coconut Grove and Coral Gables properties shared among his family included magnificent bay-front estates (one of which was eventually bequeathed by son Malcolm for the home of the president of the University of Miami). There are other lands and landmarks as well, including Lignum Vitae Key, now a state botanical site near Indian Key. W. J.'s children, Hugh, Malcolm, and Nan, shared the property on Key Biscayne.

In normal times, Matheson's Island had seemed to be a fantasy island to its many worldwide visitors who had come by yacht. Following W. J.'s death, in the early 1930s as the Depression deepened, the Matheson estate plantation seemed like an anomaly where imported peacocks still strutted in a magically restored and flourishing South Sea setting.

Across the clear waters of the bay, there was still much gloom; recovery was painfully slow on the mainland following two severe blows from nature: the 1926 hurricane and a second killer storm in 1928 that grazed the Miami area, striking Lake Okeechobee and sending flood waters into the Everglades basin that killed eighteen hundred people, many by drowning. Both real estate prices and spirits plummeted. The ripple effect of the late-1929 crash on Wall Street sent more businesses and banks into bankruptcy.

Key Biscayne, however, was still a separate world. On the plantation, work continued as nine hundred acres were replanted and thirty thousand healthy coconuts were growing once again. Resident plantation workers were envied as their Eden-like environment was restored. After the cleanup from the storms and rebuilding, they lived on their idyllic island much as they had before—with a well-stocked commissary of their own supplementing the food they grew or fished—except that mechanization and modernization offered more conveniences.

Hugh continued to manage the plantation while he and Liguori raised their family in Coconut Grove and hosted events at Mashta; Malcolm and his wife, Julia, moved to Virginia, and for many years only wintered in Florida; Nan and her husband, Willis Delano Wood, came seasonally, but made their home at the Fort Hill estate. By the mid-1930s, they discussed the possible future of the Key Biscayne land, especially when they heard that the enthusiastic Democratic Congressman Claude Pepper in Washington, D.C., was working with Miami planners and promoters who, from their downtown offices, were eyeing offshore islands for major expansion. The closest was Virginia Key.

For Virginia Key, spring of 1938 became high noon. In a strange turn of history, and a never-ending reminder that the military often forgets its past maneuvers, the U.S. government turned its attention to this barely noticed slip of a barrier island located across Bear Cut at the north end of Key Biscayne. Once set aside as a military reservation, the island that had been sunbathing for years was called to active duty.

The U.S. Navy gave full approval to the Virginia Key Harbor Project, opening the way for $5 million in federal funding toward developing a multi-million-dollar combination airplane base and ship anchorage. Lapped by the clear bay waters to the west and the Atlantic to the east, Virginia Key was about to lose its virginity, even as so many Pacific islands were losing their innocence and idyllic settings.

Unknown Virginia Key was suddenly viewed as a strategic island, a potentially significant unit of defense, a pivotal point for hemispheric action. Congressman Pepper, a young elected official from the area, was acting upon it in the spirit of patriotism. The Mathesons were advised the north end of Key Biscayne might become an air base as well. But there was opposition. Key Biscayne was incorporated into Coral Gables and its commissioners were angered by the machinations of Miami and federal officials.

During a meeting in 1939, the city of Coral Gables, ever concerned over autonomy, controlled revenues, and strict zoning, had one of its commissioners request the city to "take formal action disapproving proposed Naval Air Station of Key Biscayne."

Subsequently, Dade County leaders would join the competition over both islands as private and public parties would fight for possession for years to come.

Charles Crandon, Ed Ball, A. D. Barnes (left to right) were instrumental in making Crandon Park a reality. (Blank Collection)

Crandon Park: A Gift

Even while these maneuvers were taking place, negotiations began between the county and the Matheson family. Few knew the behind-the-scenes activities headed by Charles H. Crandon, a county commissioner, who persuaded W. J.'s heirs to donate 808.8 acres to Dade County. In fact, it was Crandon who made a bold offer to the Mathesons to build a causeway to the Key. In the spring of 1940, a jubilant Dade County Board of Commissioners accepted the prime Key Biscayne land from bay to ocean, including two miles of palm-lined Atlantic beach, for a public park (now called Crandon Park).

The deed was signed April 25, 1940: "This conveyance is made upon the express condition that the lands hereby conveyed shall be perpetually used and maintained for public park purposes only." The restrictive clause states that "in case the use of said land for park purposes shall be abandoned . . . the heir(s) . . . shall be entitled upon their request to have the said lands reconveyed to them" (Deed Book 2139). The north end of Key Biscayne was no longer available for military purposes or other commercial construction, no matter the fate of Virginia Key. Revenue bonds would be forthcoming in support of county-wide park development.

A. D. Barnes, the founding director of the Dade County Parks and Recreation Department, welcomed the terms of the Crandon Park deed, which stipulated that the land reverted to the heirs of the donors if commercial-sector activities were given the go-ahead. During his leadership of the department from 1929 to 1969, Barnes recorded that "entrepreneurs and promoters began making requests for park land." Many "were tempting . . . [and] sounded good for increased revenues, but" he wrote, "Crandon park deed restrictions quickly finished any further consideration." This held true until the definition of public-park usage was changed about forty years later by county officials intent on increasing revenue.

There was still the matter of jurisdiction of the land.

Coral Gables city fathers were furious and felt betrayed by the Matheson gift to the county, whereupon the Matheson family requested Key Biscayne's independence, asserting the islanders had not received municipal services, although they had paid municipal taxes. For their part, the Board of County Commissioners of Dade County called for the exclusion of Key Biscayne from the city of Coral Gables, leaving the property subject to the jurisdiction of the county only. In retaliation, the city resolved "its vigorous opposition and objection to any movement on the part of Dade County . . . to exclude or remove Key Biscayne or any part thereof" from Coral Gables.

The fight was on, with the Dade County Board of Commissioners maneuvering as the Mathesons and Coral Gables entered into litigation which continued for seven years.

Following the Matheson philanthropic gift to Dade County, there was a new surge of interest in developing Virginia Key. The twelve-hundred-acre complex, blueprinted by the Greater Miami Port Development, included an air base and seaport ringed by hangars, shipping berths and dock facilities, channels, and approaches. Runways were laid out to replace estuaries and rookeries.

The $11.3-million project boasted a Concourse of the Americas with consular headquarters for Latin American countries. A signature building to be called the Dade County Auditorium was designed by the New York firm of Stewart and Skinner. The little barrier island was to have offices and a hotel; warehouses, fuel tanks, hangars, runways; a fishing pier; an outdoor auditorium; tennis courts and grandstand; golf course and dance pavilion; a railroad to the mainland; passenger ferries and car ferries. Here was a project!

In addition, in late 1941, a causeway from the mainland to Virginia Key was under way. Materials for construction worth $800,000 arrived: twenty-seven thousand barrels of cement, fifteen-thousand tons of sand, and twenty-two thousand tons of crushed rock. Pilings were driven out into the bay.

Suddenly, with the bombing of Pearl Harbor in the Pacific, the nation was plunged into war. Construction was abruptly halted. Some say it was due to the unavailability of manpower and supplies. With the nation actively at war, the favored status of the project changed. It slipped from the priority list. For the duration, thirty thousand linear feet of corroding guard rail and a lot of efforts and dreams were left by the wayside and the bayside. Neither Virginia Key nor Key Biscayne went to war during Franklin D. Roosevelt's presidency or thereafter, although both became movie sets for Hollywood war films.

During World War II, German submarines lurked offshore; in May 1942 an unarmed Mexican oil tanker was torpedoed near Fowey Rocks, detonating fifty thousand barrels of oil in a fiery blast that shook the island. From the mainland, Miamians suddenly looked to the island of Key Biscayne as a protective barrier. Local fishermen and others, rallied by Wirth Munroe, assisted the Coast Guard Reserve and Hugh Matheson to form a submarine-chase patrol and a rescue operation with a lookout station on Key Biscayne. There was little time for talk of a bridge.

Although there was a delay, nonetheless, there was tacit agreement between Dade County and the Matheson family that the generous prewar gift of parkland ultimately would be made accessible to the people. Even as Henry Flagler had built his railroad in exchange for gifts of land from prominent citizens Julia Tuttle and William Brickell, Miami pioneers, thereby opening up the "Magic City" of Miami to settlers and tourists, so the Dade County commissioners would build a bridge to Key Biscayne after the war.

This was a major construction project. Old-timers watched, remembering the revolutionary bridge built in 1912 when John Collins, with financing from Carl Fisher, had built the first bridge across Biscayne Bay, the two-and-a-half-mile planked bridge to Miami Beach. It had been hailed as the longest wooden vehicle bridge in the world, and opened up the area as a luxury winter resort and playground.

The acquisition of the Key Biscayne parkland from the Mathesons was based on Charles H. Crandon's commitment: the chairman of the committee, intent on creating a grand county-wide park system, Crandon had promised "on his own pledge to the heirs that the county would build the causeway from Miami to the island," according to John Pennekamp, *Miami Herald* editorialist. To back his pledge he called on financier Edward Ball, administrator of the duPont interests, to assume $4 million (later increased to $6 million) in thirty-year bonds which would finance the construction and be repaid "from a special fund" to come from "revenue derived from causeway toll charges."

Land on the mainland for the toll plaza and causeway entrance, purchased from the Deering estate, was included. The building of causeway and entrance "did not constitute a general debt to Dade County or taxpayers." Ed Ball would carry that load as the premier toll collector.

All parties came under criticism in a 1946 *Miami Herald* story, "Rich City May Rise on Island," when it was revealed that the same law firm, Hudson and Cason, "represented both the county commmission and the Matheson heirs in the park-causeway swap . . . as well as being the local counsel for the Deering estate."

In order to span Biscayne Bay to Virginia Key and on to Key Biscayne, truck- and bargeloads of materials were required. The amount of fill used in the causeway totaled more than three million cubic yards, dredged not only from the bay bottom but also from inland sites to form excavations such as Lake Osceola on the University of Miami Coral Gables campus. Structural steel that had been unavailable during the war was delivered to the site, and fifty-five hundred tons were used for bridge work and reinforcement. For the first time, Key Biscayne was connected to the mainland by 1.2 miles of over-water bridge structures and 2.7 miles of fill.

When the causeway was named for airline pioneer Eddie Rickenbacker and finally opened in November 1947, a charmed public paid the toll, drove the "four-mile arc from the Miami mainland across sparkling Biscayne Bay," and found they concurred with the dedication brochure: "Yes, here is a new Florida pleasure land—for the nation's enjoyment—the realization of a pre-war dream, which transforms the sun-splashed beach of Key Biscayne far beyond the grandeur of Cannes, Nice or Waikiki."

The Dade County brochure continued with a prophetic but cautionary note: "With proper planning and zoning, that area of Key Biscayne south of Crandon Park can be made the finest, most beautiful and most enjoyable residential community in the world. . . . That is the future of this new land unless ruined by those into whose hands its future development will be placed."

The causeway had opened, but the matter of disassociation with Coral Gables was still not settled. In fact, the attorney for the city of Coral Gables "expected to argue the Biscayne Key ouster suit before the Florida Supreme Court on the fourteenth of October 1948." Coral Gables did not win; the attorney debated appealing the decision to the U.S. Supreme Court, for he knew that with the completion of the causeway, land values were bound to soar. The following April, however, he regretfully advised his colleagues that the court decision ousting Key Biscayne "excluded (it) from tax rolls of the City in the future." Coral Gables no longer had any hope of collecting revenues from Key Biscayne.

It was at this time that the Matheson and Deering estates began to be subdivided, and development of the once-private island ushered in a new era (Malcolm Matheson had, in fact, sold his tract in 1943, before the bridge). Key Biscayne property owners were free to proceed without the benefits or the constraints of the strict zoning and building-construction codes of Coral Gables. For better or for worse, the island returned to a less-regulated status as part of unincorporated Dade County.

Populating the Island

With these developments, the status, the availability, and the vulnerability of the island changed. Now, it seemed, the entire island was imperiled. It had known other invasions in its long history: its sands had been marked by footprints of native people followed by conquistadores; shipwrecked sailors, pirates, and smugglers had come ashore, as had pilots and wreckers. Early grant holders, lighthouse keepers, military men, and others had been relatively few, and their area of building, encampment, or cultivation was too small to upset the harmony of nature.

The Cape Florida land, the site of the original Royal Land Grant, looked much as it had when Pedro and Mariana Tuduri Fornells first came ashore in 1805. Some areas had been disturbed, but most of the native vegetation, natural contours, and beach ridges remained; except for the introduction of selected tropical plants and trees on the southernmost acreage (some of which had eroded into the sea), the flora and fauna were native. The natural maritime forest, which defines the borders of a healthy barrier island, was continuing to build as it had for thousands of years. But change was coming.

North of the Cape Florida boundary line, where the Matheson property began, running from the midsection of the island north to Bear Cut, native growth had been grubbed and removed on much of the land to create a plantation; the dominant planting was coconut palms, followed by exotic shade and fruit trees imported from the tropics. By the 1940s, the island looked like a location for a South Sea island film, according to a scout from Hollywood, California. Word spread, and many movies, including *They Were Expendable* (set originally in the South Pacific), were filmed on Key Biscayne.

But the opening of the bridge meant that the settlers did not have to come ashore in PT boats as John Wayne had done; they could drive in their automobiles. For the first time in history, Key Biscayne was easily accessible from the mainland. The area south of Crandon Park to the Pines Canal was destined to become the village and resort of Key Biscayne. From New York, Baltimore, and the heartland of America, GIs and their families, along with a diversity of others seeking the dream of a peaceful island in the sun at affordable prices, formed the first flow of

Coconut trees on the plantation.
(Blank Collection)

traffic over the drawbridge, where revenues were encouraged by the principal bond holder, the financier Ed Ball. They drove along the causeway and across Bear Cut bridge to two-mile-long Crandon Park, with its towering coconut palms and unique subtropical setting. Many of the young World War II veterans had military training on Miami Beach or had been assigned to the Pacific during their war duty, and now they and their families found Paradise in the Atlantic. On the sandy shores and everywhere were tropical wading birds; upland were songbirds. New people flocking in were joined each spring and fall by migrating flocks along the eastern flyway.

For $500 down, in 1951, veterans could move into a homestead, owing only $9,450, in the first modestly priced subdivision or development a half mile from the ocean and the bay. Other new settlers were given liberal financing. Built by the Mackle Company and Investors Diversified Services, the first 289 houses were eagerly bought. They came with Beach Club access. They were cement-block structures, sturdy, side by side, and if they were not designed for architectural awards, the setting among rows of graceful coconuts and other palms, and the magnificent flowering and fruiting trees from the Mediterranean, Africa, India, Central and South America, some established for forty years, made up for their plainness.

During the subsequent phase of development, the Mackles pumped and filled the wetlands to expand the community by laying streets, constructing houses, and sprigging the fill with grass. Additional gardening, especially tropical planting close around the houses, would be done by early residents and by the hundreds of families who followed as the streets were paved, telephones installed, and services increased. Merchants set up shop; a U.S. Post Office branch was opened inside Vernon's Drug Store next door to a hardware store and a grocery. The Community Church held its first service in the Mathesons' old coconut-husking shed in 1951, and later met at Mashta House on the loggia overlooking the bay. Just finishing his residency, John Handwerker, M.D., enthusiastically became the village doctor, making house calls, delivering babies, and whatever else was necessary. The Key Biscayne Elementary School began classes in portable buildings in 1952; the Little Island Playhouse, a preschool, opened in the old plantation commissary-schoolhouse, made available by the Matheson heirs. The Key Biscayne Bank and Trust Company was the island's first financial institution, and a weekly newspaper, forerunner of *The Islander News*, was soon in print.

The first developers who bought land from the Mathesons laid out the west-side residential community with its own oceanside Beach Club and the first island resort, The Key Biscayne Hotel and Villas. They were brothers: Robert, Elliot, and Frank Mackle; locally they became known as the Brothers Saint Mackle, as if they were Saint Peter opening the Gates of Heaven as they unlocked the wooden gate at the circle marking the beginning of the village. Others have called them different names and said they had swung open the floodgates of an island that never should have been developed for residential or commercial use.

Hugh Matheson's sons participated in the growth south of the park lands. Finlay offered an exclusive and architecturally award-winning hideaway of cottages on the ocean (the original Key Colony with a nine-hole golf course), which drew national and international guests who liked to keep a low profile; Hugh, Jr. offered a place to dine, the Jamaica Inn, built around an enclosed atrium filled with tropical palms and plants, parrots and monkeys, and connected to a rather British pub with a south Florida maritime flavor, filled with ship models and salvaged finds from Florida waters and elsewhere. Robert (Hardy) and William (Bill) continued minimal operations of a palm nursery on the remnant of the coconut plantation where the big barn still stood; Hardy took a first-hand interest in maintaining the groves with the help of a full-time caretaker, Mackfield Mortimer, who had originally landed on the key from Long Island, Bahamas, in 1918, and one helper, David Dean. They were the last of the original plantation workers still on the key. Five vintage plantation cottages on the ocean were rented to tenants who knew they had found Bali-hái. On the bay side of the island, the grand Moorish-style mansion, Mashta House, known well by many prominent yacht owners and other guests of the Mathesons who had partied there in the Roaring Twenties, was offered by Nan Matheson Wood as a community yacht club. Residents, however, did not believe they could afford its upkeep. When eventually she sold the property, Mashta House, with its imported tiles and marble, great wooden beams, and carvings and gilt walls, was crumbling into the sea. It was not restored.

In the 1950s, the days were filled with brilliant sunlight, the rhythmic sounds of lapping waves, the songs of birds, the rustle of palm fronds; idyllic hours were spent beachcombing and walking barefoot in the sand, wading in the tidal pools within a short distance from colonies of long-legged birds who shared the open spaces under the great sky which seemed to stretch to infinity. Families spent lazy days swimming, boating, and fishing.

Islanders gathered for sunrises and sunsets. They lighted great bonfires on the beach, sharing fish and conch chowders, barbecues and spirits, telling tales, singing ballads and songs. In the rainy season they experienced torrential downpours and thunderous afternoon storms, and hoped there would be no hurricanes. During the long summers they watched for waterspouts and lightning strikes, and in the evenings the black sky flashed with lightning.

On clear nights sitting out under the magnificent canopy of stars, with no glare from street or city lights, Key Biscayners listened to an amazing concert of night sounds. They could imagine they were with Rudyard Kipling, Somerset Maugham, or Isak Dinesen in the jungle regions of India or deepest Africa. The sounds were those of owls, hooting one to the other, of nighthawks diving, of bats flying in a flurry of wings, of crickets chirping, of frogs croaking in the ponds, of night herons and other birds and creatures of the night. And over all the soft sweet music, the roar of lions sounded out from the jungle.

Key Biscayne lions did not roam free. They were part of the first county-owned zoo, started when a circus broke up, leaving a small menagerie. The early zoo collection included lions, an elephant, and a rhinoceros, among others. The zoo was a beneficiary of the Galapagos turtles that the Mathesons had protected, and some monkeys and pheasants they had imported to the plantation. Under pressure of the causeway bond holder to increase traffic through the toll gates, a children's amusement area, with a merry-go-round and miniature railroad, was added, and more exotic animals were shipped to Key Biscayne, including a white Bengal tiger, as the zoo became a major south Florida attraction. Originally located on a forty-eight-acre site in Crandon Park, the zoological and botanical garden concept was created as an integral part of the park by the renowned landscape architect William Lyman Phillips. He designed parks and cityscapes, including Fairchild Tropical Garden in Miami and the city of Balboa in Panama. Phillips studied landscape architecture and city planning at Harvard with Frederick Law Olmstead, Jr., whose father was a co-designer of Central Park in New York City and, in Chicago, the World's Columbian Exposition of 1893. Later, when the barrier island was judged to be too vulnerable a hurricane target, the zoo was moved to the mainland deep in south Dade. Ironically, the new location at Metrozoo was closer to the eye of Hurricane Andrew in 1992.

The 1960s census lists 3,103 people on the island. Unsold properties on the Atlantic Ocean between Crandon Park and the Cape Florida boundary—some zoned for agricultural purposes and lined with row upon row of healthy coconut palms—became highly sought after for ocean-front development. More than a century after Dr. Henry Perrine proposed that $100,000 would put Key Biscayne on the map as a health resort and mecca for sun-seeking tourists, investors began to notice its potential. "Miami's El Dorado," as proclaimed in a 1951 *Miami Herald* headline, was in the making; the building of condominiums and hotels on the ocean front was inevitable.

One by one, the Matheson heirs sold the tracts that had been originally laid out by W. J. in rectangular slices, like ribbon farms across the island from ocean to bay, but which now were divided among players on the Island Monopoly Board.

The forerunner of the island resorts was the Mackles' own Key Biscayne Hotel and Villas. Over the years, many celebrities were guests, among them America's favorite composer Irving Berlin along with other visitors including statesmen, scientists, writers, and politicians of some note including Jack Parr, Jim Bishop, Billy Graham, Werner Von Braun. Later John Foster Dulles, Henry Kissinger, and Lyndon Johnson were among visitors. The Eddie Rickenbackers took up residents in a seaside villa. Eight years after their resort was built and following the 1960 presidential election, President-elect John Kennedy drove from his winter home in Palm Beach to shake hands with the loser, Richard Nixon, who, with his wife, Pat, and children, Julie and Tricia, were staying in one of the villas. The press called the meeting the Sunshine Summit. When Nixon became president, he chose the key as his Winter White House, using a bayside compound made available by his friends banker Charles (Bebe) Rebozo, Senator George Smathers, and Robert Abplanalp, inventor of the aerosol spray can. One member of the White House press corps remembers that flying in from Washington to cover the president on the key was a boring assignment; excluded from his

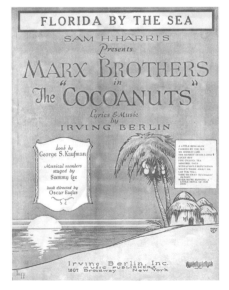

"Cocoanuts," lyrics and music by Irving Berlin. America's favorite composer stayed at the Key Biscayne Hotel and Villas. (Blank Collection)

house next to the communications center, the reporters waited for breaking news or a chance interview under palm trees in the blazing sun; when they saw him "going fishing," it was time to seek cover in the dim interiors of local "watering holes." [In the 1990s, tour leaders point out the current house on the site of the one-time Winter White House, volunteering, "This is the house where Watergate was planned."]

Up in Washington, D.C., those concerned with the integrity of the nation's capital and determined to preserve its historic and national landmarks passed a zoning law that no building could block the view or equal the height of the Washington monument. No such regulation controlled heights on Key Biscayne when high rises began to be built. The dominance of the lighthouse as the tallest building on the ocean ended.

The first high rise was Island House, a ten-story apartment building built in 1964 precariously close to the high-tide line. When a twenty-seven-story condominium was constructed later, its extreme height dwarfing the lighthouse, it aroused citizen indignation. Residents protested the county's laxity; the Key Biscayne Property Taxpayers' Association was founded in 1969.

Construction on the island continued to increase. The county reviewed many plans and builders presented projects that were granted permits, many with zoning variances. Some parcels of land went through many hands before the property usage was determined. It was only a matter of time before contractors' cranes competed with long-legged wading cranes along the shoreline. Much of the west side of the island was seawalled, and custom-designed homes began to be built on formerly "overflowed land" laced with canals, as the size and diversity of the community increased.

Key Biscayne was feeling the impact of the population migration to the coast and to sun-belt destinations; the tropical-looking island was particularly inviting because of its magnificent Atlantic beach. Moreover, the revolution in nearby Cuba sent exiles fleeing Castro's regime to refuge and to buy homes on Key Biscayne and in Miami. Latin Americans bought safe second homes on the island. Europeans were attracted to the new residential and resort community close to a city that supported international trade and Edge-Act banks in the 1970s. Ocean-front buildings rose like castles in the sand. Before long, the hotels and motels, including the Key Biscayne Hotel and Villas (forerunner of the Ocean Club), the Silver Sands, the Sonesta Beach Resort, and the Sheraton Royal Biscayne (forerunner of the Grand Bay Resort) were attracting national and international visitors and conventions to the Island Paradise. Key Biscayne had become a magnet for the rich and famous fulfilling their tropical fantasy.

President-elect John F. Kennedy and defeated-opponent Richard M. Nixon meet at the Sunshine Summit on Key Biscayne. Later as President, Nixon made Key Biscayne his Winter White House.

SIXTEEN

Cape Florida Stands Sentinel

I n 1948, a Cuban exile, José Manuel Áleman, and his wife, Elena Santeiro Garcia Áleman, bought Cape Florida for $1.5 million, a substantial increase over the purchase price of $20,000 that James Deering had paid in 1913. The tract was one of Áleman's many Florida land investments.

After the island was connected to the mainland by a causeway, property values had soared. At Cape Florida, lying in the sun almost a quarter of a century since James Deering's death, no improvements had been made. In fact, the abandoned lighthouse had been boarded up for protection against trespassers or vandals, and the keeper's cottage was merely a pile of bricks. Cape House was sometimes occupied by the caretakers, but more often shuttered closed. The outbuildings had become dilapidated. The once-cultivated "Davis Park" was wild and overgrown; native plants and many palms had survived the storms and hurricanes. The erosion of the mile-long beaches and shores on either side was advanced. The water was lapping close to the foundation of the elevated Cape House. The windswept and sandblasted lighthouse, which had been built originally about three-quarters of a mile from the high-water line, stood precariously close to the ocean. No road cut into the property, which was accessible only by boat or on foot along the beach.

With his wife, Áleman had arrived in Miami that year, fleeing Cuba in the wake of a scandalous two years as education minister during the regime of President Ramón Grau-San Martin, his intimate friend. They left behind "thousands of caballerías of land, sugar mills" and other properties (later nationalized by Fidel Castro). Moreover, he was said to have "$20 million in notes in his suitcase."

Áleman, who had been secretary of war in Cuba during the Spanish-American War when the Cape Florida lighthouse had been activated as a signal station, contacted U.S. authorities and offered the historic tower and adjacent ten acres to the National Park Service. The offer was declined. Local preservationists had supported his offer, although a few international politicians later questioned his motives when in 1951, following Áleman's death, former President Grau was indicted along with ten of his ministers (who had included Áleman) for the theft of $40 million. The widow of Grau's former secretary of education was charged and notified. When subsequently a Cuban judge issued a writ of attachment to Grau's Fifth Avenue New York house, perhaps Mrs. Áleman envisioned the Cape Florida property and other interests were threatened. Should she try to sell the Key Biscayne property or risk holding it?

She was faced with an interesting dilemma. Before her husband's death, the exiled Álemans had laid plans for an elegant subdivision, some say their own Varadero Beach on Key Biscayne. They wasted no time. By 1949, Cape Florida was swarming with surveyors and engineers, contractors and crews. The lush overgrown subtropical jungle and virgin forests were facing an unprecedented calamity. Preliminary work "concentrated on building dikes preparatory to pumping in sand fill." Hydraulic dredging and dragline construction proceeded as workers prepared to build a seawall about a mile and a half long to wrap the cape from the lighthouse around the west to the boundary line. Only the ocean beach was not to be seawalled.

Heavy equipment and materials were barged across the bay. Filling and dredging followed cutting and bulldozing as crews efficiently cleared vegetation. Few humans, except an occasional boater, were bothered by the sound of chain saws and the rumbling of earth movers. Wildlife scattered in all directions. One of the few visitors allowed inside the grounds as work began was Hodge J. Hanson, a landscape architect on a site inspection relating to Áleman's offer of the lighthouse to the National Park Service; he said that thick undergrowth and mangroves made many areas impenetrable and they "could be expected to be deeply inundated by the sea in frequent hurricane periods." Hanson, the last recorder before the defoliation and defacement of Cape Florida, also noted that "the lighthouse is at water's edge," and about fifty feet to its west, a dense palm jungle flourished. Beside the tower, he added, "The beach drops off sharply to five feet or more of water, showing the remarkable clarity and varied pastel coloration of South Florida waters. Off to seaward, many ships in the Gulf Stream are usually visible, as well as smaller vessels using Biscayne Channel to the south."

But the clear waters off Cape Florida were about to be muddied if a startling proposal made by the Dade County Planning Board, and shared with the Álemans prior to its completion, was to be a reality. It was a bold design to connect Miami, via Key Biscayne, to the existing Overseas Highway to Key West.

The proposal was unveiled in 1950. The Dade County commissioners, already proud to own Crandon Park on the north end of the island, were eager to extend Crandon Boulevard through the Cape Florida property and across the sparkling flats to Elliott Key all the way to Key Largo. No wonder the Álemans, whose land was crucial to the plan, cleared the cape so swiftly. No wonder, following her husband's death, Áleman's widow decided to protect their investment. Assured that "the causeway project would be of such great value to owners of land on the keys along the route that they could, in general, be expected to contribute to the right-of-way . . . on the southern part of Key Biscayne the local property owners have already reserved a 120-foot [wide] strip for

A proposed new overseas highway through the island was Dade County Commissioners' 1950 plan to increase ocean and bay development by bridge connecting Miami to Key Largo and Key West. (Coral Gables Public Library)

this purpose," according to the Dade County Planning Board proposal. The Dade County commissioners embraced the project "in recognition of the need of providing for this future population growth and for the development of more ocean and bay front property."

Elena Santeiro Garcia (as she thereafter called herself in business transactions in the United States) was ready. At mid-century, she was proud to see the lighthouse towering over a flat denuded landscape that for several thousand years had managed to survive and recover from fires, floods, and hurricanes. A 1951 aerial image shows the Cape cleared and filled for development; it was as if it had simply been paved over.

With the exception of a fringe of greenery around Cape House and the light tower, and a thin coastal strand on the oceanside, every vestige of natural contours, native vegetation, and landscaping had been removed by earth-moving equipment. The length and width of the entire historic tract, rookeries and habitats were destroyed as ancient man-

This 1951 aerial photograph shows denuded Cape Florida stripped of vegetation, filled, and leveled by developers. (National Oceanic and Atmospheric Administration)

grove and buttonwood forests had been felled, and once-swollen ponds and swamps filled; dunes, ridges, mounds, and grounds had been bulldozed and leveled. All the trees and plants had been burned. The wildlife either escaped or was killed. Many rattlers and other snakes and reptiles slithered across the boundary line as did raccoons, marsh hares, and opossums; displaced birds also crossed over along with other wildlife dependent on a growing environment. The entire west side of the property had been seawalled and the small harbor enlarged as a yacht basin.

But Áleman's widow was disappointed when, as with many envisioned schemes, Dade County shelved the plan. The new overseas highway did not materialize. The view from the cape would not be altered by the proposed causeway with artificial islands between Key Biscayne and Key Largo. (Later, however, a few intrepid individuals drove pilings directly into the banks to build elevated houses over water to form a renegade community called Stiltsville.) Garcia added to her holdings a tract from ocean to bay, previously sold by Malcolm Matheson, and containing property on both sides of the private canal (present-day Pines Canal) including a three-hundred-foot strip south of the canal. The canal had been cut by W. J. Matheson in the 1920s. North of it, lots, waterways, and basins eventually became the separate, so-named Cape Florida subdivision, bought, sold, and divided in a series of transactions by American and Cuban investors and developers, among the first being the president of the Keyes Company and his client Augustin Batista and others.

Garcia had waited patiently. In 1957, the property was advertised for $9.5 million as "the only remaining large tract of undeveloped beach frontage in the Miami area . . . its value . . . increasing with the rapid growth of population." New York furrier Louis R. Ritter met the price; but the following year, after an illness and failure to meet his payments, he died. The property was returned. Then Garcia received an irresistible offer; she sold the Cape Florida property to a developer for $13 million, taking a mortgage of $12 million. Few noticed in 1957 the loss of an architectural and historic landmark when Cape House went up in flames and burned to the ground.

Once again, Cape Florida passed from Hispanic ownership back into American hands. The price was high, but it was incomparable real estate. Arthur A. Desser, president of Lefcourt Realty Corporation, subsidiary of Desser and Garfield, Inc., advertised a $500-million planned community. A model community of luxurious residences and resort properties to rival Miami Beach was advertised nationally as the Delaware firm laid roads and prepared to build, but no foundations were laid. In 1962, the widow Áleman was surprised. Foreclosure proceedings were imminent. Desser and Garfield could not meet the terms of their agreement and the property would revert to her. Legal documents pronounced this "Done and Ordered at Miami, Florida the 9th day of April, 1963." The property was returned in July.

This event was singularly important in the future of Cape Florida. Elena Santeiro Garcia, whose reputation, many say, had been sullied by her association with her husband (whose $20 million of real estate in south Florida she had inherited), needed a way to clear her name. Her volatile stepson, reported Howard Kleinberg in a *Miami Herald* column in the 1990s, had further scarred the Áleman name by becoming embroiled in American-Cuban relations, sending arms to Fidel Castro and then committing suicide when he was rebuffed by both Castro and the Miami Cubans.

A forest of fast-growing and unchecked Australian pine (*Casuarina*) had established an exotic habitat on the filled land of Cape Florida, superseding native growth. The evergreens grew tall and so dense that the lighthouse was hidden except from the open sea. But it was not forgotten.

The opportunity to put the entire tract in the public domain captured the attention of community leaders, historians, and other concerned citizens. Could this historic piece of property and irreplaceable Florida landmark be restored and preserved? Prior to the county's Metro Planning Advisory Board hearing proposals on acquiring fifty acres around the light tower for a park in 1964, *The Miami News* and its editor, Bill Baggs, raised the question of "the feasibility of acquiring this island paradise [Cape Florida] for everyone to enjoy." Why not purchase all the land? Then-County Commissioner R. Hardy Matheson, whose family once had held all of the other property on the island, said, "There isn't enough undeveloped land in South Florida to let this go." But the

A touch of paradise for sale. (Betty Rice Collection)

commissioners were not unanimous. By this time, Cape Florida was on the high-priority list of recommendations for state purchase. U.S. Interior Secretary Stewart Udall, who had flown over the property that once had been under the custodianship of the United States, urged that it be preserved, but not by the federal government. Two years later, the unofficial matchmaker, visionary Bill Baggs, brought together Áleman's widow and representatives administrating the state's new recreation land fund. In 1966, they reached an agreement and she sold the land, which included the lighthouse, for a park. Upland acreage would be increased by some 470 acres of submerged land (some of which had once been above water). The total cost was $8.5 million when federal funds of $2.3 million were added to the $6.2 million from the state.

Park rangers prepared the land for visitors; they also set about protecting the animals and their habitats. Beaches and the dunes on the ocean were patrolled to safeguard the annual nesting of sea turtles and their eggs. Native plants were identified and encouraged. Few recognized that the "piney woods" was not an integral part of a centuries-old "unspoiled natural wilderness" nor that the casuarinas had been introduced to Cape Florida in the 1890s, recommended for use as windbreakers and for attractive seaside planting by such authorities as Harvard botanist and encyclopedist Liberty Hyde Bailey. Later they would be condemned as undesirable exotic species; they sucked the soil of needed nutrients. But picnickers liked the forest shade and whispering songs of the Australian pines that had reseeded following the disastrous 1950 clearing of the cape.

The priceless property was opened to the public on January 1, 1967, as a state park. Later it would be appropriately named Bill Baggs Cape Florida State Park. Once again, this historic tract became public land to be held in trust.

The legislature in Tallahassee funded lighthouse restoration so that the landmark could at last be seen by the public, and its significance appreciated along with its spectacular overview. John Pennekamp wrote in *The Miami Herald* on October 10, 1970, "The view from the tower probably is the most spectacular land and seascape in Florida." Additionally, a replica of the keeper's cottage was built on the old compound. In 1978, after a hundred years of darkness, the tower was relighted as a stable aid to navigation and placed in the service of the U.S. Coast Guard. The exposed red brick walls were not white-washed but sandblasted.

It appeared the tower had been stabilized, and, according to one observer, "the last touch of paradise, and with it, the last virgin beach" had been saved. But, of course, on a barrier island nothing is forever.

SEVENTEEN

The Courting
of Key Biscayne

Following the designation of the ancient Cape Florida land as parklands, there was celebration. Those who lived on the island were envied because now all Key Biscayne was divided in three parts, and the 2.5-square-mile village was buffered by miles of green park to the north and south, as well as being ringed by water.

Residents might be on the front line of hurricanes, but they had survived Cleo in 1960, Donna in 1964, and Betsy in 1965 when all over the island, homes and streets had been flooded; kayaks and airboats temporarily replaced cars. Following hurricane Betsy, more than three feet of water covered and stood for many days on the low-lying island where the average elevation is less than five feet above sea level. Flood and wind damage to property caused hardship for human, animal, and plant communities. Most islanders had taken refuge on the mainland, ordered to evacuate by the National Hurricane Center, which was concerned over the adequacy of the only escape route over the drawbridge. In the bay, a storm blew a barge into the drawbridge, damaging it and making egress and access impossible by road.

After Betsy caused extensive damage, there were no storms of any consequence to hit the key for some years—at least none designed by nature.

In their place there was a rising storm surge of development. The community was viewed by county fathers as one of many mushrooming satellite communities that formed part of the Greater Miami environs. (By decade's end it would have the fifth richest tax base in the county, just behind much-larger Miami, Miami Beach, Coral Gables, and Hialeah.) But the islanders disagreed, and there was much unrest at the little village and island resort. "Residents took fierce protective pride in their village and resisted the onslaught to urban development to the point of lying down in front of bulldozers poised to rip out a swath of palm trees for a new traffic circle. . . . For sheer anti-highrise, anti-traffic, environmental militancy, there was no more hard-nosed bunch than the defenders of Key Biscayne," wrote Charles Whited in *The Miami Herald* in 1987.

All the construction on the little island was taking place at the same time that federal and state coastal-land- and water-management acts were being enacted Ironically, there was not only dialogue, but there were new laws concerning the endangered coastal barrier islands and protection of their special ecosystems and resources. But even the Development of Regional Impact statements (DRIs), which should have slowed the removal of some sand ridges, wetlands, woodlands, and wildlife habitats, did not end the building boom on the island.

By 1985, there were "100 businesses between the ocean and toll-booth . . . along the ten miles of land and sand from the lighthouse to the mainland," according to a story in *The Miami Herald* reporting on traffic problems caused by four million cars traveling to and fro annually along the causeway. Besides the beaches, there were attractions en route on Virginia Key such as the Seaquarium, Planet Ocean (replaced later by the MAST Academy), and the City of Miami Marine Stadium; also government and university laboratories including the Bureau of Commercial Fisheries with its Tropical Atlantic Biological Laboratory, NOAA's Atlantic Oceanographic and Meteorological Laboratories, and the University of Miami's Rosenstiel School of Marine and Atmospheric Sciences with major facilities for tropical and subtropical studies. Across the Bear Cut Bridge from the world-renowned oceanographic complex was the Crandon Marina with docks for pleasure boats and yachts, and home port to the deep-sea charter fishing fleet. Just beyond was the county's Key Biscayne championship golf course, The Links, site of the PGA Tour and the annual Royal Carribean Classic.

Traffic jams had become such an issue that beachgoers and islanders were relieved when the county announced that after four years of study, with $2 million in hand, they were ready to replace the old drawbridge. In an unusual offering of $25.4 million of revenue bonds that had no secondary backing but were sold in anticipation of proceeds from future causeway tolls, they proceeded. The system would meet the criteria for evacuation in times of hurricanes or other emergencies. Traffic projections had been considered to the year 2003 and beyond, according to the Dade County Public Works Department.

The magnificent $27-million multi-laned causeway soared like a rainbow over Biscayne Bay. It even had a bicycle path. The William Powell Bridge rose to a height of seventy-six feet, ten inches, its high arch one thousand feet long over the Intracoastal Waterway. And over the rainbow, on either side, were pots of gold.

Upon completion of the bridge, almost before the concrete had dried along the length of the widened causeway, heavy earth-moving equipment rumbled across Biscayne Bay into the park to breach an entrance into the west-side wilderness that lay adjacent to the Biscayne Bay Aquatic Preserve and Crandon Boulevard. Upon the historic "overflowed land," on the west side of the island between the aquatic preserve and the highway, an area designated by the master plan as highly stressed and environmentally sensitive, a project was under way. In the process, wildlife habitats, marine nurseries, bird rookeries, and barrier-island ecosystems were eliminated as $3 million of taxpayers' money brought the land up to sea level in preparation for building a major sports facility and stadium for professional tennis tournaments.

The Matheson family, who believed their deed more firmly planted in the laws of the land than the trees being uprooted in the wetlands and woodlands, objected when they became fully aware that the public officials had committed themselves to a multi-million-dollar development with a private corporation to build a for-profit professional tennis complex and a wished-for fourteen-thousand-seat stadium with commercial space. [In May 1993, *The Miami Herald* reported the county had, as of that date, spent $27.35 million building the facility, scheduled for completion for the March 1994 games—the same cost as building the new bridge in 1985.]

The first legal objection, *White vs. Metro Dade County,* was filed by sixty-nine litigants, and soon a separate suit was also filed by the family who held a reverter clause that the park would return to them if it were used for other than public-park purposes. The county was charged with violating its own Comprehensive Master Plan for Development as well as the deed to Crandon Park. As in other parts of the world, private citizens, alarmed by commercialization, were seeking solutions to *reclaim the parks for the people.*

Nearly half a century earlier, in private correspondence, visionary and practical naturalist David Fairchild had cautioned his philanthropic friend W. J. Matheson, whose gift of land gave rise to an aspiring parks department:

> I have heard with the keenest pleasure that you have deeded the wonderful hammock which you have guarded all these years from destruction, to the County.
>
> I trust that the terms will be sufficiently binding to prevent any political manipulation of it years hence. The drift of public opinion is so strongly toward the preservation of natural scenery that I think there is little likelihood of there being any change made for a generation at least, in the wild character of the hammock. By that time we may know more about how to maintain such a spot in its original wilderness condition. Allow me to thank you in behalf of all my friends and lovers of the wild hammocks for what you have done.

Dr. Fairchild's hopes are still shared by many citizens concerned with preserving natural places and with changing definitions of the use or abuse of public park spaces. Many in Dade County had believed the Mathesons would wave their reverter clause like a red flag in front of a bull. But in the corridors and chambers, the ardor of legal matadors was not forthcoming. As litigation quietly proceeded, construction of the "professional sports franchise facility" continued. Moreover, the politicians who might have chosen a more suitable mainland site seemed not to see the incompatibility of tennis being played over tropical wetlands on a barrier island.

In 1987, the fledgling Tennis Center on Miami's tropical island attracted worldwide attention as the games of the Lipton Championships were played in a temporary stadium at Crandon Park surrounded by a newly landscaped tract just south of The Links at Key Biscayne, the number-one-rated public-owned golf course in the United States. The financial players were good financiers; founding chairman Earl "Butch" Buchholz with his brother, tournament director Cliff Buchholz, and the International Players Championship, Inc. received high praise as the tournament attracted major sponsors, global spectators, and top seeds to Miami's new five-star annual event.

The singles women's Lipton Champion in the first year of island games was Steffi Graf defeating Chris Evert; Martina Navratilova and Pam Shriver were doubles winners. The same year, the singles men's champion was Miloslav Mecir who defeated Ivan Lendl. Thereafter, ninety-six men and ninety-six women would compete annually at "Wimbledon West," and one of the players would be Key Biscayner Mary Joe Fernandez. Major networks beamed celebrity photographs from Key Biscayne. Joyful promoters were over the rainbow.

Projections of record attendance at the ten-day event of 20,000 a day prompted traffic and parking concerns (by 1992, attendance topped 200,000 spectators, and by 1995 the record would increase to nearly 216,000). The county commissioners blessed the Metro-Dade Parks solution: A $1.2-million pedestrian underpass connecting the Tennis Center to the east-side parking lots of Crandon Park. In order to construct the tunnel, the plan was to cross the boulevard median. Aroused environmentalists said the proposal showed no understanding of the nature of a sedimentary barrier island at sea level where winds and water continually undermined and redistributed the shifting sands— without the help of man. But the county moved rapidly. In October 1987, islanders and Dade County beachgoers, arriving for a relaxing time at the sea, were shocked to become witnesses to clear-cutting of the dense jungle in the median between the ocean and the bay. Opposite the new entrance to the tennis complex, mahoganies, gumbo-limbos, and other tropical and subtropical hardwoods and palms were being bulldozed in a two-acre area.

Even one of the county commissioners, summoned to the scene by angered citizens and environmental groups, called it an "unconscionable massacre of trees." Protestors planted hundreds of bare stakes signifying the loss, the tunneling project was aborted, and the Parks Department replanted the median strip. Shortly thereafter, the state legislature showed its concern and, on July 7, 1988, designated Crandon Boulevard a protected State Historic Highway. The construction of the tennis complex continued.

Following another four years of wrangling, negotiations ensued whereby the county made sufficient concessions for the Mathesons to agree to an out-of-court settlement. Crandon Park would have a new master plan: development would be curbed in remaining spaces, and the stadium would be shielded from view by generous landscaping of native plants. Some believed a step had been taken for preserving the passive use of public park space. Disappointment, however, among those fighting commercial use and "mass recreational marketing" of American parklands contrasted with the excitement radiating from the

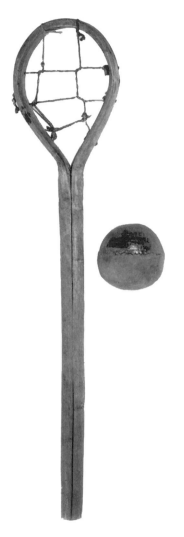

Racket of pine wood, strung with rawhide, with buckskin ball used in games by nineteenth-century Seminoles. (Smithsonian Institution)

Greater Miami Visitor and Convention Bureau, as well as national and international tourism and sports circles. From the top of the bleachers there was a new vantage point for viewing Miami's sparkling, ever-rising skyline across the waters of Biscayne Bay.

The Lipton Championships had a highly photogenic and unique home, and the 1994 games, carrying $3.3 million in prize money, offered "The World's Best Tennis" to its millions of fans. Miami's tropical beauty and the island's state-of-the-art stadium would be seen in sixty-six countries on six continents through live and taped worldwide broadcasting.

Village of Key Biscayne Inc.

Before the arrival of the The Lipton, there was a movement among islanders toward self-government. With one of the richest tax bases in the county, island leaders and taxpayers became increasingly fed up with what they believed to be county laxity, audacity, and the perceived disregard of the public trust and neighborhood needs. There was talk of secession. "Before they moved in earnest toward incorporation," reported Associate Editor Joanna Wragg in the *Miami Herald* "they researched the law, crunched the numbers . . . created an advisory council . . . and waited for Metro to respond to community issues." Instead the rising current of indignation built up as the County Commission yielded public roads to private oceanside development causing many residents to feel increasingly ignored and excluded from far-reaching decisions. The levees opened wide to incorporation.

On June 18, 1991, voters went to the polls to take charge of their own destiny. Citizens on the half-mile-wide section of sandbar reaffirmed their separate island identity. A month later, on the occasion of the annual Fourth of July celebration—with its parade of floats and flag-waving residents and merchants, civic and service organizations and others strutting to the syncopation of trumpets, tubas, and drums of the Chowder Chompers Band—and in the flare and splendor of skyrockets and Roman candles, the community's own Independence Day dawned. Official incorporation took place on July 19, 1991.

The first business was the election of a mayor and council. A nationwide search brought in an experienced village manager. Land was at a premium; density must be considered. The environment of a water-flanked island resort and the character of a small village were priorities. At the same time the Chamber of Commerce was pleased to welcome visitors to traditional fairs and events, sponsored by community groups, such as the annual Key Biscayne Art Festival and the Lighthouse Run (the oldest in south Florida). The 1990 census showed 8,854 persons, 42.8% or 3,790 Hispanic (1,576 of Cuban origin) and 57.2% or 5,064 non-Hispanic (of which 4,998 were white). In the preliminary master plan of future land use, Key Biscayne would list as its first goal to "protect and enhance the residential, commercial, resort and natural resource areas of Key Biscayne"; its second goal, relating to community character, states, "Key Biscayne should be a residential refuge from the outside world."

The new officers prepared to move forward, but it was not to be easy. Thirteen months after incorporation, as the village was trying to carefully craft its self-governing organization and goals, red-and-black hurricane flags went up.

The Great Hurricane of 1992

"It is on the sand islands of the long coasts that hurricanes eternally work their greatest change," Marjory Stoneman Douglas had written in 1976 in her book *Hurricane*. Since the mid-1830s (specifically in 1835 and then in 1876, 1878, 1893, 1896, and 1926), reports of hurricanes describe details of changes and permutations to Key Biscayne beaches, plants, and wildlife, as well as to submerged lands, and also damage to buildings and structures, including ships. Dreaded cyclical events, hurricanes bring great destruction to populated communities. In a natural community such as the coastal ecosystems of unsettled barrier islands, great havoc may be experienced, but nature, if left undisturbed, will gradually restore the balance.

One hundred years earlier in 1893, a powerful hurricane struck the Florida east coast, and Ralph Munroe watched its assault on Key Biscayne from his home six miles across the bay. He related a dramatic account of seeing "the white flash of breakers on the outerbeach of Key Biscayne, *over the trees*, and throughout the entire length of the key." Waters S. Davis was troubled that the cape was "so liable to destruction by storms" after the 1893 hurricane destroyed new structures and his new plantings.

And so it was in 1992 that the future plans for the island were put on hold during the third week of August; anxieties rose as the barometer began to fall ominously. The director of the National Hurricane Center, broadcasting from Coral Gables, warned coastal residents of impending dangers and cautioned them to take measures to protect their lives and property. Winds howled across the Atlantic from Cape Verde off the African coast toward Cape Florida. Faced with a mandatory evacuation, residents fled to the mainland. In the black, predawn hours of August 24, Hurricane Andrew struck the barrier island with sustained winds of more than 130 miles per hour, driving water across the beach and uplands. Once again waves crashed over the low-lying island.

A Category Four hurricane with winds from 130 mph in excess of 164 mph, the storm came roaring in off the Gulf Stream. The lighthouse was blasted by rain, sea, and sand and pounded by immense waves and winds. The venerable tower withstood the attack. The keeper's cottage was battered but withstood the storm surge and kept its footing. After the worst of the storm had passed, helicopter pilots reported Key Biscayne awash but proclaimed that the Cape Florida tower had survived. In fact it could be seen for miles around as it had not been viewed since the Australian pine forest had grown around it just after mid-century. It could be seen from the mainland as a landmark of great consequence— a symbol of south Florida's survival.

Many felt the hurricane had been the most harrowing event of their lives. Ironically, some islanders had fled to shelters in south Dade directly in the path of the unpredictable eye, where entire neighborhoods or communities were destroyed. Although no lives were lost on the island, returning islanders were shocked by the massive devastation. The storm surge was not as high as expected, but the force of the winds and rising water had caused billions of dollars in damage and uprooted much of the tropical jungle. It was only in the wake of the fury of the hurricane that islanders and others who had watched the development in previous years took notice of the dangers and long-term environmental and economic consequences of overbuilding and overpopulating an exposed sand island. Federal emergency funds and other aid were offered for recovery and planting as the fledgling community was faced with a new mandate to take full measure of the opportunities, regulations, and laws that govern the management of municipalities as unique and vulnerable as Key Biscayne. The master plan, when approved by the state, would take into consideration that barrier islands are coastal *high hazard* zones and natural resources must be protected and replenished.

With spirited leadership and a renewed sense of neighborhood, the Village repaired and replanted along hurricane-ravaged streets and public places as did private landowners on their property. Volunteers and service clubs, especially garden clubs, beautified church, school, and other grounds including the prominent site of the Dade County Public Library on Key Biscayne. With private contributions, the area surrounding the library was transformed into a sanctuary of flowering trees and tropical plants around a historic pond.

The islanders' painful initiation-by-hurricane had created a more enlightened citizenry, more attentive to the demands and necessity of human, environmental, and fiscal responsibilities. In a reordering of priorities, the community was rebuilding.

Until it incorporated as an independent village in the summer of 1991, the community of Key Biscayne was governed for forty years by Dade County. Today it boasts its own Mayor and Council members, a manager, police, and fire departments. (Village of Key Biscayne)

EIGHTEEN

Coastal Guardians

Beyond the lighthouse compound at Cape Florida, hurricane destruction was extensive. The eye of the storm passed fifteen miles to the south but meteorologists explained that the leading edge of the eye wall "swiped" Key Biscayne. "But what a swipe it was!" exclaimed a park ranger as he looked at the swift and effective timbering of at least a million board feet of Australian pine. It tore up and flattened almost all of the growing plants and trees on the ancient tract of land. The animal habitats were destroyed. The park was declared a catastrophe.

In the aftermath of Hurricane Andrew, with nearly four hundred acres of nonindigenous Australian pines deforested by the force of the storm winds and waves that swept overland, the state recognized an environmental opportunity of almost overwhelming size. First, scientists and experts from the Florida Department of Natural Resources (DNR) urged the removal of exotic trees. Federal Emergency Management Administration (FEMA) funds were granted. The Army Corps of Engineers directed the removal and mulching of the casuarinas and other exotics. Once more, earth-moving equipment rumbled across the ancient tract where the mulch was spread over the once-green parkland which looked like a barren moonscape.

Before and after. August 1992 the god *Jurakan* smote the entire length of the island. At Cape Florida 400 acres of tall "Australian" pine forest lashed by wind and water were distroyed. In the light of day, the lighthouse towered over a denuded landscape. The tower could be seen for miles as it had not been seen for many years. The Division of Recreation and Parks began immediately to study protecton of the remaining natural biological communities and an extensive restoration project to restore native vegetation, such as wetland mangrove communities and coastal strands, but first the badly scarified land had to be prepared. (Photos © by Barry Howe)

Natural ecological systems were undisturbed as shown in this previously
unknown survey of the Mary Ann Davis
tract, 1895. One hundred years later,
Cape Florida would initiate a major
ecological restoration of tract and thus
joins the global movement toward
environmental and historic landscape
rehabilitation. (Davis Collection)

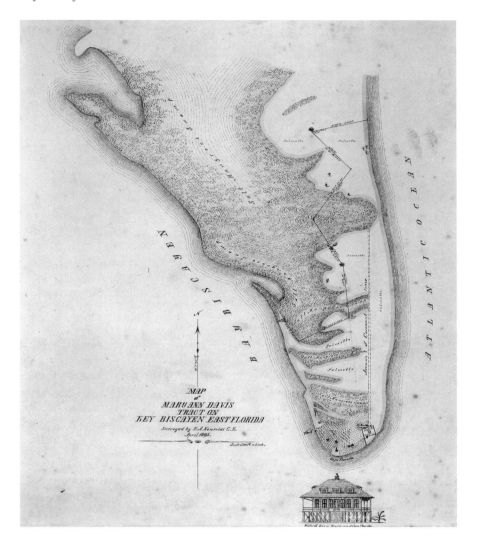

Preliminary research by state biologists and other investigators suggested that an unsuspected richness of native flora had existed prior to
the irreversible 1950 clearing and filling of the tract. A forward-looking
Florida Department of Environmental Protection (DEP), working with
its Division of Recreation and Parks, proposed a major ecological
restoration initiative based on botanist Robin B. Huck's study of
1992–1993. It called for rebuilding ridges and swales, reseeding and replanting four biological communities: "the beach dune, coastal strand,
maritime hammock, and marine tidal swamp with impounded wetlands." It called for removing areas of fill that had been pumped in with
three to five feet of bay bottom at mid-century. The object was to
reestablish "historic natural communities" of both botanical and
wildlife habitats so that the recontoured land would look much as it did
in the days of the Tequestas and later settlers and, in time, appear as if
it had returned to its natural roots.

In the state's final plan, this model ecological restoration of a size not
previously attempted swung into operation as new administrators and
rangers were joined by on-site biologists, ecologists, and resource-
management personnel. Professional excitement and public interest
mounted as state-of-the-art satellite technology arrived at Cape Florida

including the Global Positioning System (GPS), facilitating swift and exact tree inventories, and the Geographic Information System (GIS) for advanced precision map technology.

Concerned with the conservation and protection of coastal ecosystems, the American Littoral Society, with headquarters in Sandy Hook, New Jersey (four miles from Red Bank, New Jersey, where Key Biscayne's early coconut planters had originated in the 1880s), became an active partner with the state of Florida to supervise volunteers and help implement the plan, named the Cape Florida Project. In 1993 the U.S. Congress made $4 million available to the Department of Agriculture for reforestation and restoration at Cape Florida following Hurricane Andrew. Additional monies, including those from the state's Coastal Zone Management Fund, surpassed the $10 million goal. It is ironic that appropriations of the 103rd U.S. Congress are helping to finance a program in the 1990s to eliminate all exotic tropicals except the coconut, when the 25th Congress in the 1830s encouraged the introduction of foreign plants at Cape Florida "as highly desirable to promote the peace and prosperity of the Union."

The ambitious plan to replant one hundred thousand native plants and trees, from seedlings and saplings to forty-foot-tall palms, moved forward rapidly in 1994 and 1995. Volunteers helped remove exotics and also assisted in establishing an on-site native plant nursery. As wetlands and freshwater ponds were being recreated, expectant birders would celebrate the return of long-displaced tropical and migrating birds. Park goers soon found picnic shelters, walkways, bikeways, nature trails, and additional facilities to complement sunning, ocean swimming, and bayside fishing; boaters began to rendezvous once again at No Name Harbor.

Lighthouse restoration gained support. Well before the storm, a partnership between DNR and the Dade Heritage Trust had been forged to bring together private and public funds to protect the lighthouse. In the late 1980s, to halt its deterioration, Dade Heritage Trust, with the support of the Florida Bureau of Historic Preservation, led a million-dollar campaign to restore the tower to its 1856 condition. Viewed as a centerpiece of the Miami Centennial in 1996, the lighthouse and its relighted beacon will again serve as a navigational aid, as well as a national visitor destination and focal point at Key Biscayne, according to park manager Lee Niblock. The DHT Lightouse Committee's continuing objectives will be to maintain and preserve the historic landmark and lighthouse compound. The tower—with its red bricks painted white as it was in George Meade's design—and the keeper's cottage and grounds will become part of an educational, cultural, and historical center, a core component of the Cape Florida park. Toward this goal, the Village of Key Biscayne and also The Villagers, Inc. of Miami have committed resources.

In addition, the county archaeologist Robert S.Carr proceeded on archaeological investigations begun in the 1980s of prehistoric, Seminole War period, and pioneer settlement sites. In the Archaeological and Historical Conservancy Technical Report #91 in 1994, a post hurricane archaeological survey and assessment of the cape underscored the ur-

A fresh-water pond photographed at the cape, for James Deering in 1915. (Vizcaya Museum and Gardens)

gency of protection and management of sensitive areas and the need for cultural resource guidelines during reconstruction, restoration, and increased traffic and attendance. Archaeological monitoring "to prevent the loss of artifacts and data from significant sites" and to identify new sites was initiated.

Carr and his staff also work in Crandon Park to safeguard their discovery of a string of ancient village sites, the largest yet found of the extinct Tequesta tribe. The charred post holes of houses as well as potsherds, bones, and tools were exposed by the winds and water of Hurricane Andrew so that examinations on the surface revealed new discoveries. Further archaeological studies await funding, but preliminary work suggests a promising yield of artifacts and information on how the earliest people lived on Key Biscayne.

On the ocean side at the south end of the county-owned Crandon Park, the forty-eight-acre site of the original zoo, renamed The Gardens at Crandon Park, was redesigned and relandscaped. With some specimen tropical trees remaining from the past, the quiet garden is encircled by new palm glades and palm groves, laced with foot trails, and planned waterways for canoes. It serves as a green buffer zone between the active recreational area and the village, as does Calusa Park on the bayside.

At the northern end of Crandon Park, opposite the marina, Metro-Dade County is pursuing its own restoration of wetlands and sand ridges at the Bear Cut Preserve under the watchful eye of naturalists including those at the Marjory Stoneman Douglas Biscayne Nature Center which is located on adjoining land. Along with the Nature Center's educational programs that teach coastal island ecology to south Florida schoolchildren, there is hope that cooperative efforts will be able to create an interpretive nature and archaeological community on the north end of the island not far from the petrified-fossil mangrove forest. A reconstructed Tequesta village site could be studied and celebrated as are other Southeastern Indian cultures.

Village Green

The dedication of the Village Green was a community event held on April 22, 1995. Mayor John F. Festa, Vice Mayor Betty Sime, and other Council members Raul Llorente, Michele Padovan, Hugh T. O'Reilly, Raymond Sullivan, and John Waid, as well as Village Manager C. Samuel Kissinger, officiated at the celebration that coincided with Earth Day, as reported by the weekly paper, The Islander News.

Even as the Tequestas had been the first villagers on the island using but not overusing its natural resources, whether on- or offshore, those who formed a twentieth-century community in the center of the island began to realize the importance of preserving Key Biscayne's heritage. Hurricanes had visited and changed the island, its habitats, and contours since the beginning. In the 1990s the islanders who knew little about the events and cultures that preceeded them learned about the power of tropical hurricanes. They began to realize the meaning of stewardship.

A far-sighted village council proposed purchasing a central 9.5-acre tract, thereby removing it from development. Its grounds were historic. Tequestas sites were close by; the historic Matheson nursery had been located on this land where trees from the world's tropics were first introduced into the United States in the early part of the century. A few remain from Africa and the South American rain forest. The land was raised to meet federal flood standards as thousands of cubic yards of sand fill from the state park were trucked out of the cape and recycled to the new site. Landscaped and sodded, watered by an irrigation system for the dry winters, and drenched by the tropical rainy season, the village had regained and preserved the last remaining open space for a public park. With areas for recreation, playgrounds, and community gatherings, the new Village Green was dedicated in 1995 to be held in trust.

It was becoming evident that there was a need for community cooperation to preserve and restore historic landscapes and structures such as the Calusa Playhouse. The island's many important historical sites and wonders were waiting to be identified and discovered by residents and visitors of all ages along the Key Biscayne heritage trail.

Natural Reef Gardens

The earliest divers and spear fishermen were the Tequestas, who found an inexhaustible source of fishes among the reefs off Key Biscayne. Only traces of the tropical coral gardens remain today. The northernmost reaches of the continent's living tropical reef were dazzling. As late as the 1960s, snorkelers and scuba divers enjoyed the sight of thousands of colorful fishes and undersea creatures in their magnificent habitat; the marine aquarium was a rainbow of color as parrotfishes and angelfishes flashed by. Backed up in crevices and holes were crustaceans, crawfish, and stone crabs. Close to the beach at low tide, "honeycomb rock formations" built by sabellariid worms revealed communities of waving anemones, scurrying hermit crabs, and darting little tropical fishes.

Islanders never needed to sail to the upper keys for recreational diving because off the island between Fowey Reefs and Water Witch Shoals, east of Crandon Park, the waters were alive, and the coral growth on the uppermost fringes of the Florida reef tract was healthy. Close to shore on sandy shoals, star, brain, finger, and rose coral colonies (typical of the Key Largo limestone area where John Pennekamp Coral Reef State Park is located) supported animals and plants of the living reef system. In the 1920s, William J. Matheson, then owner of much of Key Biscayne, sent written invitations to friends, including botanist David Fairchild, to sail along the shore for private viewings "of my underwater gardens."

During the past quarter of the twentieth century, serious divers, as well as viewers in glassbottom boats, head further offshore, close to the dark line of the Gulf Stream, to visit artificial reefs created by the purposeful sinking of derelict ships and, in one instance, an airplane. Commercial and sport fishermen also head for deep waters since much of the underwater life near the shore has vanished.

Until recent years, on the west side of the island in Biscayne Bay, north of Florida Bay that runs inside the coral-rock and limestone keys, the water was crystal clear. Sailors, fishermen, and shrimpers attested to its variety of sea life. Today the area is heavily boated and fished and surrounded by urban activity; government funding is under way to restore and clean up the bay. Sea grasses are being replanted, but the permissiveness continues as shoreline mangroves are removed, leaving fewer and fewer intertidal nurseries at the bay's edge. On- and offshore ecosystems are as intricately entwined as the roots of the mangrove trees, and the laws governing their protection are just as tangled in disputes. As a result of development on shores and beaches, spillover and spill-offs result in "cultural eutrophication," threatening underwater habitats, reefs, grazing grounds, and associated marine animal and plant life in oceans, bays, and lakes. The natural aging processes of bodies of water, salt and fresh, are speeded up by the accidental seepage of nutrients (from pesticides to gasoline to sewage) causing decay or stagnation and depleting oxygen. Pollution by degrees is more subtle than massive sewage or oil spills, but no less disastrous. The restoration of the appropriate flow of fresh water from the Everglades to Biscayne Bay and Florida Bay is being offered as one means of recovering the imbalance in the endangered marine environments.

There are more than a hundred coral reefs from Fowey Rocks to Tortugas that must be better managed and protected to survive the impact of urbanization, which causes over-stress that has seriously endangered the health of the reef system and the seas around them. It is all part of the new challenge to effectively care for tropical marine ecosystems to prevent their destruction.

Agassiz's 1850s fieldwork on corals is carried on by those who realize that irreplaceable resources must be managed.

Fisheries

Coastal and fisheries management is not a new concept, but the need for regulating the competition for regional and global resources is increasingly urgent due, in part, to the demands of a growing world population, which results in over-harvesting and over-use of marine habitats.

In 1799, Andrew Ellicott, who surveyed the boundary between the United States and Spain (Florida), sailed around south Florida and visited Key Biscayne, observing that the marine resources were abundant: "Along the Florida Reef and among the Keys, a great abundance and variety of fish may be taken: such as hog-fish, grunts, yellow tails, black, red and gray snappers, mullets, bone-fish, amber-fish, margate-fish, barracoota, cavallos, pompui, groopers, king-fish, siber-fish, porgys, turbots, stingrays, black drum, Jew fish, with prodigious variety of others, which in our situation we found excellent."

He also wrote of the Florida lobster or crawfish (now protected except in season): "We found a remarkable species of prawns . . . in great numbers in holes in the rocks, they frequently weigh up to three pounds a-piece, and are improperly called lobsters; they want the large claws that lobster have. Their meat is harder, and less delicate than that of the lobsters of the northern states." He added, "Key Biscanio is much frequented by the privateers, wreckers and turtlers from the Bahama Islands."

As far back as the English ownership of Florida (1763–1783), there are documented feuds over the rights to fish the waters north of Cuba, along the string of keys to Cape Florida. James Grant, governor of the Crown colony in St. Augustine, was angry at the aggressors from Havana, but contrary officials in Cuba issued permits to fishermen to continue working the waters as they had when Spain held title.

Whether Spanish or British, they were bold seamen and over the years some were spies in disguise. Their works of espionage were apparent during the Turnbull settlement when Cuban fishermen carried messages to the oppressed Minorcans to keep faith, implying the Spaniards would return to Florida, which they did in 1783. As late as the nineteenth century, when the Americans were in charge, men from Havana traded ammunition and arms with Florida Indians for assistance in maintaining fisheries.

In the early 1800s, when Spain again held Florida and Pedro Fornells came to settle Key Biscayne, American and English wreckers and fishermen with ties to the Bahamas claimed the bay, the island, and the mainland as their fishing and hunting grounds. Sometimes called the "Men from New Providence," they defied the Spanish Crown. They not only fished but shot deer, alligators, bear, and panther, taking the time necessary on shore to skin and cure them before sailing back across the Gulf Stream with their illicit cargo. They knew the waters well. Three of them—Pent, Lewis, and Hagen (Egan)—were called "respectable pilots at Cape Florida" by Charles Vignoles in the early 1820s. They or their families laid claim or held title to much of the historic land upon which present-day Miami stands.

Today international laws of the sea are defining national boundaries to prevent poaching and disputes, but the search for the best fishing grounds, and the results of over-fishing, pit Bahamians, Cubans, and Floridians against each other in an ongoing war over diminishing marine resources.

USCGC Key Biscayne, commissioned in 1991, patrols U.S. waters including duty from the Gulf of Mexico to the Florida Straits. (U.S. Coast Guard)

Sea Turtles

As on other subtropical and tropical beaches, the ancient sea turtle comes to lay her eggs, one hundred to a clutch, during the hot summer months in a ritual often performed under a full moon.

Sea turtles have been coming ashore on Key Biscayne for thousands of years. The native people watched them digging their nests and laying their eggs above the high-water line in the soft sand. When the young turtles mature, they swim great distances to return to the beach of their birth to lay their own eggs and continue the cycle.

Loggerhead turtles are predominant on Key Biscayne beaches, with

Turtling on beach in 1800s. (*Harpers New Monthly Magazine*)

green turtles a less frequent second. In the 1950s and 1960s, occasional hawksbills, leatherbacks, and the rare Kemp's ridley were seen. Complete turtle skeletons, long buried on the beaches, were frequently found by beach walkers in the 1950s, reminders of earlier years when turtlers turned the nesting mothers on their backs and butchered them. Now capture is permitted only for tagging. In 1980, the Tropical Audubon Society began the first of ongoing sea-turtle conservation programs on the island to protect hatchlings under the guidance of the Florida Department of Natural Resources. When they break through their round eggs, baby sea turtles still face natural predators—raccoons, crabs, and sea gulls—although the small black bears are no longer a threat as hatchlings race across the sands into the welcoming ocean where their life journey begins, not without hazards of the deep. The serious depletion of sea turtles by nest raiders and coastal development disrupting their nesting sites prompted state and federal laws. The Endangered Species Act protects sea turtles in U.S. waters; on shore, eroded beaches continue to threaten historic nesting habitats as the sandy continental coastline loses its edge.

A Golden Resource

Key Biscayno...produces many mangroves, some hammocks...and much sand.
    —JOHN C. WILLIAMS, 1837

The most important resource of Key Biscayne is its sand. A barrier island, it is primarily composed of sand which must be protected as a golden resource.

Barrier islands are inextricably bound to the sea, and their destiny follows the currents and tides of wind and water. Positioned at the edge of continents where land and ocean interact, barrier islands help deflect threatening atmospheric and marine forces from environmentally endangered coastlines. Sometimes hurricanes blow the islands away; other times they reshape them; storm scars and scarification are part of nature's cycle.

Man-made alterations to seaboards are contrary to nature's cycle of nourishing and renourishing and can prevent the littoral drift of sand that assures island replenishment. When natural coastal dynamics are obstructed, shore-zone disruption is inevitable.

The barrier beach is constantly changed by the action of the restless sea. If the beach's natural and physical features are altered or considerably modified, it loses its natural resiliency. On Key Biscayne the first oceanside buildings were constructed along the fragile dune lines where native vegetation had previously helped protect the ever-changing shore. At that time, too few realized the key was a true barrier island of unconsolidated sand. It was some years before coastal laws and regulations mandating setback lines for coastal construction were put into a master plan. National protection ultimately given to pristine or undisturbed barrier islands came too late for Key Biscayne.

With coastal management would come unexpected data. Along the entire East Coast and around the Gulf of Mexico, inlet and port dredging federally mandated and conducted by the Army Corps of Engineers was contributing to accelerated erosion. The seaward jetties at port openings and the constant dredging and deepening of channels interrupted the *natural river of sand* that for millennia had flowed to "downdrift beaches." Billions of cubic yards of sand had been blocked from reaching beaches on barrier islands, and so it was on Key Biscayne.

During the 1980s, many beachgoers and coastal dwellers expressed mounting concern as the once-broad beach eroded, threatening property and human and animal life on this island resort and sanctuary. The daily pelican patrols flew over the shrinking ribbon of sand without pause, but herons, egrets, ibis, terns, and sea gulls, looking for a place to feed along the shallows, now had little sand to stand on, and the generous ancient nesting ground for sea turtles was virtually washed away.

In studies by marine scientists and geologists, including Harold R. Wanless of the University of Miami, sand transport comparisons along the East Coast showed that specifically in Miami, just north of Key Biscayne, "Government Cut has served as a complete block to the southward drift of sand during the past 67 years, 1927 to 1994." Key Biscayne and the barrier-island system that includes Virginia Key has thus "been deprived of 14,600,000 to 24,300,000 cubic feet of sand," according to Wanless.

In 1987 private money was joined with public funds of $2.6 million to restore 2.7 miles of sand from Cape Florida to the beginning of the county park. The critically starved Atlantic beach on the Island Paradise was renourished by offshore dredging of sand not far from Cape Florida. Some years earlier, an alert county park, which counted on beach attendance revenues, began its own renourishment program to preserve its beautiful beach, ranked in a University of Maryland study as one of the ten best beaches in the world in 1994. It plumped its beach by dredging bottom sand from Bear Cut and continuing to build adjacent offshore sandbars. There was some concern about disturbing the off-shore bottom and the channel at Bear Cut. The ocean and bay waters were becoming increasingly murky as activity and traffic increased in the waters. Two hundred years earlier, the Royal Surveyor General of

View through sea oats along beach.
(Joan E. Gill)

East Florida, F. G. Mulcaster, had described Bear Cut in 1772 as the entrance to the bay: "At the North End of Key Biscayne [is] a channel of above a quarter mile wide, with above thirteen feet water, without a breaker, and the water so clear that you might see to pick a sixpence at the Bottom."

Ongoing dredging of the Port of Miami and channel deepening are contracted well into the twenty-first century. Dodge Island, Miami's world-famous seaport facility for cargo and cruise lines, is built with sand diverted from Key Biscayne. Recent studies report that the sites along the Atlantic Seaboard are running out of sand suitable for beach renourishment. Although investment in beach rebuilding is controversial, Florida could hardly afford to ignore the problem—in 1992, beachgoers funneled $7.9 billion into the state economy. It was suggested that sand might be barged in from the Bahamas. It was also suggested that at Government Cut a sand-transfer system should be constructed so that the diverted sand blocked by the parallel stone jetties, some three thousand feet long, and a percentage of the quality sand brought up from the channel deepening should be used to replenish the downdrift beaches. On the southernmost barrier island, Key Biscayners want to declare: *The sand stops here.*

An erosion prevention strategy, introduced into Florida during the last decade of the twentieth century by the Division of Beaches and Shores (DEP), includes funding by federal, state, and local governments for "inlet management/sand by-passing programs" and also "dune reconstruction and protection." Recontouring and revegetating dunes with plants well adapted to flooding will help collect and hold wind-blown or storm-driven sand. It is not a new idea. It traces back at least to early settlement of Cape Cod. According to author and naturalist Henry David Thoreau (1817–1862), "The inhabitants at Truro were formerly regularly warned under the authority of law in the month of April to plant beach grass, as elsewhere they are warned to repair the highways."

From Cape Cod to Cape Florida, in the 1990s, hardy sea grasses such as sea oats (*Uniola piniculata*), along with other wild dune flowers, vines, and shrubs, are being replanted. And so it is that latter-day Thoreauvians attempt to repair the eroding margins of continents and shores, of fragile capes and coastlines, where land and water meet.

The journey toward an understanding that human beings are the custodians of every piece of this planet, a concept known by its earliest people, is coming round. It is a long journey and there has been much tragedy along the way with great loss of plants, animals, and human life, pristine land, clean water, and clear air. The concept of stewardship is essential as the twenty-first century dawns. For most of the globe it is a matter of protecting, recovering, restoring, and caring for treasures that go back eons.

The barrier island passage is shorter. Rippling ribbons of sand along the continental body are land-in-motion washed over by the sea. Their age is measured in mere thousands of years because they are made of sand: a medium unstable, nimble, and easily scattered.

Key Biscayne, the southernmost sand barrier island of the United States, is only four thousand years old. For more than a thousand years, people have walked its beaches and trails and, on it, put down posts and pilings to build their homes and towers. The latest island dwellers, living on ancient village sites, are learning about their environmental and historic heritage, but it is at high risk as building and paving continue. If it is not to vanish, then they, like the earliest people, must keep watch upon the island and not lose it through oversight or dalliance. They must be coastal guardians of the deep beach and wind-swept sand.

Acknowledgments and Private Sources

Primary sources of unexpected worth in private collections enriched the information available from other sources.

Thanks to the following people for allowing me into their libraries and homes to search private papers, journals, notes, and albums and allowing me to use the materials as I wished.

Eleanor and Tom Catlow of Galveston, Texas, invited me into the attic of the house (now the Virginia Point Inn) originally built by Waters S. Davis for his daughter Sarah where I discovered a nineteenth-century photograph of the lighthouse and an oil painting in an oval frame of Mary Ann Channer Davis. The Catlows put me in contact with a living Davis, of whom there are many who helped, especially Jeremy S. Davis in Texas; Waters S. Davis IV of Massachusetts; the late Catherine Davis Gauss of Connecticut; and her sons Jack Gray of Connecticut and David H. Gray of Vermont. I am most grateful for the generosity and interest of Davis descendants Sarah (Sally) C. Larroca, and her brother Paul Creson, both in Texas, and Caverly Gonzalez Day in Florida and her sister Elena G. Millie of Washington, DC.

In 1987 Eris Henry (Hank) DuBose (present-day family members spell their name with a capital B) in San Antonio, Texas, directed me to his cousins in Gonzales when we visited him in search of his late sister, Lucille, who had become interested in the Texas-Florida connection. Then Josephine DuBose Johnson in Hammond County, Texas, not only opened her archives and papers but introduced me to a multitude of helpful relatives, including Earl Wyatt, who took us to the overgrown homestead where the first lighthouse keeper and his wife had retired, and where they are buried. Additionally John Charles DuBose was generous with his collection of memorabilia also in Gonzales.

Thanks also to members of other lighthouse families, especially descendants of the Frows, including Marilyn Warner and Julie Perry in Florida.

It was my good fortune to find untapped sources of fresh materials on the early coconut planters, Field and Osborn. This was made possible with the interest and assistance of Randall Gabrielan, the director of the Middletown Historical Society in New Jersey. Also, Lothian Lyons at the library of the New York Botanical Garden was helpful.

Thanks to the Mathesons, especially to R. Hardy Matheson, my landlord when I lived on the coconut plantation, and many thanks to Finlay B. Matheson, keeper of the copyrights to family photographs in Miami. Thanks to the late William M. Preston of Massachusetts, who shared time and materials, and to his two daughters (Anna [Nan] Matheson's granddaughters), Sarah Preston Carleton, and Jean Preston Guyton in Colorado who was especially interested and helpful.

Thanks to the family of David Fairchild including his son Graham Bell Fairchild and grandson David Mueller. Special thanks to Bertram Zuckerman who gave me full access into the Fairchild Tropical Garden Research Center to pursue my search for the Matheson-Fairchild connection and other matters.

My appreciation to Wirth and to Mary Munroe who welcomed me to the Barnacle on the bay across from Key Biscayne in the 1950s, broadening my vision. Thanks also to their son William Middleton Munroe who carries on the family tradition of ship-building in Coconut Grove.

I am indebted to Doris Littlefield, the curator of Vizcaya Museum and Gardens, for allowing me to use materials long in the vault to better understand the James Deering era at Cape Florida.

Thanks also go to Helen Clark Mitchell and William Evans Thomas who shared experiences as children of superintendents on the Matheson plantation before I moved there at midcentury; and to Mackfield (Mack) Mortimer who sailed to the island in the early days from his home on Long Island in the Bahamas to work there, and stayed as caretaker on the plantation until the Mathesons sold the property.

Jane Quinn, author of an authoritative book on the Minorcans and their Florida experience, who like other scholars was unaware of the Fornells family Key Biscayne holdings, gave me an introduction to Victoriano Seoane Pascuchi of Mahon (Majon) in Minorca. He generously assisted during my 1988 research visit to the Mediterranean island. Thanks also to Father Fernando Marti for permitting me access to the Cathedral Archives in Ciudadela to trace the ancestry of Pedro Fornells back to the thirteenth century. And to the university scholars at the *Seminario*

who in 1988 enabled me to find records of the Tuduri, Fornells and other related Minorcan families.

So very many persons have been generous with their knowledge and encouragement including our good friends Maxine and Bruce Alspach, Linda Thornton, Janet Eaglstein, Therold Lindquist, Dorothy Zinzow, Sharyn Richardson, Joe Podgor, Jim Hirschman, Don Sackrider, Betty Rice, Ann Black, John Keasler, Anne Owens, Mary Ordaye, Stephen Lynch III, Gilbert Voss; also Allen and Joan Morris, Nixon and Evelyn Smiley, Gloria Anderson, William (Toby) Muir, and Joel Chrycy. I would like to express thanks to my friend Jim Woodman who visited me on the plantation in the late 1950s when he was gathering information for Key Biscayne's first chronicle, which he aptly subtitled, "The Romance of Cape Florida."

Throughout the text, in sources, and in the bibliography, scholars are cited with appreciation. To the many unnamed including Key Biscayners who have contributed in untold ways, I give my thanks.

For her expertise, I thank Jean Fowler for technical support, loyalty, good humor during long hours, and unflagging spirits. Thanks to my family for their individual contributions, patience, and belief in me.

For use of the Boyer Gonzales watercolors, special thanks to friends at the Rosenberg Library in Galveston, Texas.

Heartfelt thanks to Jean Bradfisch, former editor of *Sea Frontiers* of the International Oceanographic Foundation, for keen assistance and editorial prowess, during the past several years of manuscript preparation.

And I am grateful for invaluable exchanges with my two remarkable friends, Joseph (Joe) Campbell and Marjory Stoneman Douglas, collectors and superb interpreters of the human condition, origins, and natural phenomena. They guided me from becoming too "islandcentric," and urged me to complete the work in the direction I had chosen. I smile upon recalling the words of the ancient Greek poet, Pindar, who wrote that at the nod of Zeus "the island sprang from the watery sea."

Neither islands nor books spring so easily into existence. When we measure the creation of the barrier island, we sift each grain of sand and measure each wave. We must reckon with each discovery to build the facts and uncover island folklore. My journey has been more than what the lexicographer Samuel Johnson observed in the 1700s, when he said that an author "must turn over half a library to make one book."

Public Collections and Research Facilities

Government and Church Documents

Invaluable public sources include American state papers, territorial papers of the United States, East Florida papers, Spanish land grants in Florida, church and parish records, plus federal, state, county, and municipal government records. Original documents of historical government materials are safeguarded and held at the National Archives in Washington, DC, in civil and military divisions (such as relevant record groups 23, 24, 26, 43, 45, 49, 64, 94). Across the Atlantic in England, in the Public Record Office, are original treaties and hand-written correspondence and other papers in the British Colonial Office related to America, the West Indies, and Florida (C.O. 5 and 23), as well as to Minorca (C.O. 174 and 175). In Minorca, seminary, cathedral, and other records kept prior to 1768 are of inestimable worth.

Sources

Library, museum, and research facilities as well as corporate and public collections provided useful information and materials:

American Littoral Society/Sandy Hook, NJ

American Philosophical Society/Philadelphia, PA

Audubon Society, Tropical/Miami, FL

Bahamas Title Research/Nassau, Bahamas (William Holowesko)

Baltimore Public Library/Baltimore, MD

Baylor University/Waco, Tx.

Bill Baggs Cape Florida State Recreation Area/Key Biscayne, FL (Lee Niblock and park staff; John Frostbutter)

Boston Public Library/Boston, MA

British Library/London, England

Cathedral Archives/Ciudadela, Minorca

Charleston Public Library/Charleston, SC

Cold Spring Harbor Laboratory/Long Island, NY

Dade County Parks and Recreation Department/Miami, FL

Dade Heritage Trust/Miami, FL

Daughters of the American Revolution (DAR) Library/Washington, DC

Duke University/Durham, NC

Fairchild Tropical Garden, Research Center/Miami FL (Bertram Zuckerman)

Florida Atlantic University/Boca Raton, FL (Daniel F. Austin, Sandy Norman)

Florida Department of Environmental Protection (formerly Florida Department of Natural Resources)/Tallahassee, FL

Florida Department of State: Division of Archives, History and Records Management/Tallahassee, FL

Florida Historical Society/Tampa, FL

Florida State Archives/Tallahassee, FL

Florida Museum of Natural History/Gainesville, FL (Jerald T. Milanich)

Florida State Museum/Tallahassee, FL

Florida State Photographic Archives/Tallahassee, FL (Joan Morris)

Friends of the Everglades/Miami, FL

Galveston County Court House/Galveston, TX

Gonzales Public Library/Gonzales, TX

Guildhall Library/London, England

Harvard University Library, Archives/Cambridge, MA

Historical Association of Southern Florida, Charlton W. Tebeau Library/Miami, FL

Historical Society of
Pennsylvania/Philadelphia, PA
Huguenot Society of South Carolina/Charleston, SC
Huntington Library, Huntington Historical Society/Long Island, NY
Kalamazoo Nature Center/Kalamazoo, MI
Key West Public Library/Key West, FL (Betty Bruce, Thomas Hambright)
Library of Congress/Washington, DC
Mariners' Museum/Newport News, VA
Marjory Stoneman Douglas Biscayne Nature Center/Key Biscayne, FL
Metropolitan Dade County, Historic Preservation Division/Miami, FL
Miami-Dade Public Library, Coconut Grove branch/Coconut Grove, FL
Miami-Dade Public Library, Coral Gables branch/Coral Gables, FL
Miami-Dade Public Library, Key Biscayne branch/Key Biscayne, FL (Wayne Powell)
Miami-Dade Public Library/Miami, FL
Middletown Historical Society/Middletown, NJ (Randall Gabrielan)
Museum of Early Southern Decorative Art (MESDA)/Charleston, SC
Museum of Natural History of the Florida Keys, Florida Keys Land and Sea Trust/Marathon, FL
National Archives/Washington, DC (Jim Rush, William F. Sherman, Stuart Butler, Jerry Hess)
National Museum of Natural History, Smithsonian Institution/Washington, DC (William Sturtevant)

National Oceanic and Atmospheric Administration (NOAA)/Rockville, MD, and Virginia Key, FL
National Portrait Gallery, Smithsonian Institution/Washington, DC
National Press Club, H. L. Mencken Library/Washington, DC
New York Botanical Garden Library/Bronx, NY (Lothian Lynas)
Pascagoula Public Library/Pascagoula, MS
Philadelphia Public Library/Philadelphia, PA
Public Record Office/Kew and London, England
Rosenberg Library, History Center Special Collections/Galveston, TX (Casey Greene, Lise Darst, Margaret Schlankey, Harry F. Taylor)
South Carolina Historical Society Library/Charleston, SC
Southeast Texas Institute/San Antonio, TX
St. Augustine Historical Society/St. Augustine, FL (Page Edwards, Jacqueline Fretwell and staff)
Sub-Tropical Horticulture Research Station/Miami, FL
Tulane University/New Orleans, LA
United States Department of Agriculture/Washington, DC
United States Department of Commerce/Washington, DC
United States Department of the Interior/Washington, DC
United States Division of Foreign Plant Introductions, Chapman Field/Miami, FL
United States Navy, Library and Museum/Washington, DC
University of Florida, P. K. Younge Library/Gainesville, FL

University of Miami Luis Calder Memorial Medical Library/Miami, FL
University of Miami Otto G. Richter Memorial Library, Archives and Special Collection/Coral Gables, FL (Helen Purdy, William Brown, John McMinn, Esperanza Varona, Gladys Ramos)
University of Miami Rosenstiel School of Marine and Atmospheric Science/Virginia Key, FL (Gilbert L. Voss, F. G. W. Smith, C. Richard Robins, Harold R. Wanless, Donald R. Moore)
University of Pennsylvania Museum/Philadelphia, PA
U.S. Lighthouse Society, San Francisco, CA (Wayne C. Wheeler)
University Seminary/Ciudadela, Minorca
Village of Key Biscayne/Key Biscayne, FL (Manager and staff; mayor and council)
Vizcaya Museum and Gardens/Miami, FL (Doris Littlefield)
Yale University/New Haven, CT

Map Collections

American Philosophical Society; British Library; British Public Record Office; Florida State University; Library of Congress; Louisiana State University; National Archives; Rosenberg Library; Historical Society of Pennsylvania; Historical Association of Southern Florida; University of Miami; Antique Maps & Prints (J. Rubini).

Bibliography

Books

Amos, William H., and Stephen H. Amos. *Atlantic and Gulf Coasts.* New York: Alfred A. Knopf, 1989.

Armstrong, John. *The History of the Island of Minorca.* London: Printers to the Royal Society, 1756.

Bailey, Liberty Hyde. *The Standard Cyclopedia of Horticulture.* Vol. I–III. London: Macmillan, 1927.

Barbour, Thomas. *That Vanishing Eden: A Naturalist's Florida.* Boston: Little, Brown, 1944.

Bartram, John. *A Description of East-Florida, with a Journal.* 3rd edition. London: W. Nicoll, 1769.

Bartram, William. *Botanical and Zoological Drawings, 1756–1788.* Philadelphia: American Philosophical Society, 1968.

Bartram, William. *Travels through North and South Carolina, Georgia, East and West Florida.* Philadelphia: James and Johnson, 1791. Reprint, Mark Van Doren, ed. New York: Dover, 1928.

Bellamy, Jeanne. "Naming the Land." in *The Florida Handbook.* 21st edition. Tallahassee: Peninsular, 1987–1988.

Benét, Stephen Vincent. *Spanish Bayonet.* New York: George H. Doran, 1926.

Browne, Jefferson B. *Key West: The Old and the New.* Facsimile of the 1912 edition. Gainesville: University of Florida Press, 1973.

Campbell, Joseph. *The Way of the Animal Powers: Historical Atlas of World Mythology.* London: Times Books, 1984.

Carr, Archie. *So Excellent a Fische: A Natural History of Sea Turtles.* Garden City: Natural History Press, Doubleday, 1967.

Carr, Archie. *The Everglades.* The American Wilderness. New York: Time-Life Books, 1973.

Carson, Rachel L. *The Edge of the Sea.* Boston: Houghton Mifflin, 1955.

Carson, Rachel L. *The Sea Around Us.* New York: Oxford University Press, 1951.

Catesby, Mark. *The Natural History of Carolina, Florida, and the Bahama Islands.* London: G. Edwards, 1754.

Chapin, Henry, and F. G. Walton Smith. *The Ocean River: The Story of the Gulf Stream.* New York: Charles Scribner's, 1962.

Clark, John, ed. *Barrier Islands and Beaches.* Washington, DC: The Conservation Foundation, 1976.

Corse, Carita Doggett. *Dr. Andrew Turnbull and the New Smyrna Colony of Florida.* Jacksonville: Drew Press, 1919.

Dau, Frederick W. *Florida Old and New.* New York: G. P. Putnam's, 1934.

Davis, Britton. *The Truth about Geronimo.* Lincoln: University of Nebraska, 1929.

De Brahm, John Gerar(d) William. *The Atlantic Pilot, Terra Incognita.* London, 1772.

De Dorsey, Louis, Jr., ed. *de Brahm's Report of the the General Survey in the Southern District of North America, 1790.* Columbia: University of South Carolina Press, 1971.

Dewhurst, W. W. *The History of St. Augustine, Florida.* New York: G. P. Putnam, 1886.

De Wire, Elinor. *Guide to Florida Lighthouses.* Sarasota, FL: Pineapple Press, 1987.

Douglas, Marjory Stoneman. *Adventures in a Green World: The Story of David Fairchild and Barbour Lathrop.* Coconut Grove, FL: Field Research Projects [limited edition], 1973.

Douglas, Marjory Stoneman. "A Civilization beyond Belief: Ancient Man in Florida" in *The Florida Handbook.* 15th edition. Tallahassee: Peninsular, 1975–76.

Douglas, Marjory Stoneman. *Florida: The Long Frontier.* New York: Harper & Row, 1967.

Douglas, Marjory Stoneman. *Hurricane.* With an Afterword by Dr. Neil Frank, Director, National Hurricane Center. New York: Reinhart, 1958.

Douglas, Marjory Stoneman. *The Everglades: River of Grass.* Rivers of America. New York: Rinehart, 1947. Rev. ed., Sarasota, FL: Pineapple Press, 1988.

Driver, Harold E. *Indians of North America.* Chicago: University of Chicago Press, 1969.

Ellicott, Andrew. *The Journal of Andrew Ellicott, Late Commissioner on Behalf of the United States . . . for Determining the Boundary of the United States and His Catholic Majesty. . . .* Philadelphia: Budd and Barthram for Thomas Dobson, 1803.

Fairbanks, George R. *Florida, Its History and Its Romance.* Jacksonville: H. and W. B. Drew, 1898.

Fairbanks, George R. *The History and Antiquities of the City of St. Augustine, Florida.* Facsimile of 1858 edition. Gainesville: University Presses of Florida, 1975.

Fairchild, David. *The World Grows Round My Door.* New York: Charles Scribner's, 1947.

Fairchild, David. *The World Is My Garden.* New York, Charles Scribner's, 1938.

Federal Writers Project. *Florida: A Guide to the Southernmost State.* New York: Oxford University Press, 1939.

Fontaneda, Hernando d'Escalante. *Memoir of Hernando d'Escalante Fontaneda.* (c. 1575). Translated by Buckingham Smith. David O. True, ed. Coral Gables: University of Miami Press, 1945.

Forbes, James Grant. *Sketches, Historical and Topographical of the Floridas, More Particularly of East Florida.* New York: C. S. Van Winkle, 1821.

Gaby, Donald C. *The Miami River and Its Tributaries.* Miami: Historical Association of Southern Florida, 1993.

Gannon, Michael V. *The Cross in the Sand.* Gainesville: University of Florida Press, 1967.

Gantz, Charlotte Orr. *A Naturalist in Southern Florida.* Coral Gables: University of Miami Press, 1971.

Giddings, Joshua R. *The Exiles of Florida.* Columbus, OH: 1858. Facsimile of the 1858 edition. Gainesville: University of Florida Press, 1964.

Gifford, John C. *The Everglades and Other Essays Relating to South Florida.* Miami, 1911.

Gill, Joan E., and Beth R. Read. *Born of the Sun.* Hollywood, FL: Worth International Communications, 1975.

Gilliland, Marion Spjut. *Key Marco's Buried Treasure, Archaeology and Adventure in the 19th Century.* Gainesville: University Presses of Florida, The Florida Museum of Natural History, 1988.

Gilliland, Marion Spjut. *The Material Culture of Key Marco, Florida.* Gainesville: University Presses of Florida, 1975.

Goggin, John M. *Indian and Spanish Selected Writings.* Coral Gables: University of Miami Press, 1965.

Griswold, Oliver, and Charles M. Brookfield. *They All Called It Tropical.* Miami: Data Press, 1949.

Griswold, Oliver. *The Florida Keys and the Coral Reef.* Miami: Greywood, 1965.

Hannaway, Patti. *Winslow Homer in the Tropics.* Richmond: Westover, no date.

Harper, Roland M. *Natural Resources of Southern Florida.* Tallahassee: State Geological Survey, 18th Annual Report, 1927.

Harvey, Karen. *St. Augustine and St. Johns County: A Pictorial History.* Design by Barbara Buckley. Norfolk, VA: Donning, 1980.

Harwood, Kathryn Chapman. *The Lives of Vizcaya: Annals of a Great House.* Miami: Banyan Books, 1985.

Henshall, James A. *Camping and Cruising in Florida.* Cincinnati: Robert Clarke, 1884.

Hoffmeister, John Edward. *Land from the Sea: The Geological Story of South Florida.* Coral Gables: University of Miami Press, 1974.

Holland, F. Ross, Jr. *Great American Lighthouses.* Washington: Preservation Press, National Trust for Historic Preservation, 1989.

Hurley, Neil E. *History of Cape Florida Lighthouse.* Camino, CA: Historic Lighthouse Publishers, 1989.

Hurley, Neil E. *Keepers of Florida Lighthouses 1820–1939.* Alexandria, VA: Historic Lighthouse Publishers, 1990.

Kingston, W. H. G. *In the Wilds of Florida.* London: T. Nelson, 1880.

Kleinberg, Howard. *Miami Beach: A History.* Miami: Centennial Press, 1994.

Leavenworth, Payne. *Historic Galveston.* Photographs by Richard Payne. Houston: Herring Press, 1985.

Lyon, Eugene. *The Enterprise of Florida: Pedro Menéndez de Avilés and the Spanish Conquest of 1565–1568.* Gainesville: University Presses of Florida, 1976.

Macmillan, H. F. *Tropical Planting and Gardening with Special Reference to Ceylon.* 5th edition. London: Macmillan, 1949.

Matthiessen, Peter. *Indian Country.* New York: Viking, 1992.

McCarthy, Kevin M. *Florida Lighthouses.* Gainesville: University of Florida Press, 1990.

McComb, David G. *Galveston: A History.* Austin: University of Texas Press, 1986.

McIver, Stuart. *One Hundred Years on Biscayne Bay 1887–1987.* Coconut Grove: Biscayne Bay Yacht Club, 1987.

Menard, Henry W. *Islands.* New York: Scientific American Books, 1986.

Milanich, Jerald T., and Samuel Proctor, eds. *Tecachale: Essays on the Indians of Florida and Southeastern Georgia during the Historic Period.* Gainesville: University of Florida Press, Florida Museum of Natural History, 1978.

Milanich, Jerald T., and Susan Milbrath, eds. *First Encounters, Spanish Explorations in the Caribbean and the United States 1492–1570.* Gainesville: University of Florida Press, 1989.

Milanich, Jerald T., and Charles H. Fairbanks. *Florida Archaeology.* New York: Academic Press, 1980.

Miller, Mable Fentress. "A Sense of Place: Key Biscayne" in *The Dade County Environmental Story.* Miami: Environmental Information Service, Friends of the Everglades, 1987.

Morison, Samuel Eliot. *The European Discovery of America. The Northern Voyages, A.D. 500–1600.* New York: Oxford University Press, 1971.

Morison, Samuel Eliot. *The European Discovery of America. The Southern Voyages, A.D. 1492–1616.* New York: Oxford University Press, 1974.

Morris, Allen, compiler. *The Florida Handbook.* Tallahassee: Peninsular, published biennially.

Morton, Julia F. *500 Plants of South Florida.* Miami: Fairchild Tropical Garden, 1981.

Morton, Julia F. *Wild Plants for Survival in South Florida.* Miami: Fairchild Tropical Garden, 1962.

Muir, Helen. *Miami, USA.* New York: Henry Holt, 1953.

Munroe, Ralph M., and Vincent Gilpin. *The Commodore's Story.* Ives Washburn, 1930.

Myers, Ronald L., and John J. Ewel. *Ecosystems of Florida.* Orlando: University of Central Florida Press, 1990.

Nash, Charles Edgar. *The Magic of Miami Beach.* Philadelphia: David McKay, 1938.

Niering, William A. *Wetlands.* New York: Audubon Society, Borzoi Book, Alfred A. Knopf, 1989.

Nolan, David. *50 Feet in Paradise.* San Diego: Harcourt Brace Javonovich, 1984.

Ochse, J. J. *Fruits and Fruit Culture in the Dutch East Indies.* English edition. Batavia-C., Java: G. Kolff, 1931.

Parks, Arva Moore. *Miami: the Magic City.* Tulsa: Continental Heritage Press, 1981.

Parks, Arva Moore. *The Forgotten Frontier: Florida through the Lens of Ralph Middleton Munroe.* Miami: Historical Association of Southern Florida, 1977.

Peters, Thelma. *Biscayne Country 1870–1926.* Miami: Banyan Books, 1981.

Peterson, Roger Tory, and Virginia Marie Peterson. *Audubon's Birds of America. The Audubon Society Baby Elephant Folio.* New York: Artabras Book, Harrison House, 1985.

Pierce, Charles W. *Pioneer Life in Southeast Florida.* Coral Gables: University of Miami Press, 1970.

Pilkey, Orrin H., Jr., Dinesh C. Sharma, Harold R. Wanless et al. *Living with the East Florida Shore.* Durham: Duke University Press, 1984.

Pla, José. *Mallorca, Menorca e Ibiza.* Tercero edicion. Barcelona: Ediciones Destino, 1970.

Popenoe, Wilson. *Manual of Tropical and Subtropical Fruits.* Facsimile of the 1920 edition. New York: Hafner Press, Macmillan, 1974.

Proby, Kathryn Hall. *Audubon in Florida.* Coral Gables: University of Miami Press, 1974.

Quinn, Jane. *Minorcans in Florida: Their History and Heritage.* St. Augustine: Mission Press, 1975.

Redford, Polly. *Billion-Dollar Sandbar, A Biography of Miami Beach.* New York: E. P. Dutton, 1970.

Riley, Sandra. *Homeward Bound: A History of the Bahama Islands to 1850.* Miami: Island Research, 1983.

Romans, Bernard. *A Concise Natural History of East and West Florida.* New York, 1775. Facsimile of the 1775 edition. Gainesville: University of Florida Press, 1962.

Schwartz, Maurice L., ed. *Barrier Islands.* Benchmark Papers in Geology, vol. 9. Stroudsburg, PA: Dowden, Hutchinson and Ross, 1973.

Secretary of the Navy. *U.S. Navy Annual Report for the Year 1898.* Washington: U.S. Government Printing Office, 1898.

Sewell, John. *Memoirs and History of Miami, Florida.* Miami: Privately printed, 1933. (Pictorial edition *Miami Memoirs: John Sewell* by Arva Moore Parks) Tulsa: Arva Parks, 1987.

Simmons, William H. *Notices of E. Florida, etc.* Facsimile of the 1882 edition. Gainesville: University of Florida Presses, 1976.

Simpson, Charles Torrey. *In Lower Florida Wilds.* New York: Macmillan, 1920.

Small, John Kunkel. *Eden to Sahara: Florida's Tragedy.* Lancaster, PA: Science Press, 1929.

Small, John Kunkel. *Flora of the Florida Keys.* Lancaster, PA: The New Era, 1913.

Smiley, Nixon. *Yesterday's Miami.* Miami: E. A. Seemann, 1973.

Smiley, Nixon. *Knights of the Fourth Estate.* Miami: E. A. Seemann, 1974.

Sprague, John Titcomb. *The Origin, Progress, and Conclusion of the Florida War.* Facsimile of the 1848 edition. Gainesville: University of Florida Press, 1964.

Stork, William. *An Account of East-Florida with a Journal Kept by John Bartram of Philadelphia, Botanist to His Majesty for the Floridas.* London: Nicoll and Woodfall, 1766.

Stork, William. *A Description of East Florida.* London, 1769.

Sutton, Imre, ed. *Irredeemable America: The Indians' Estate and Land Claims.* Albuquerque: University of New Mexico Press, 1985.

Tasker, Georgia B. *Enchanted Ground: Gardening with Nature in the Subtropics.* Miami: The Miami Herald, 1994

Taylor, Thomas. Florida Territorial Lighthouses, 1821–1845 Allendale: TWT, 1995

Tebeau, Charlton. *A History of Florida.* Coral Gables: University of Miami Press, 1971.

Tebeau, Charlton. *Man in the Everglades: 2,000 Years of Human History in the Everglades National Park.* Coral Gables: University of Miami Press, 1968.

Thomas, Hugh. *Cuba: The Pursuit of Freedom.* New York: Harper & Row, 1971.

Thoreau, Henry David. *Cape Cod.* 1865. New York: Norton, 1951.

Vignoles, Charles B. *Observations upon the Floridas.* New York: E. Blis and E. White, 1823. Facsimile of the 1823 edition. Gainesville: University Presses of Florida, 1977.

Vogel, Karl. *Aloha Around the World.* Introduction by Arthur Curtiss James. New York: G. P. Putnam, Knickerbocker Press, 1923.

Voss, Gilbert L. *Coral Reefs of Florida.* Sarasota: Pineapple Press, 1988.

Williams, John Lee. *The Territory of Florida.* Facsimile of the 1837 edition. Gainesville: University of Florida Press, 1962.

Windhorn, Stan, and Wright Langley. *Yesterday's Key West.* Key West: Langley Press, 1973.

Woodman, Jim. *The Book of Key Biscayne: Being the Romance of Cape Florida.* Miami: Miami Post, 1961.

Wright, J. Leitch, Jr. *British St. Augustine.* St. Augustine: Historic St. Augustine Preservation Board, 1975.

Zuckerman, Bertram. *The Dream Lives On. A History of the Fairchild Tropical Garden 1938–1988.* Miami: Fairchild Tropical Garden, 1988.

Journal articles, unpublished papers, and reports

Arana, Eugenia B., and Doris Wiles. "The Don Pedro Fornells House." *El Escribano,* no. 48 (July 1963): 8–13.

Amidown, Margot. "The Wagner Family: Pioneer Life on the Miami River." *Tequesta* VLII (1982); 5–37.

Arnade, W. Charles. "Who Was Juan Ponce de Leon?" *Tequesta* XXVII (1967): 29–55.

Austin, Daniel F. "The Coconut in Florida." *Principes Journal of the Palm Society* 22, no. 3 (July 1978): 83–87.

Bagur, J. D. "Barrier Islands of the Atlantic and Gulf Coasts of the U.S.: An Annotated Bibliography, 1978." Biological Services. Fish and Wildlife Service. U.S. Department of Interior.

Barnes, A. Douglas. "History of Dade County Park System, 1929–1969: The First Forty Years." Unpublished, 1986.

Bartlett, Captain John Russell. "Watching for the Enemy in the Spanish War." *The Century Magazine* LXII (1901): 907–915.

Bell, Frederick W., and Vernon R. Leeworthy. "An Economic Analysis of the Importance of Saltwater Beaches in Florida." Florida Sea Grant College, Report SGR 82, February 1986: 1–166.

Beeson, Kenneth H., Jr. "Fromajadas and Indigo: The Minorcan Colony in Florida." Master's thesis, University of Florida, P. K. Yonge Library, Gainesville, FL, 1960.

Black, Hugo, III. "Richard Fitzpatrick's South Florida 1822–1840." Part II, Fitzpatrick's Miami River Plantation. *Tequesta* XLI (1981): 38–68.

Blank, Harvey. "Henry Perrine: Pioneer Physician, Scientist and Citizen." *Bulletin of the University of Miami School of Medicine, Jackson Memorial Hospital* 12, no. 1 (March 1958): 24–28.

Brookfield, Charles M. "Cape Florida Light." *Tequesta* IX (1949): 5–12.

Camps, Pedro. "The Golden Book of the Minorcans, 1768–1784." Parish records of Diocese of St. Augustine. Microfilm. St. Augustine Historical Society.

Carr, Robert S. "An Archaeological Survey and Investigations at Bill Baggs State Park, Key Biscayne." Miami-Dade Historic Preservation Division Office of Community and Economic Development and State of Florida Department of Parks and Recreation, March 1987.

Chardon, Roland E. "North Biscayne Bay in 1776." *Tequesta* XXXV (1975): 37–74.

Chardon, Roland E. "The Cape Florida Society of 1773." *Tequesta* XXXV (1975): 1–26.

Chulamanis, Sherry and Christopher. "Fossil Mangrove Reef of Key Biscayne." *Sea Frontiers* 24, no. 2 (March–April 1978): 108–114.

Curtis, Muriel. "Key Biscayne—An Isle of Palms." *South Florida History Magazine,* Winter 1989: 6–9.

Damon, Marilyn M. "Beach Revegetation Guideline Manual." Broward Soil and Water Conservation District, 1987: 1–37.

Davis, T. Frederick. "Juan Ponce de Leon's Voyages to Florida." *The Quarterly, Periodical of the Florida Historical Society* XIV (July 1935): 1–69.

Darrach, William et al. "Epidemic Encephalitis." Report of a survey by the Matheson Commission. New York: Columbia University Press, 1929.

Dieterich, Emily Perry. "Birds of a Feather: The Coconut Grove Audubon Society, 1915–1917." *Tequesta* XLV (1985): 5–27.

Dodd, Dorothy. "The Wrecking Business on the Florida Reef, 1822–1860." *Florida Historical Quarterly* XXII (April 1944): 170–199.

Donselman, Henry, and Randy McCoy. "Lethal Yellowing—Recent Development." *Fairchild Tropical Garden Bulletin* 40, no. 1 (January 1985): 19–25.

Emerson, Ralph Waldo. "Emerson's Little Journal at St. Augustine, March 1827." *Florida Historical Quarterly* 18: 84–93.

Fairchild, David. "The Makapuno Coconut of the Philippines . . . Its Introduction into Florida." Fairchild Tropical Garden, Occasional Paper No. 17, August 1947.

Florida Department of Natural Resources. "A Proposed Compre-

hensive Beach Management Program for the State of Florida." Department of Natural Resources, Division of Beaches and Shores, Tallahassee, FL, March 1986.

Florida Department of Natural Resources. "Beach Restoration: A State Initiative." Division of Beach and Shore with the Assistance of Restore Our Coast Task Force, August 1985.

Forry, Samuel. "Statistical Researches Relative to the Etiology of Pulmonary and Rheumatic Diseases, illustrating the application of the Laws of Climate to the Science of Medicine: based on the Records of the Medical Department Adjutant General's Office." *American Journal of the Medical Sciences* 1, no. 1 (1841): 2–54.

Gaby, Donald, and Stephen Baig. "Gulf Stream Variability and Width." *NOAA, Mariner's Weather Log* 23, no. 3 (Summer 1983): 133–134.

Godfrey, Paul J. "Comparative Ecology of East Coast Barrier Islands: Hydrology, Soil, Vegetation." *Barrier Islands and Beaches,* 1976: 5–33.

Goggin, John M. "Archaeological Investigations on the Upper Florida Keys." *Tequesta* 4 (1944): 13–35.

Goggin, John M. "The Seminole Negroes of Andros Island, Bahamas." *Florida Historical Quarterly* 24 (1946): 201–206.

Goggin, John M. "The Indians and History of the Matecumbe Region." *Tequesta* X (1950): 13–24.

Goodwin, Jeffrey et al. "Crandon Park Tropical Hardwood Hammock at West Point Preserve, Key Biscayne." Draft, April 1993.

Griffin, Patricia C. "Mullet on the Beach." Master's thesis, University of Florida, P. K. Yonge Library, Gainesville, 1977.

Griffin, Patricia C. "Mullet on the Beach: The Minorcans of Florida 1768–1788." *El Escribano* 27 (1990): 1–219.

Hanson, Hodge J., and Albert C. Manucy. "Cape Florida Lighthouse." Historic Site Report, 1949.

Harrigan, Anthony. "The Charleston Tradition." *American Heritage* IX, no. 2 (Feb. 1958): 48–61.

Hawkes, J. M. "The East Coast in 1870." (from New Orleans: *Florida Gazetteer*, 1871). *Florida Historical Journal* XVIII, no. 2 (1939): 106–113.

Hecht, Jeff. "America in Peril from the Sea." *New Scientist,* June 8, 1988: 54–59.

Hoffmeister, J. Edward, and H. Gray Multer. "Fossil Mangrove Beach of Key Biscayne." *Geological Society of America Bulletin* 76 (August 1965): 845–852.

Holder, J. B. "Along the Florida Reef." *Harpers New Monthly Magazine,* vol. 42–43 (February–July 1871).

Hoyt, John H. "Barrier Island Formation." *Geological Society of American Bulletin* 78 (1967): 1125–1136.

Huck, Robin B., and Joan Gill Blank. "Historic Native Flora and Early Settlement Agriculture of Cape Florida, Key Biscayne." Association of Southeast Biologists. Abstract. Florida Museum of Natural History and Grapetree Productions, 1994.

Huck, Robin B. "Restoration Initiative for Cape Florida State Recreation Area following Hurricane Andrew." Division of Recreation and Parks. Draft. May 1993.

Hudson, F. M. "Beginnings in Dade County." *Tequesta* I, no. 3 (July 1943): 1–35.

Kersey, Harry A. "The Seminole Negroes of Andros Island Revisited. Some New Pieces to an Old Puzzle." *The Florida Anthropologist* 34, no. 4 (1981): 169–176.

Kogo, Mothohiko. "Mangrove Planting." Realistic Approaches to Environmental Issues. *The Japan Times* October 4, 1991.

Langley, Wright, and Arva Moore Parks. "Diary of an Unidentified Land Official, 1855. Key West to Miami." *Tequesta* XLIII (1983): 5–23.

LaRoe, Edward T. "Barrier Islands as Significant Ecosystems." Barrier Islands of the Atlantic and Gulf Coasts of the U.S.: An Annotated Bibliography, 1978. Biological. U.S. Fish and Wildlife Service.

Leatherman, Stephen P., ed. "Barrier Islands from the Gulf of St. Lawrence to the Gulf of Mexico, Coastal Research Symposium, Boston, 1978." New York: Academic Press, 1979.

Lockey, Joseph B. "The St. Augustine Census of 1786." *Florida Historical Quarterly* 18, no. 1 (1939): 11–31.

MacLeish, William. "From Sea to Shining Sea: 1942." *Smithsonian* 22, no. 8 (November 1991): 34–48.

Marks, Henry S. "Earliest Grants in the Miami Area." *Tequesta* XVIII (1958): 15–21.

Matheson, W. J. "William Abram Lighthall, Inventor and Engineer." Typescript, c. 1926

McAllister, Birdie. "A Study of the Flora of Key Biscayne, Dade County, FL." Master's thesis, Duke University, Durham, NC, 1938.

Meyer, Marjorie G. "Venancio Sanchez: Nineteenth-Century St. Augustine Citizen." Master's thesis, Arkansas State Teachers College, 1959.

Mitchell, Helen Arthur. "Memories of Matheson's Plantation, 1919." Typescript, 1978.

Mormino, Gary R. "The Firing of Guns and Crackers Continued Till Light: The Diary of the Billy

Bowlegs War." *Tequesta* XLV (1985): 48–72.

Nelson, Walter G. "Guidelines for Beach Restoration Projects." Part I, Biological. Gainesville: Florida Sea Grant College, July 1985: 1–66.

Niles National Register. Jeremiah Hughes, ed. Printed by the editor. Baltimore: 1826–1840.

Parks, Arva Moore. "Key Biscayne Base Marker—1855." *Tequesta* XXXIII (1973): 3–16.

Parks, Arva Moore. "Miami in 1876." *Tequesta* XXXV (1975): 89–139.

Parks, Arva Moore. "The Land across from the Light." Master's thesis, Otto G. Richter Library, University of Miami, Coral Gables, FL, 1971.

Perrine, Henry. "On the Climate of Florida." American Intelligence. *American Journal of the Medical Sciences* XIV (1834): 267–270.

Perrine, Henry. "Random Records of Tropical Florida" (from *The Magazine of Horticulture* September 1840). *Tequesta* XI (1951): 51–62.

Rasico, Philip D. "Census of 1786, Minorcans in St. Augustine." *El Escribano* 16 (1979): 43–57.

Rasico, Philip D. "Minorcan Population of St. Augustine in the Spanish Census of 1786." *Florida Historical Quarterly* 66 (October 1987): 160–184.

"Report of the Barrier Island Work Group." U.S. Department of the Interior, Heritage Conservation and Recreation Service, December 18, 1978. U.S. Government Printing Office, 1980: 1–81.

Riggs, Stanley R. "Barrier Islands as Natural Storm Dependent Systems." Barrier Islands of the Atlantic and Gulf Coasts of the U.S.: An Annotated Bibliography, 1978. Biological. U.S. Fish and Wildlife Service.

Robins, C. Richard. "Effects of Storms on the Shallow-Water Fish

Fauna of Southern Florida with New Records of Fishes from Florida." *Bulletin of Marine Science of the Gulf and Caribbean* 7 (1957): 266–275.

Schafer, Daniel L. " 'Everything Carried the Face of Spring': Biscayne Bay in the 1770's." *Tequesta* XLIV (1984): 23–31.

Shabecoff, Philip, Robert Reinhold, and Frances Frank Marcus. "How America Is Losing Its Edges." *New York Times,* May 3, 1987.

Shappee, Nathan D. "Fort Dallas and the Naval Depot on Key Biscayne, 1836–1926." *Tequesta* XXI (1961): 12–40.

Small, John Kunkel. "The Coconut Palm—Cocos Nucifera." *Journal of the New York Botanical Garden* 30, no. 355 (July 1929): 153–161.
____ Ibid. 30, no. 356 (August 1929): 194–203.

Stauble, Donald K. "Guidelines for Beach Restoration Projects." Part II, Engineering. Gainesville: Florida Sea Grant College, June 1986: 1–100.

Sturtevant, William C. "Chakaika and the Spanish Indians ." *Tequesta* XIII (1953): 35–74.

Sunderman, James F. "Army Surgeon Reports on Lower East Coast, 1838." *Tequesta* X (1950): 25–33.

Thomas, William Evan. "My Island Home, 1914." Helen Otto, ed., Typescript, 1968.

Wanless, Harold R. "A Comparison of Sand Transport Past Bakers Haulover Inlet and Government Cut." Unpublished, February 1989.

Wilson, Otto. "Coconut, Citizen of the Tropics." *Nature Magazine* March 1925: 161–166.

Wright, J. Leitch, Jr. "Notes and Documents: A Note on the First Seminole War as Seen by the Indians, Negroes, and Their British Advisers." *Journal of Southern History* 34, no. 4 (1968): 565–575.

Index